KNOCK OUT!

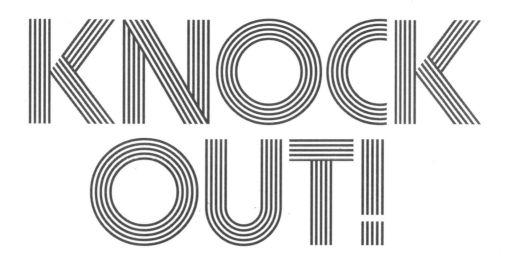

First published in English in 2021
by SelfMadeHero
139–141 Pancras Road
London NW1 1UN
www.selfmadehero.com

First published in Germany under the title "Knock Out!"
English translation © 2021 SelfMadeHero

Written and illustrated by Reinhard Kleist
Translated from the German edition by Michael Waaler

Publishing Director: Emma Hayley
Editorial & Production Director: Guillaume Rater
Publishing Assistant: Stefano Mancin
Designer: Txabi Jones
UK Publicist: Paul Smith
US Publicist: Maya Bradford
With thanks to: Dan Lockwood

The translation of this work
was supported by a grant
from the Goethe-Institut.

Copyright text and illustrations © 2019 CARLSEN Verlag GmbH,
Hamburg, Germany

Photo on page 147: Emile Griffith on November 23, 1964, in London
© Popperfoto via Getty Images
Photo on page 155: Emile Griffith on May 16, 2005, in Long Island
City, New York © Al Bello via Getty Images

A CIP record for this book is available from the British Library

ISBN: 978-1-910593-86-8

10 9 8 7 6 5 4 3 2 1

Printed and bound in China

THE TRUE STORY OF EMILE GRIFFITH

KNOCK OUT!

REINHARD KLEIST

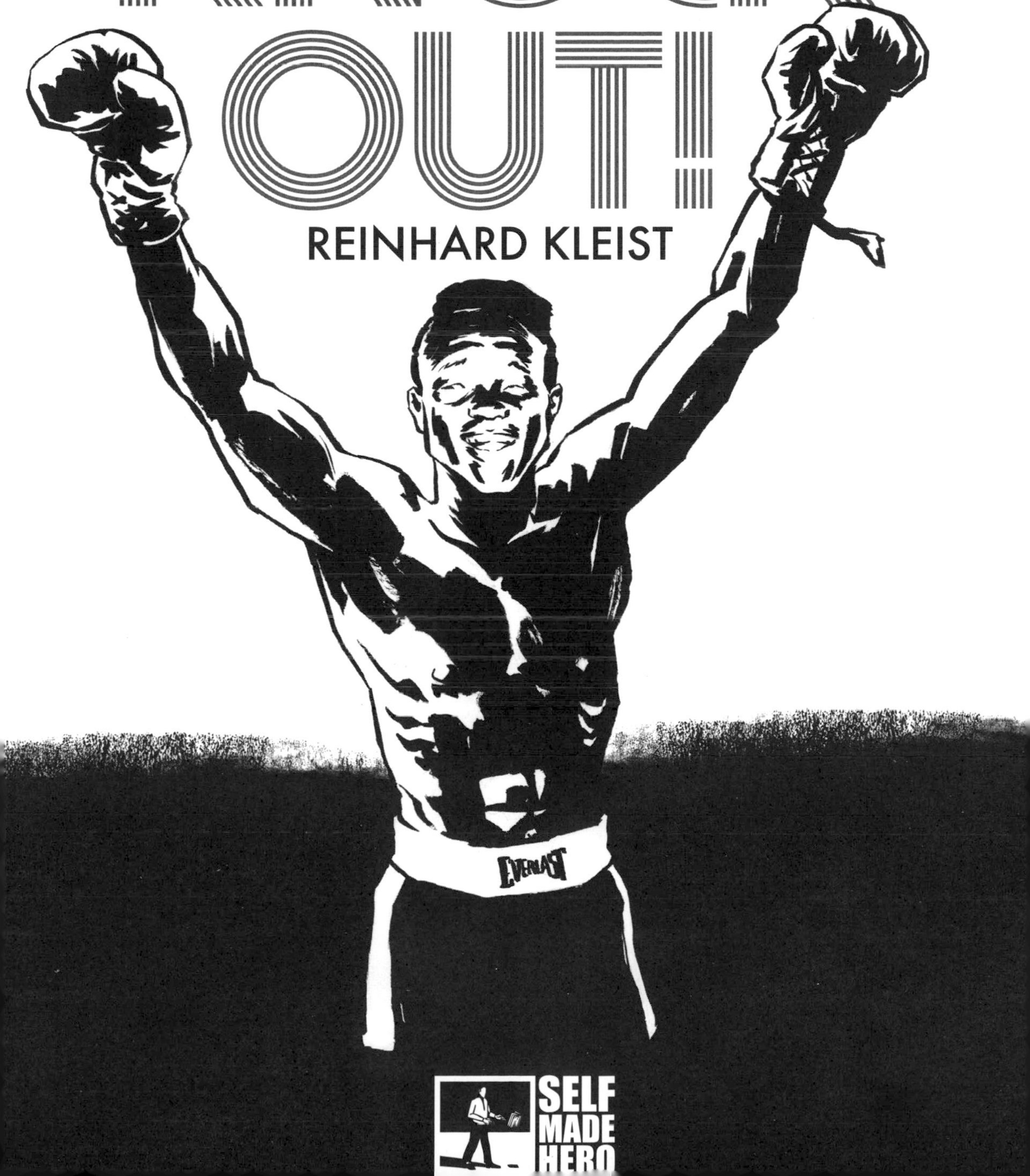
EVERLAST

SELF MADE HERO

PREFACE

I accidentally stumbled across Emile Griffith's life story while researching my book on the boxer Herztko Haft, and it hasn't let go of me since. Beyond his dramatic biography, with all of its highs and lows, something spoke to me on a much deeper level.

I have lived in Berlin for almost 25 years, and despite it being one of the most tolerant cities in the world, I have suffered homophobic insults and even threats while walking down the street hand in hand with my boyfriend. Friends of mine have been physically assaulted in the center of the city, and there are weekly reports of right-wing attacks on members and institutions of the LGBTQ community. However, any comparison to Emile's situation must always take into account my status as a privileged white European living in a time and a country where the fight for LGBTQ rights has made great advancements (although it is far from over!).

Emile was Black and from a poor background, which he boxed himself out of. He lived at a time when the gay and lesbian liberation movement had only just begun. His life and suffering left a deep impression on me. He might not have been someone you would describe as an active advocate for LGBTQ rights, but he lived a life of incredible courage. He did not hide the fact that he was a Black man who loved men, but instead celebrated life in spite of the many blows of fate. His is a story that has inspired great respect in me.

Moreover, this is without taking into account the fact that Emile Griffith was one of the greatest boxers ever seen inside the ring—and an incredible hat designer.

I would like to take this opportunity to thank Ron Ross, who wrote the book *Nine... Ten... and Out!*, which served as the primary source for this graphic novel. He was always there to answer all of my questions as I worked on it, and he replied to my e-mails promptly. I would have loved to have had the chance to meet him on a promotional tour in the US and to personally hand him a copy of this book. After everything I have read about him, he seems to have been a wonderful person and friend. He was a boxer, a boxing promoter, and an author. Ron Ross died in March 2020 following a coronavirus infection. I bow low before him.

Reinhard Kleist
Berlin, 2021

FOREWORD

The Sweet Science and Open Secrets

If you are holding this book in your hands, you already know—or are about to find out—that Emile Griffith lived an exemplary life. I do not mean to suggest that Griffith was a paragon of virtue, but that he was singular. Griffith somehow represented both the nobility and the tragedy encapsulated in the phrase "he was ahead of his time" while at the same time transcending the strictures of that cliché. That saying usually designates a figure whose experiences and desires prove incompatible with the circumstances of their life, but Griffith managed to enjoy the fullest expression of his hopes and desires at a time when this should not have been possible. And yet, in the end, those circumstances constrain his story to the point that one inevitably wonders how things might have turned out had Griffith been born ten or fifteen years later.

If you were well versed in the masculine subculture of professional boxing in New York City during the activist phase of the civil rights movement (1954–1968), then Emile Griffith's sexuality was an open secret. Unfortunately, open secrets provide neither the protection of genuine concealment nor the begrudging acceptance that might come from full disclosure. An open secret at best grants a plausible deniability which offers no defense against the rumor and innuendo that accumulates when the truth is known, but not publicly acknowledged. So it was with Emile Griffith's queerness.

This is not to say that Griffith faced overt persecution for his sexuality. Unlike another flamboyant and charismatic boxer, the powers that be did not prevent Griffith from pursuing his living as a prizefighter. He was not censured for his brief and improbably successful career as a women's hatmaker, nor for his carousing in the underground bars throughout New York City that provided a safe outlet for same-sex desire. But this was precisely because—unlike Muhammad Ali—Griffith did not feel compelled to speak out. Instead, as Reinhard Kleist's *Knock Out!* so vividly portrays, Griffith rose to fame as a Golden Gloves champion and professional boxer seemingly unburdened by a desire to engage in any form of activism.

Griffith's reticence seems to stem in part from his background as a Caribbean-born son striving to make his mother proud amid the hustle and bustle of New York City. Although he was certainly active in the scene, the galvanizing impact of the Stonewall riots—the event that granted coherence to the struggle for gay rights—occurred eight years after Griffith first became champion. Without the clarity provided by that famous Greenwich Village uprising, it is uncertain that the public would have taken Griffith seriously had he chosen to declare himself queer. Instead, that same public happily celebrated Griffith as an exemplar of the "sweet science" of boxing, the latest in a long line of exceptional athletes who would vie for recognition as the best pound for pound fighters in the world. Although these boxers lived in the shadow of heavyweight champions like Ali and Sonny Liston, fighters like Griffith enjoyed considerable acclaim and esteem. At least until Griffith fought Benny Paret.

Griffith and Paret fought twice before the events depicted in this book, with Griffith winning the first bout and the welterweight championship and Paret winning the rematch and reclaiming the title. Anticipation for their third fight attracted enough attention that novelists like Norman Mailer and Pete Hamill attended the contest even though it was to be televised nationally. Indeed, according to the account of the fight that Mailer published in *Esquire*, a tabloid gossip columnist ran a blind item about a boxing champ who liked to visit gay bars a week before the fight. Robbed for the first time of the flimsy protection of the open secret, Griffith defended himself from public scrutiny in the way he was trained to do: he struck back.

I have suggested that—thanks to the timing of his birth—there were no models for Emile Griffith, that the choices he made throughout his life were really no choices at all. But this is not quite accurate. There were two other Black men from Harlem whose sexuality was an open secret at the time: Bayard Rustin and James Baldwin. Together, they represented three paths open to queer Black men in the late 1950s and early '60s—the organizer, the orator, and the fighter. Each of them endured combat and censure, but also unqualified success born of their excellence. All three were—in their own ways—warriors. Each was exemplary.

Jonathan W. Gray, PhD
New York City, 2021

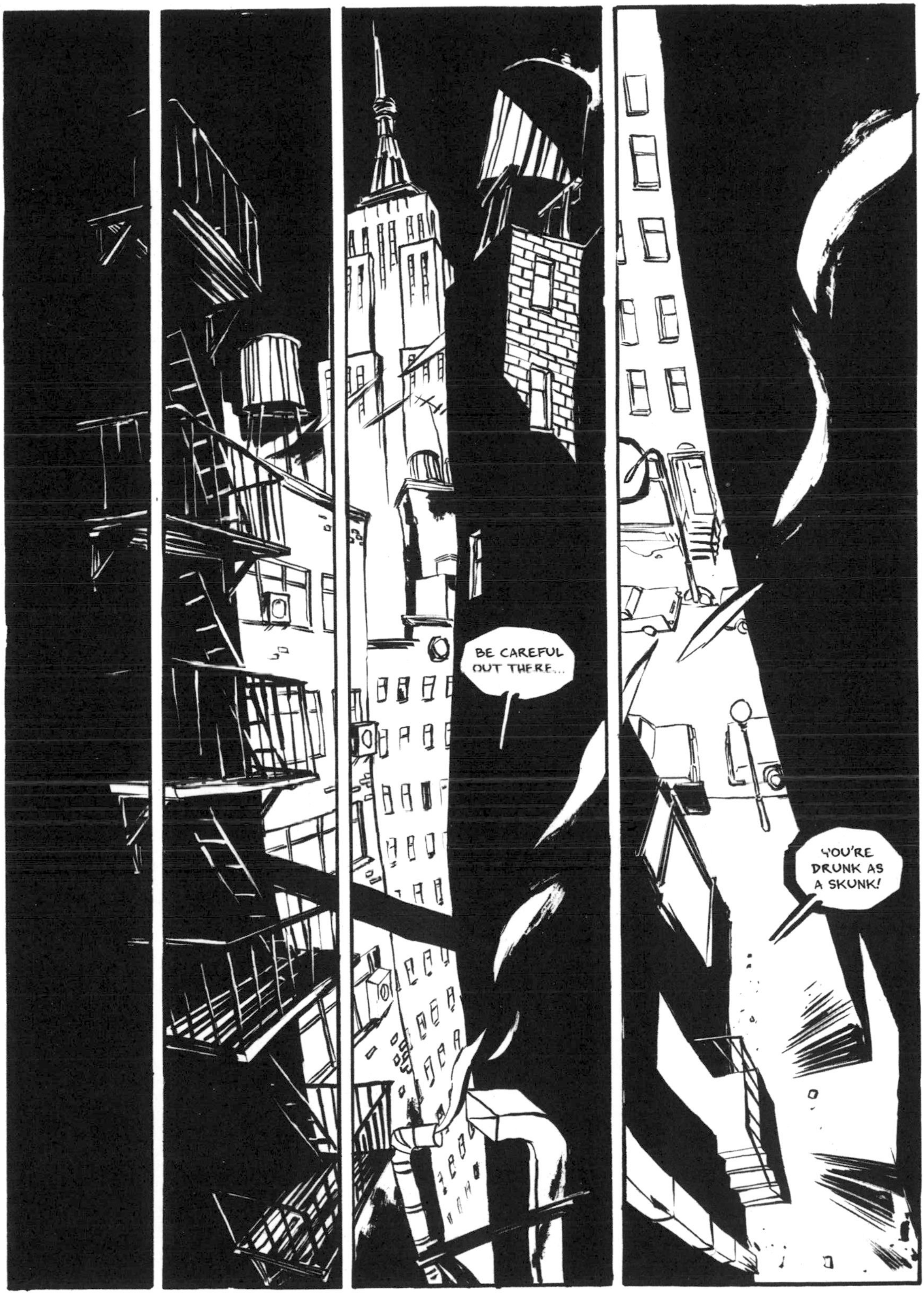
BE CAREFUL OUT THERE...
YOU'RE DRUNK AS A SKUNK!

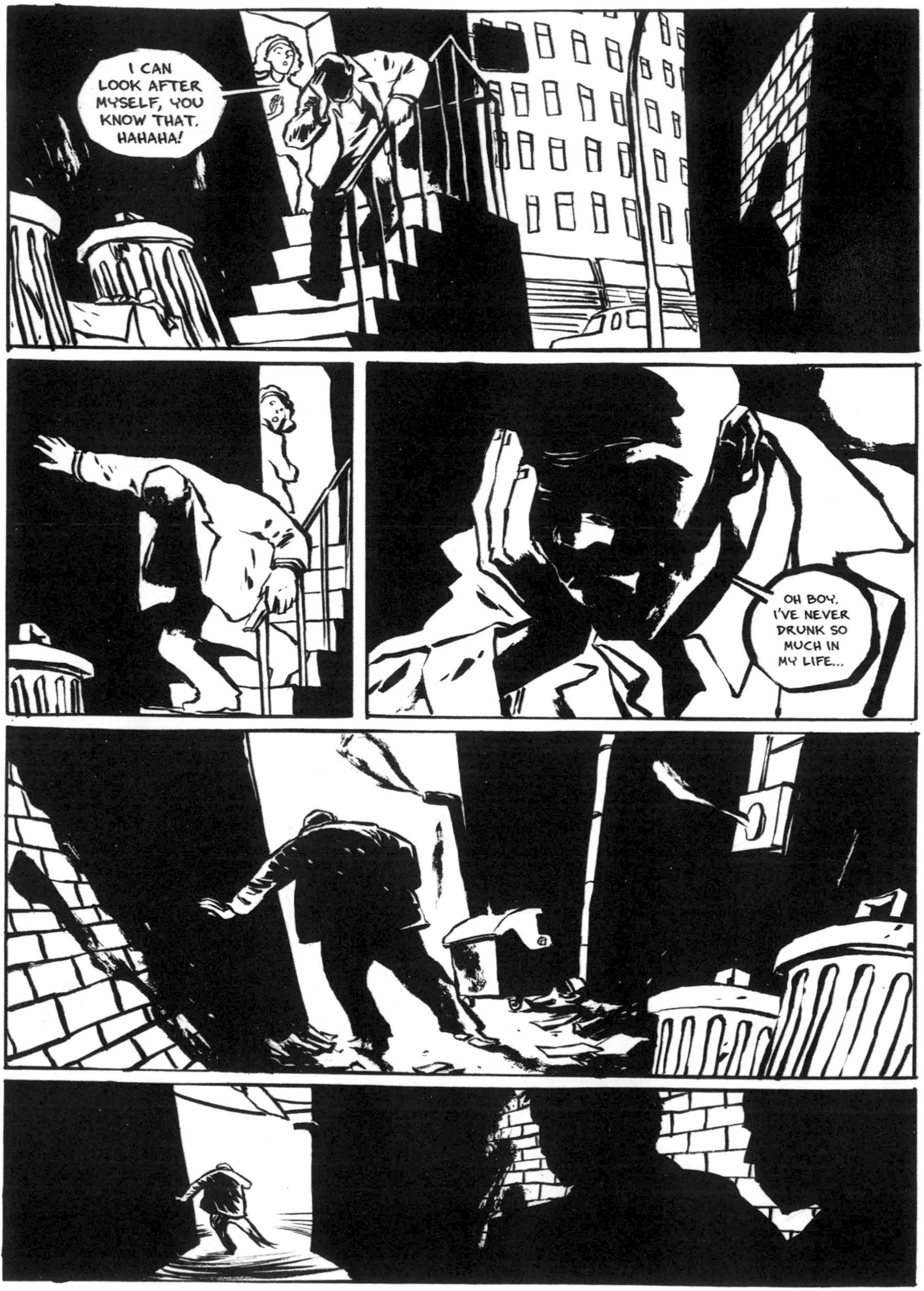
I CAN LOOK AFTER MYSELF, YOU KNOW THAT. HAHAHA!
OH BOY, I'VE NEVER DRUNK SO MUCH IN MY LIFE...

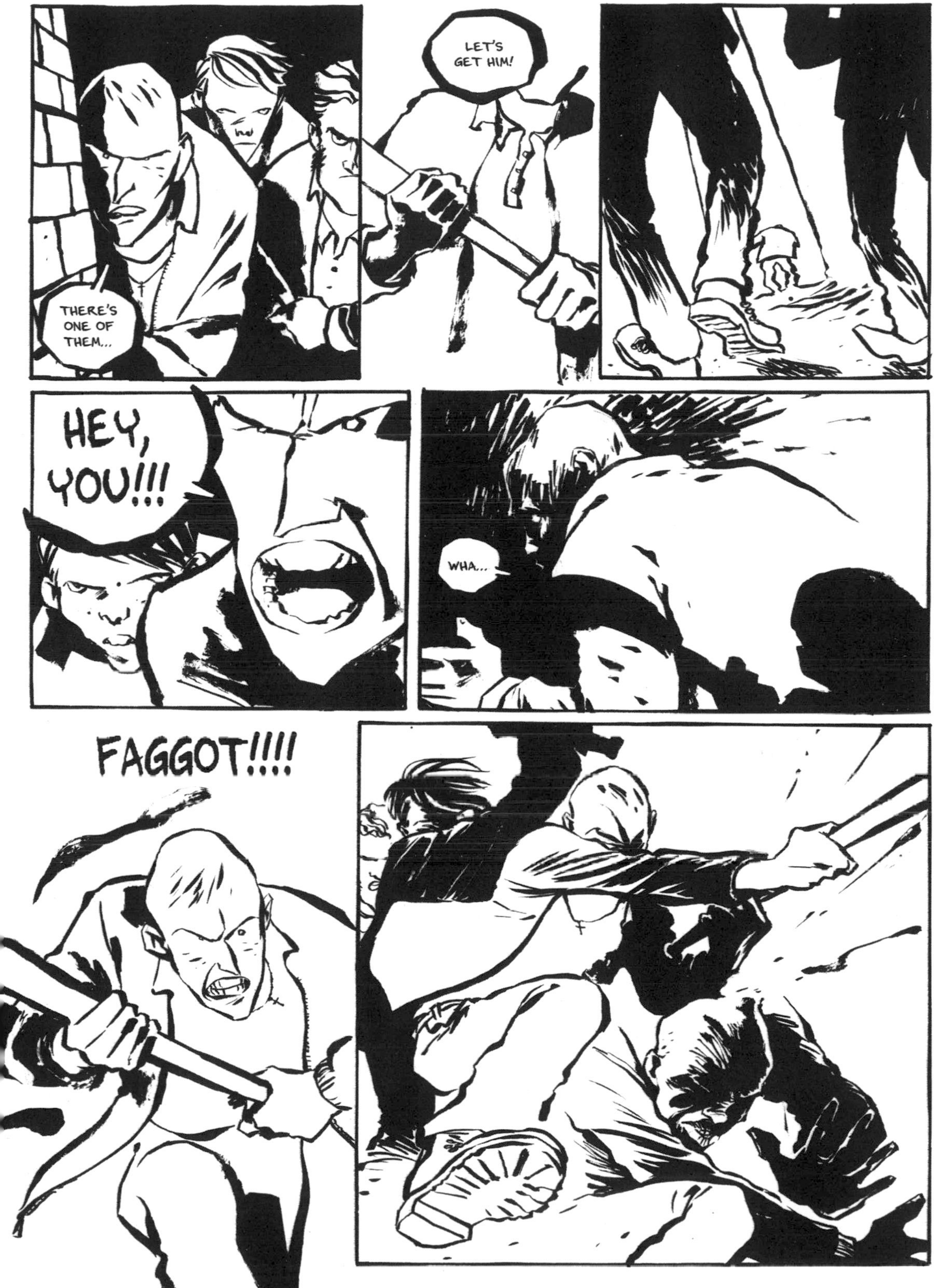
THERE'S ONE OF THEM...
LET'S GET HIM!
HEY, YOU!!!
WHA...
FAGGOT!!!!

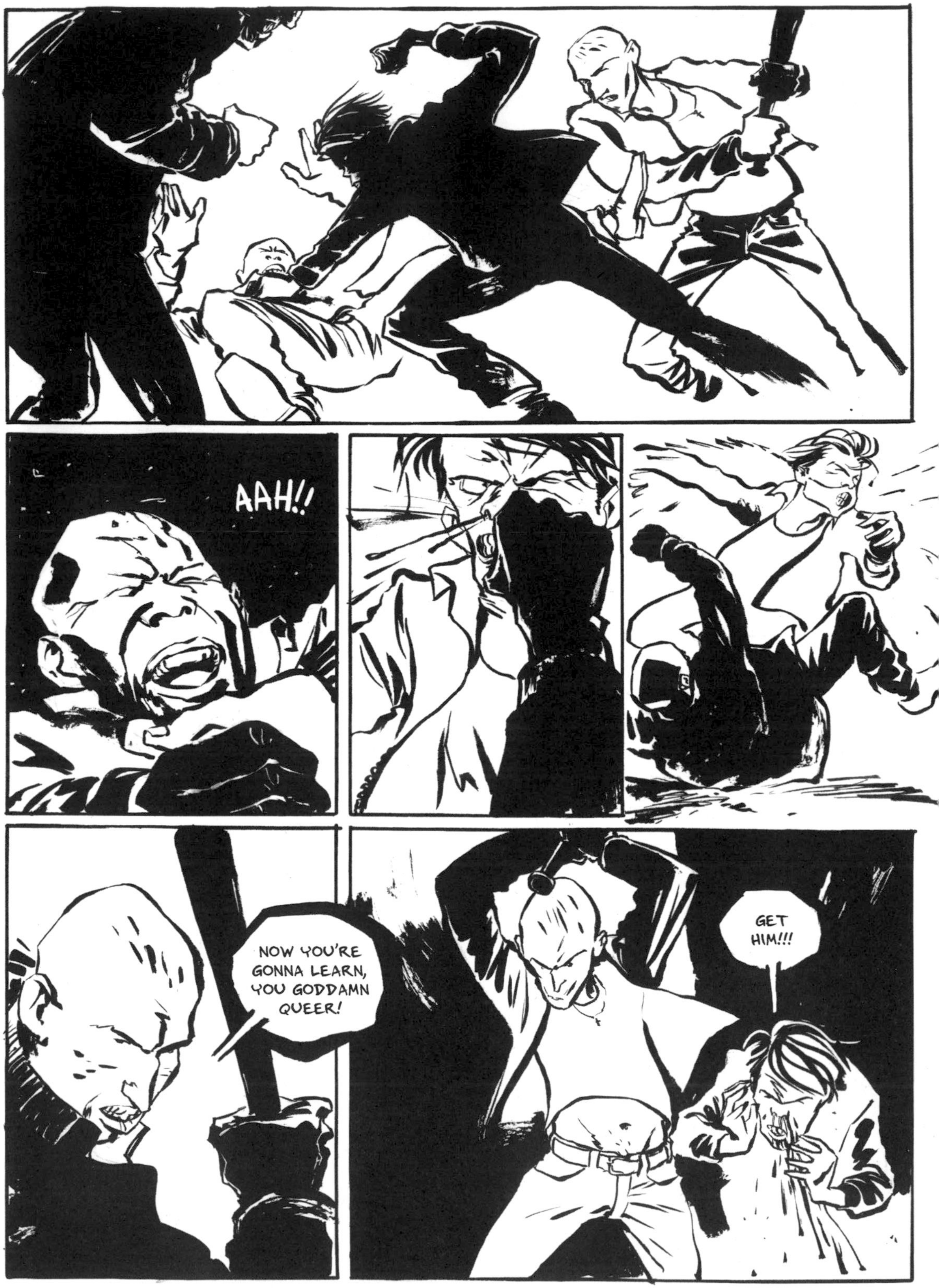
AAH!!
NOW YOU'RE GONNA LEARN, YOU GODDAMN QUEER!
GET HIM!!!

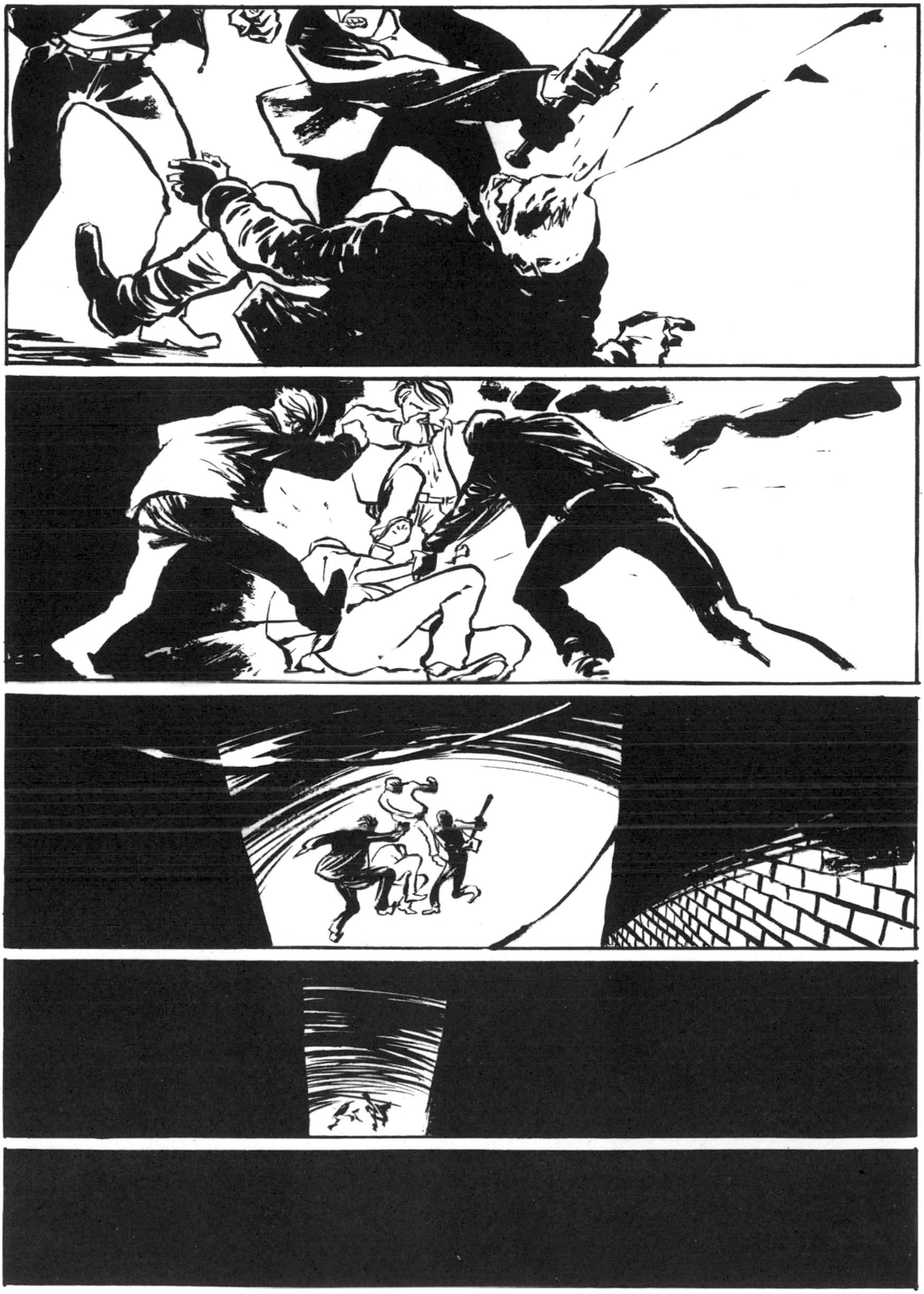

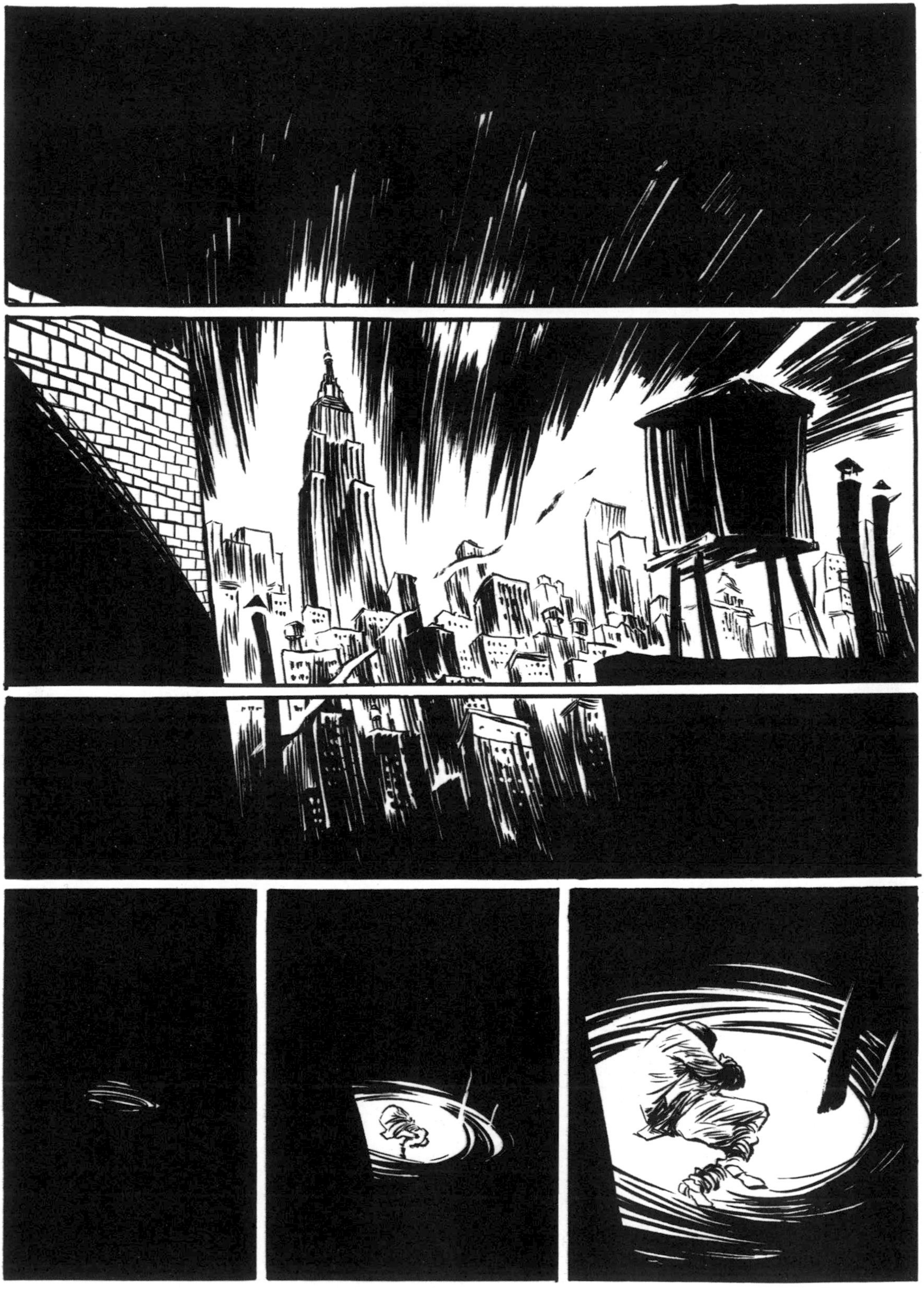

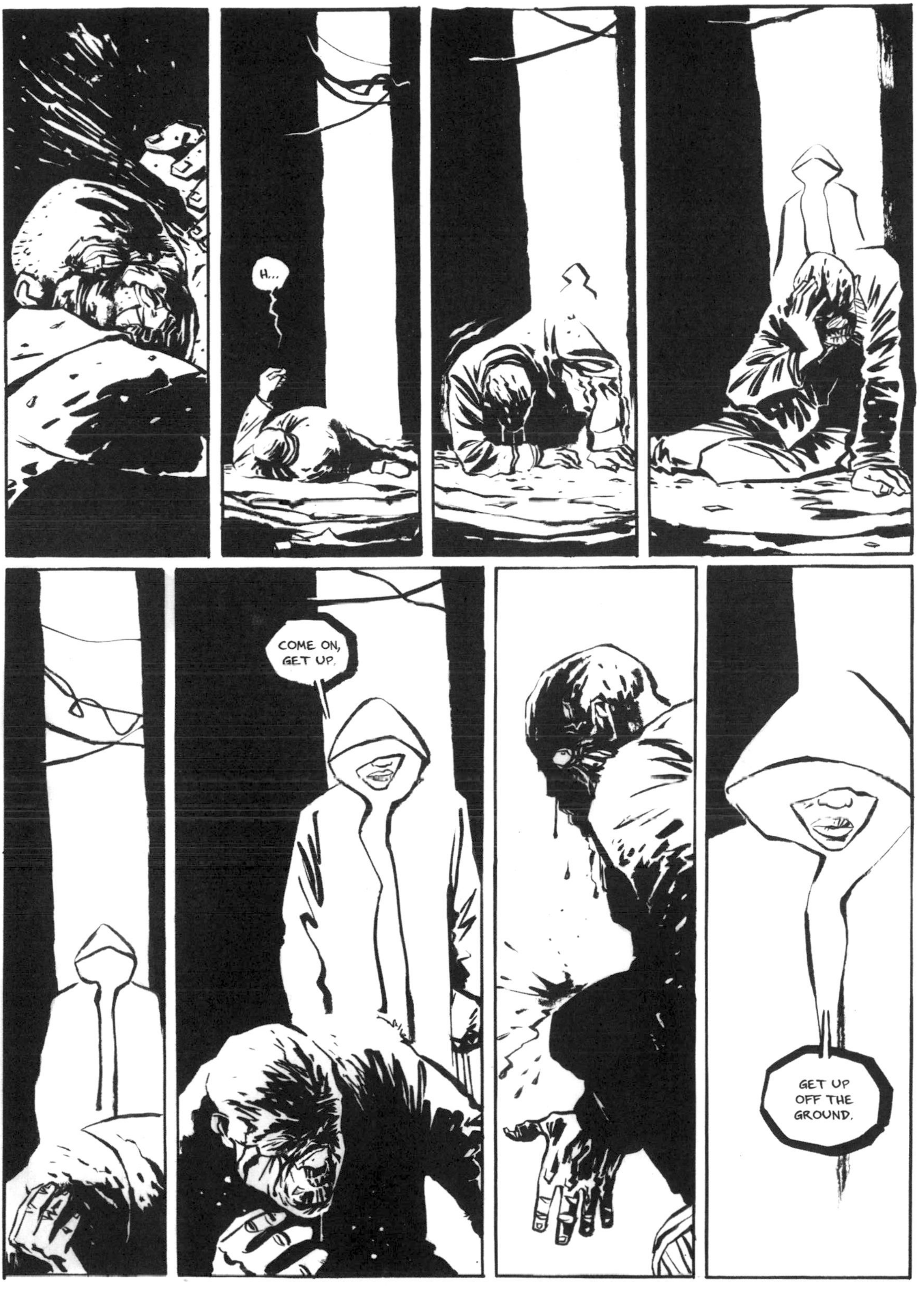
H...
COME ON, GET UP.
GET UP OFF THE GROUND.

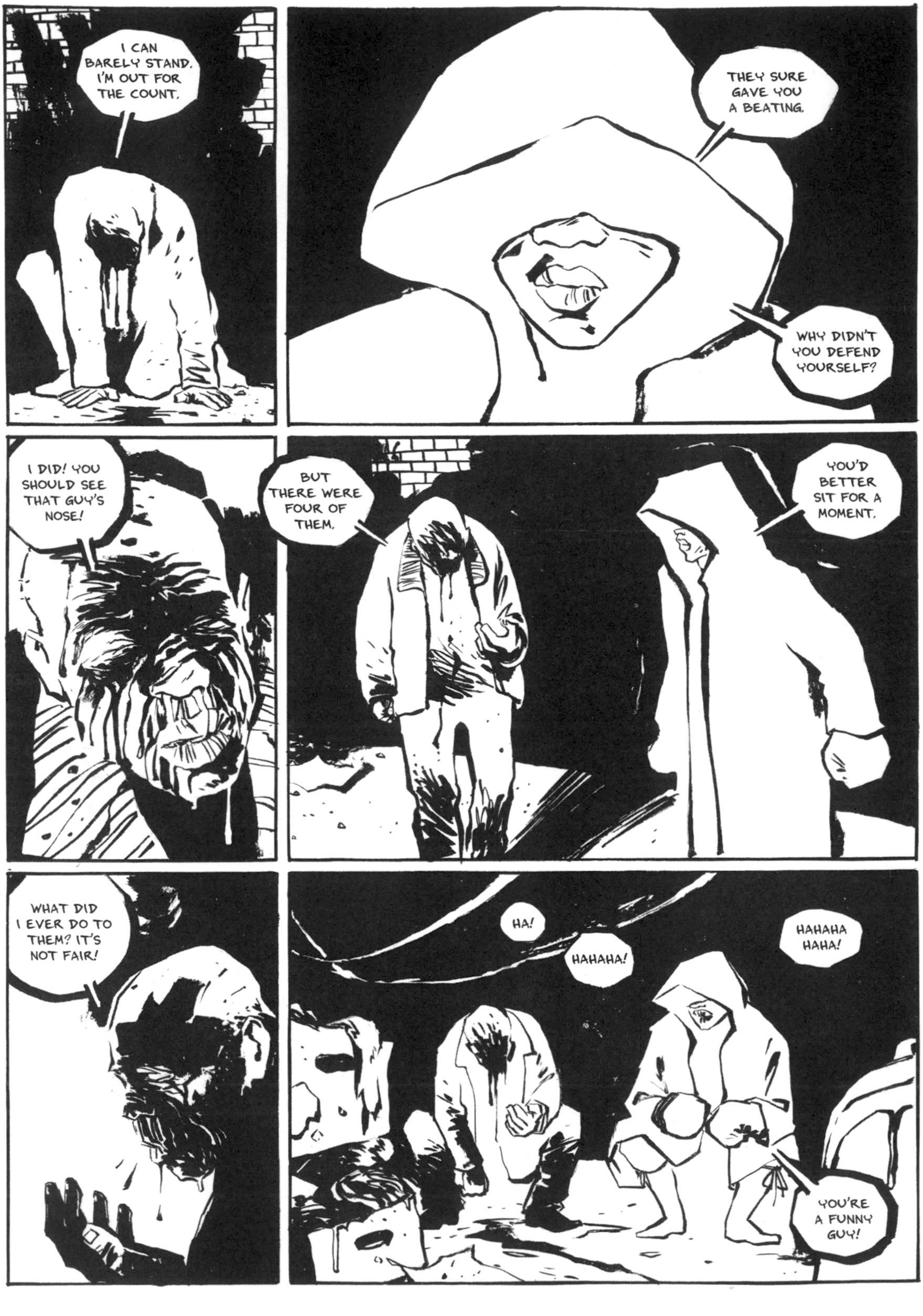
I CAN BARELY STAND. I'M OUT FOR THE COUNT.
THEY SURE GAVE YOU A BEATING.
WHY DIDN'T YOU DEFEND YOURSELF?
I DID! YOU SHOULD SEE THAT GUY'S NOSE!
BUT THERE WERE FOUR OF THEM.
YOU'D BETTER SIT FOR A MOMENT.
WHAT DID I EVER DO TO THEM? IT'S NOT FAIR!
HA!
HAHAHA!
HAHAHA HAHA!
YOU'RE A FUNNY GUY!

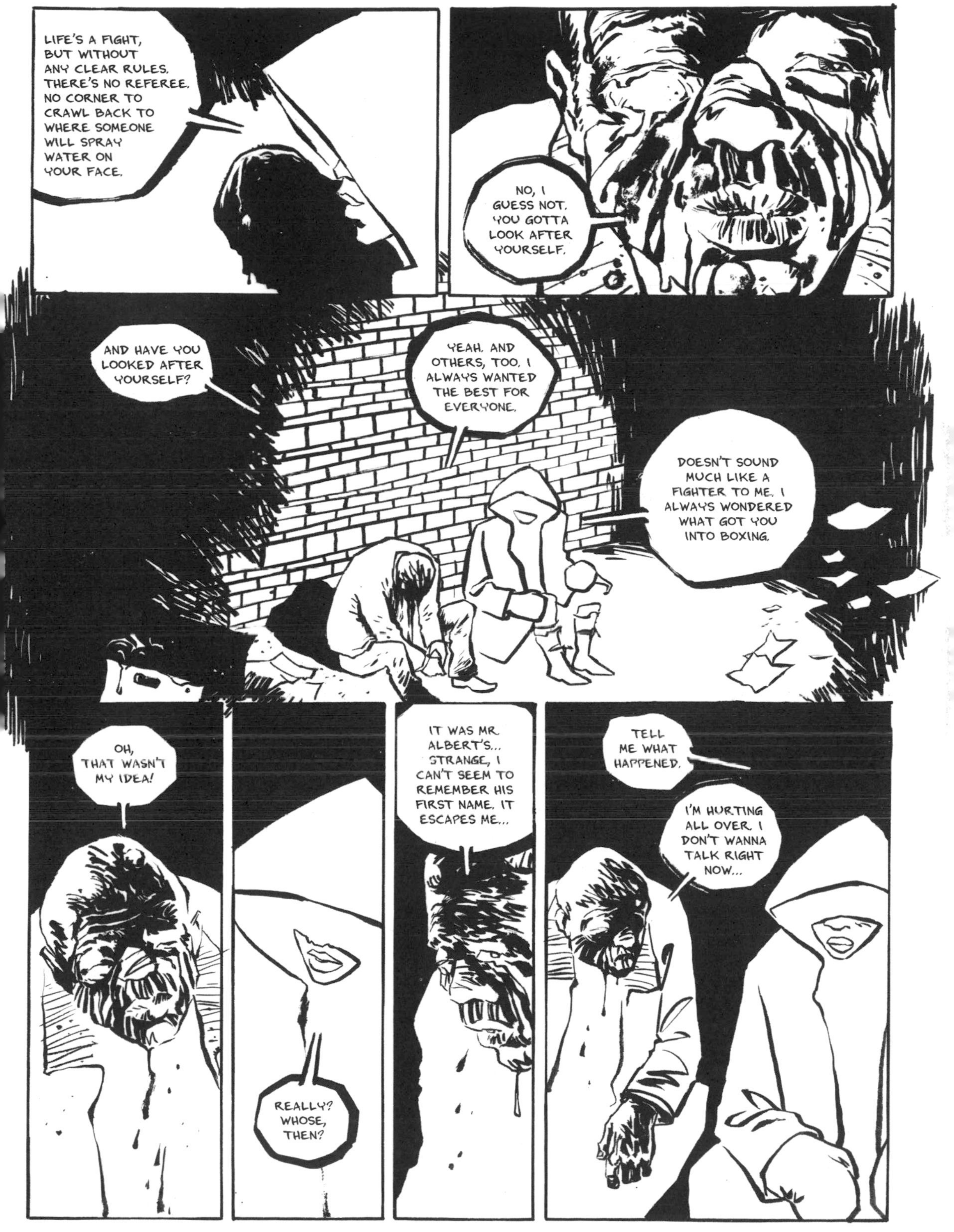
LIFE'S A FIGHT, BUT WITHOUT ANY CLEAR RULES. THERE'S NO REFEREE. NO CORNER TO CRAWL BACK TO WHERE SOMEONE WILL SPRAY WATER ON YOUR FACE.
NO, I GUESS NOT. YOU GOTTA LOOK AFTER YOURSELF.
AND HAVE YOU LOOKED AFTER YOURSELF?
YEAH. AND OTHERS, TOO. I ALWAYS WANTED THE BEST FOR EVERYONE.
DOESN'T SOUND MUCH LIKE A FIGHTER TO ME. I ALWAYS WONDERED WHAT GOT YOU INTO BOXING.
OH, THAT WASN'T MY IDEA!
REALLY? WHOSE, THEN?
IT WAS MR. ALBERT'S... STRANGE, I CAN'T SEEM TO REMEMBER HIS FIRST NAME. IT ESCAPES ME...
TELL ME WHAT HAPPENED.
I'M HURTING ALL OVER. I DON'T WANNA TALK RIGHT NOW...

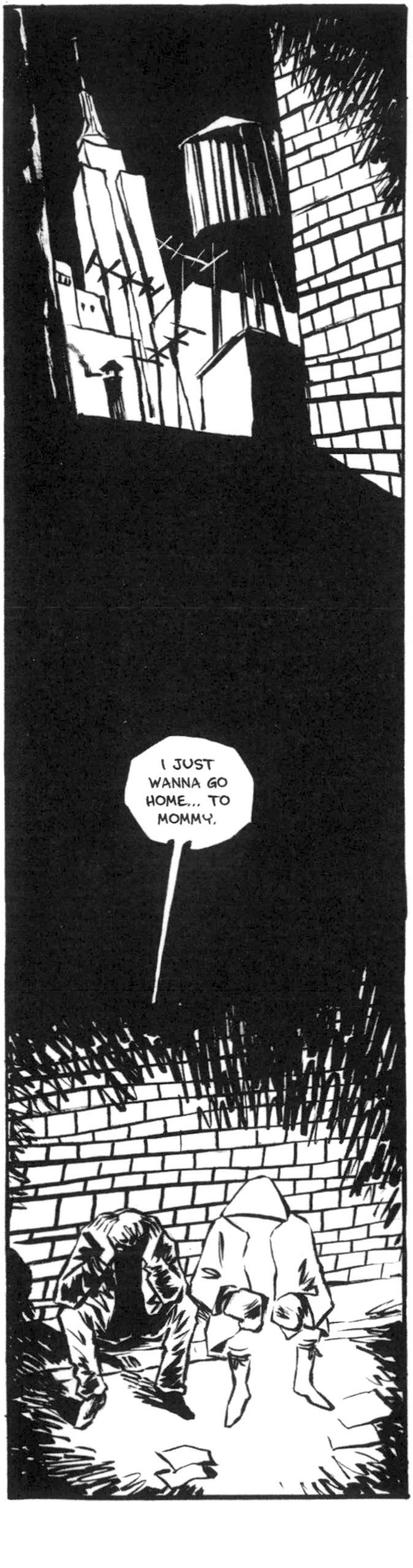
I JUST WANNA GO HOME... TO MOMMY.
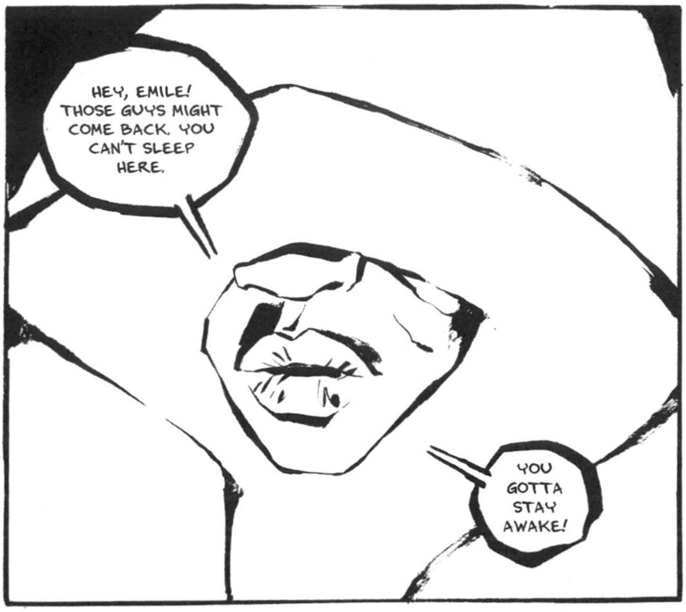
HEY, EMILE! THOSE GUYS MIGHT COME BACK. YOU CAN'T SLEEP HERE.
YOU GOTTA STAY AWAKE!
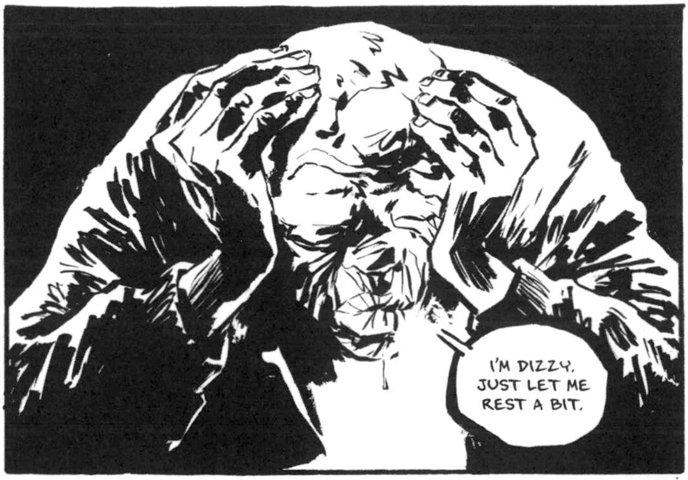
I'M DIZZY. JUST LET ME REST A BIT.
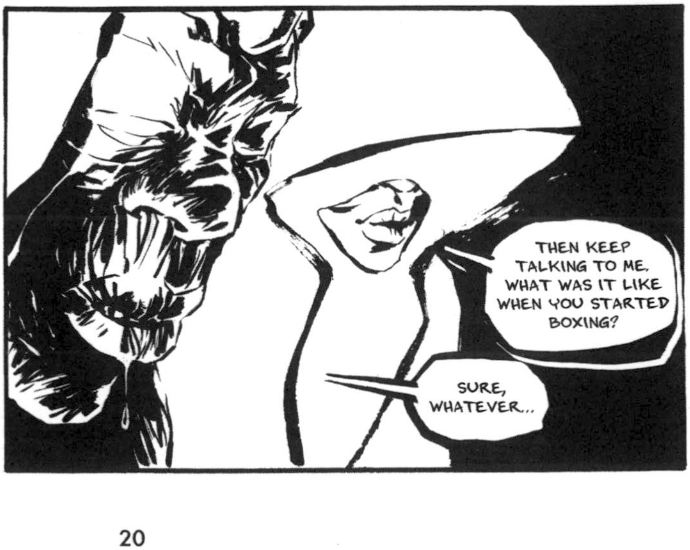
THEN KEEP TALKING TO ME. WHAT WAS IT LIKE WHEN YOU STARTED BOXING?
SURE, WHATEVER...

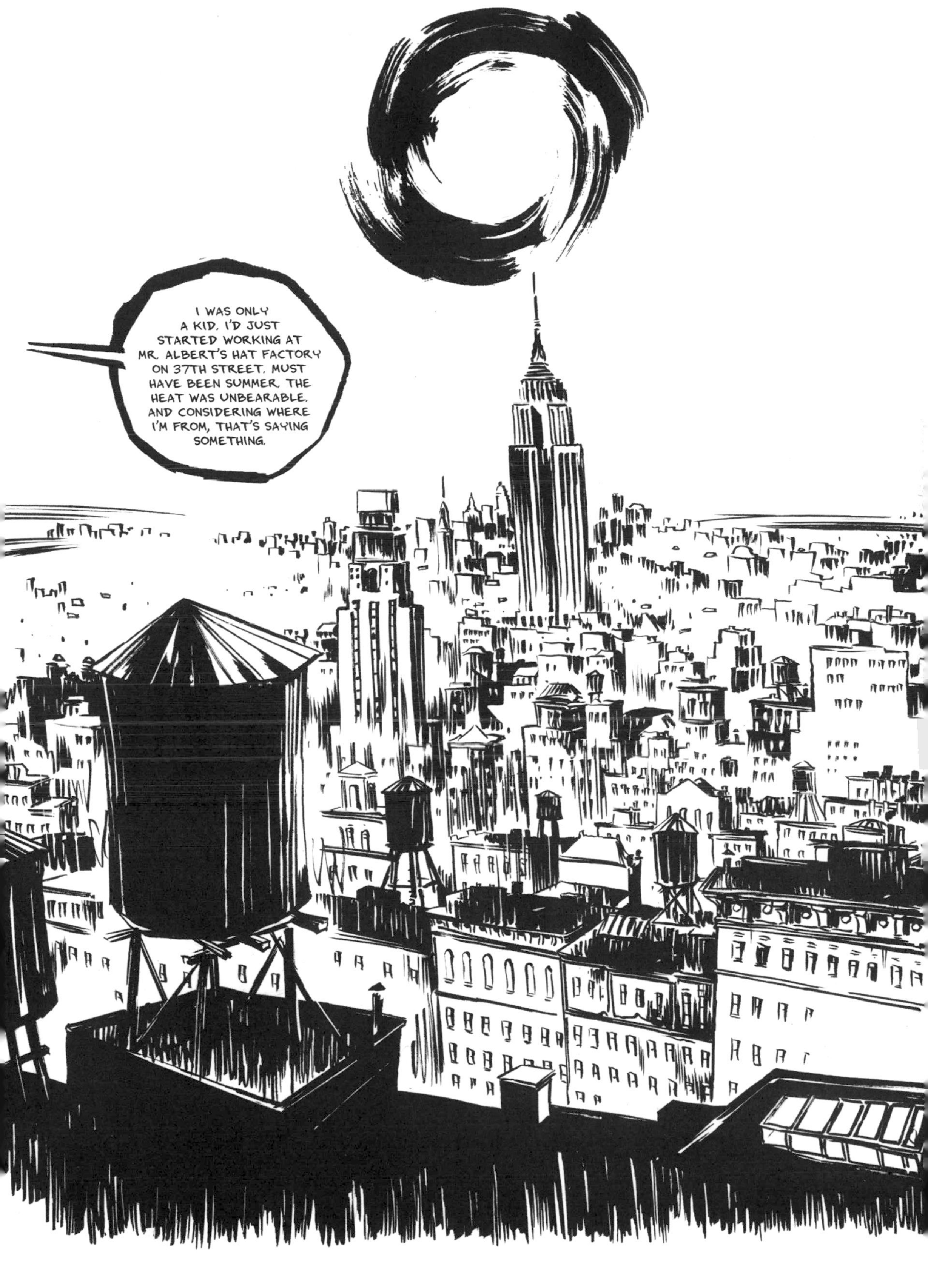
I WAS ONLY A KID. I'D JUST STARTED WORKING AT MR. ALBERT'S HAT FACTORY ON 37TH STREET. MUST HAVE BEEN SUMMER. THE HEAT WAS UNBEARABLE, AND CONSIDERING WHERE I'M FROM, THAT'S SAYING SOMETHING.

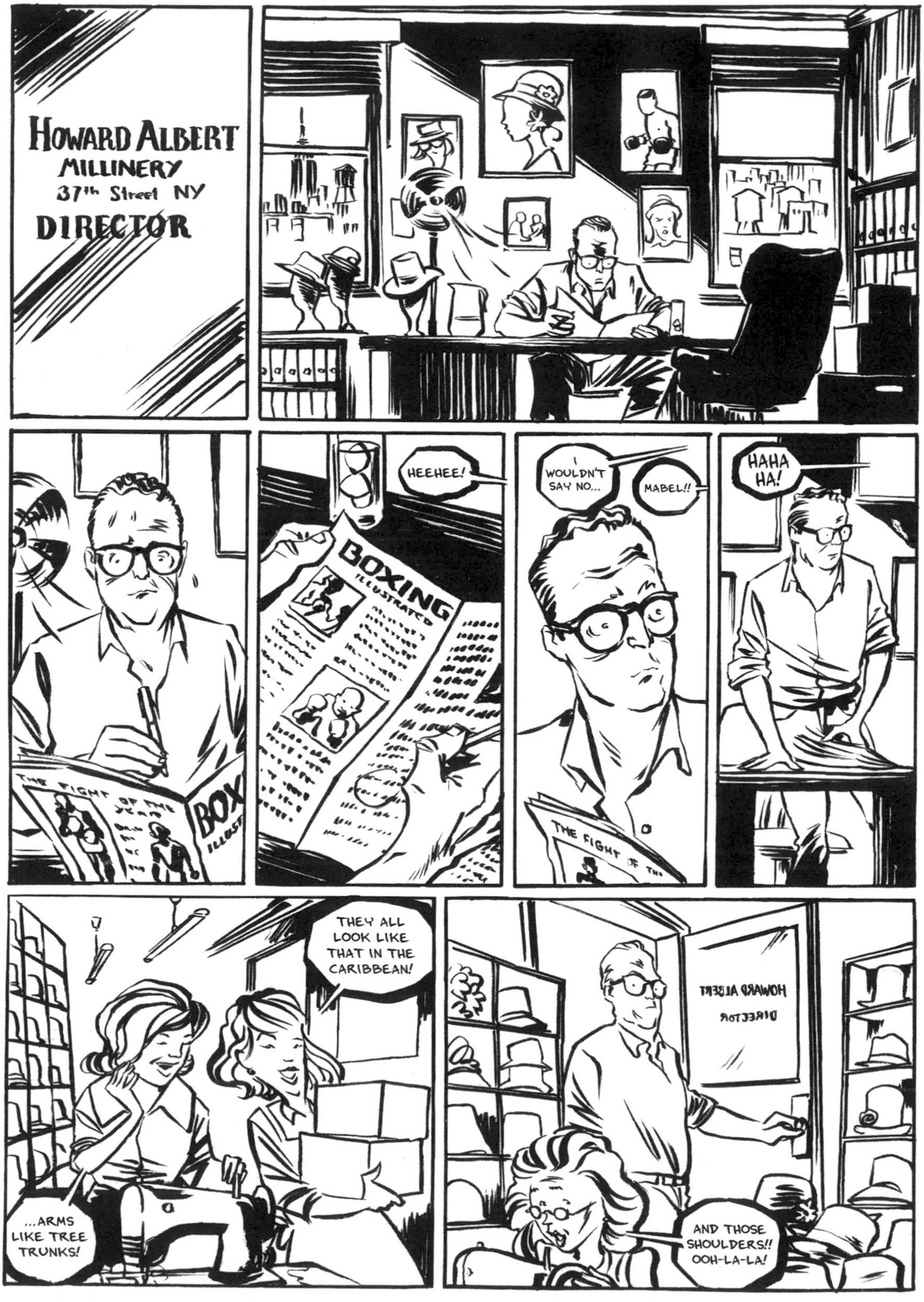
HOWARD ALBERT
MILLINERY
37th Street NY
DIRECTOR
THE FIGHT OF THE YEAR
BOXING ILLUSTRATED
HEEHEE!
I WOULDN'T SAY NO...
MABEL!!
HAHA HA!
THEY ALL LOOK LIKE THAT IN THE CARIBBEAN!
...ARMS LIKE TREE TRUNKS!
AND THOSE SHOULDERS!! OOH-LA-LA!

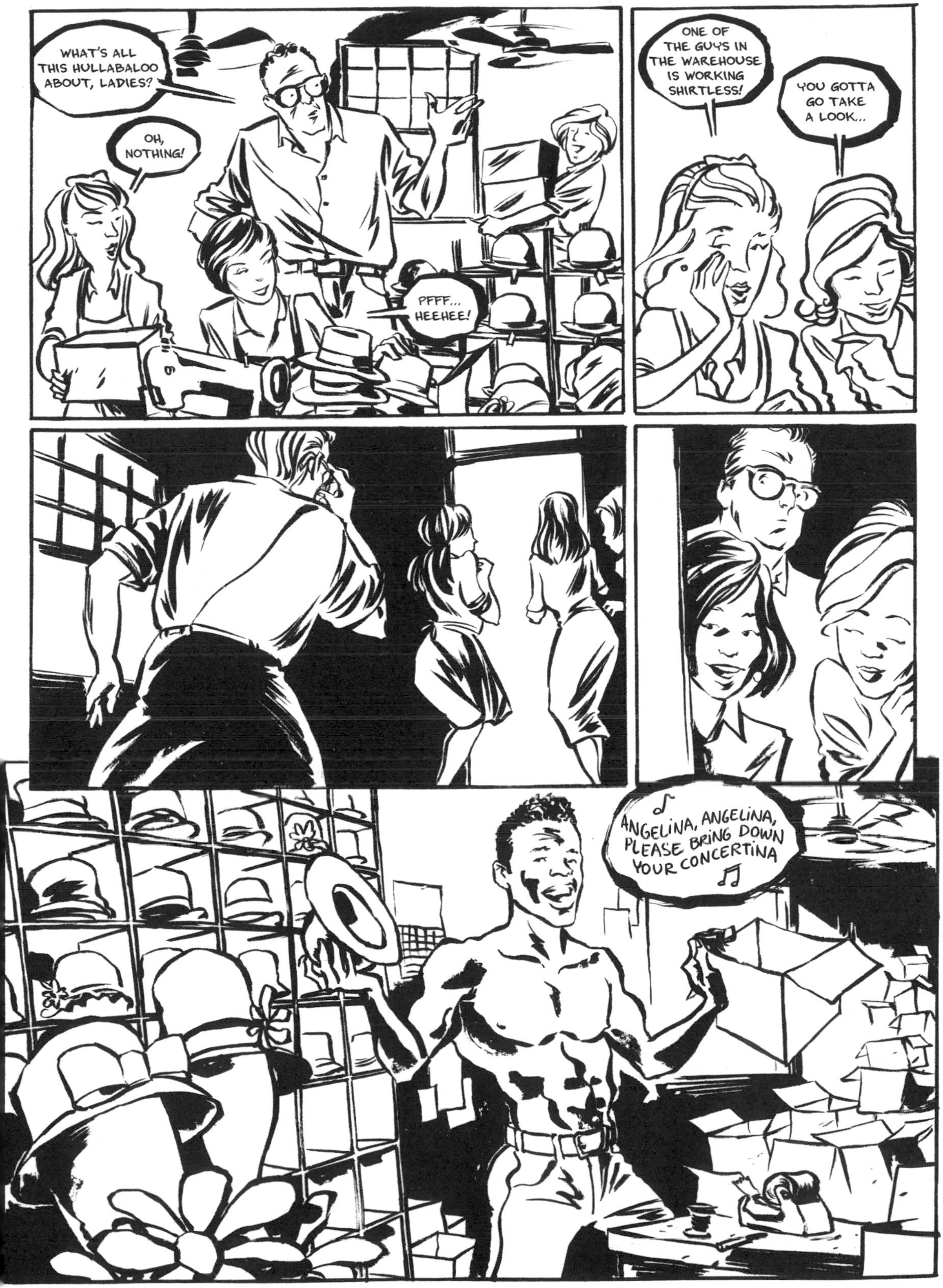
WHAT'S ALL THIS HULLABALOO ABOUT, LADIES?
OH, NOTHING!
PFFF... HEEHEE!
ONE OF THE GUYS IN THE WAREHOUSE IS WORKING SHIRTLESS!
YOU GOTTA GO TAKE A LOOK...
ANGELINA, ANGELINA, PLEASE BRING DOWN YOUR CONCERTINA

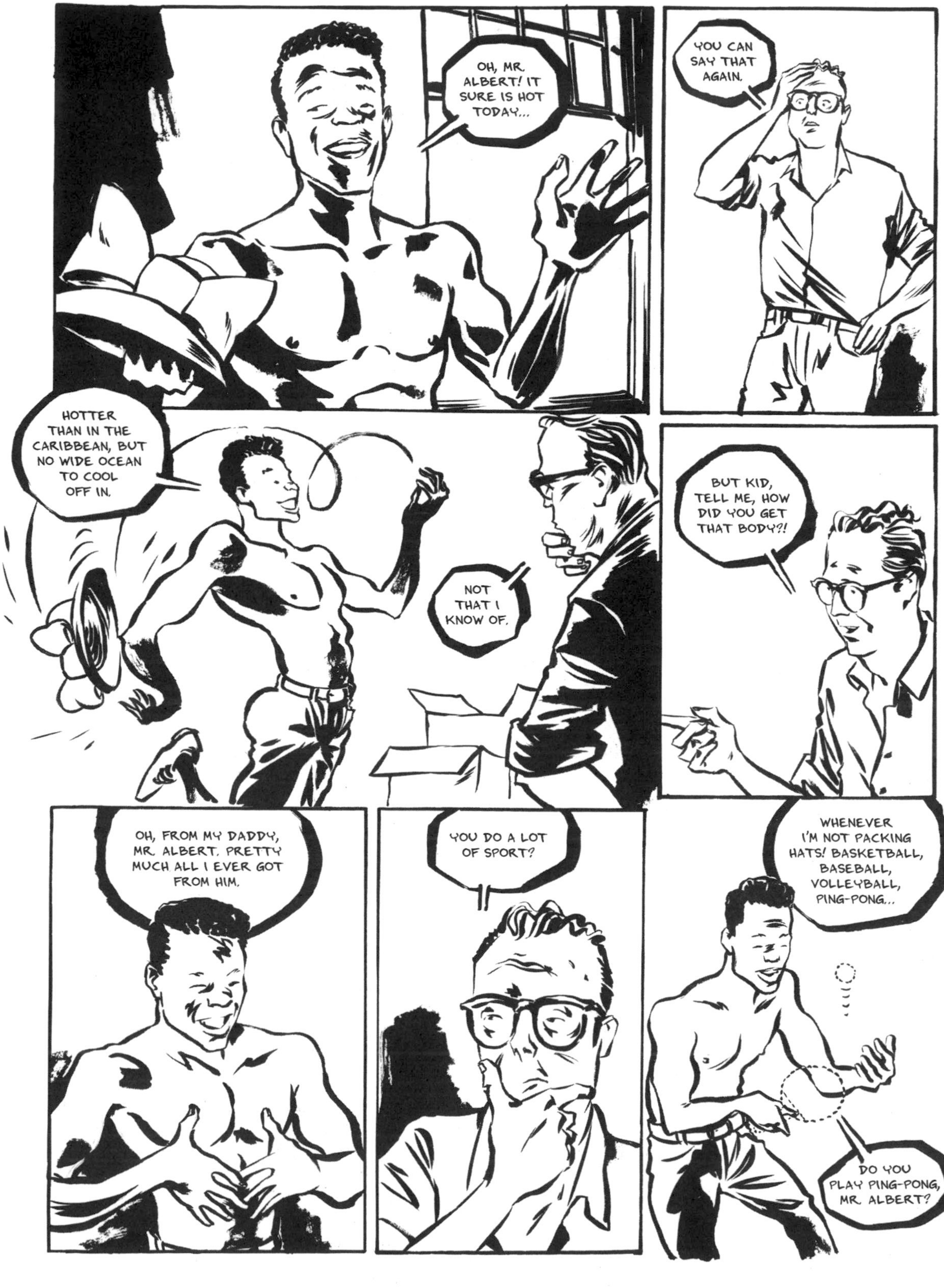
OH, MR. ALBERT! IT SURE IS HOT TODAY...
YOU CAN SAY THAT AGAIN.
HOTTER THAN IN THE CARIBBEAN, BUT NO WIDE OCEAN TO COOL OFF IN.
NOT THAT I KNOW OF.
BUT KID, TELL ME, HOW DID YOU GET THAT BODY?!
OH, FROM MY DADDY, MR. ALBERT. PRETTY MUCH ALL I EVER GOT FROM HIM.
YOU DO A LOT OF SPORT?
WHENEVER I'M NOT PACKING HATS! BASKETBALL, BASEBALL, VOLLEYBALL, PING-PONG...
DO YOU PLAY PING-PONG, MR. ALBERT?

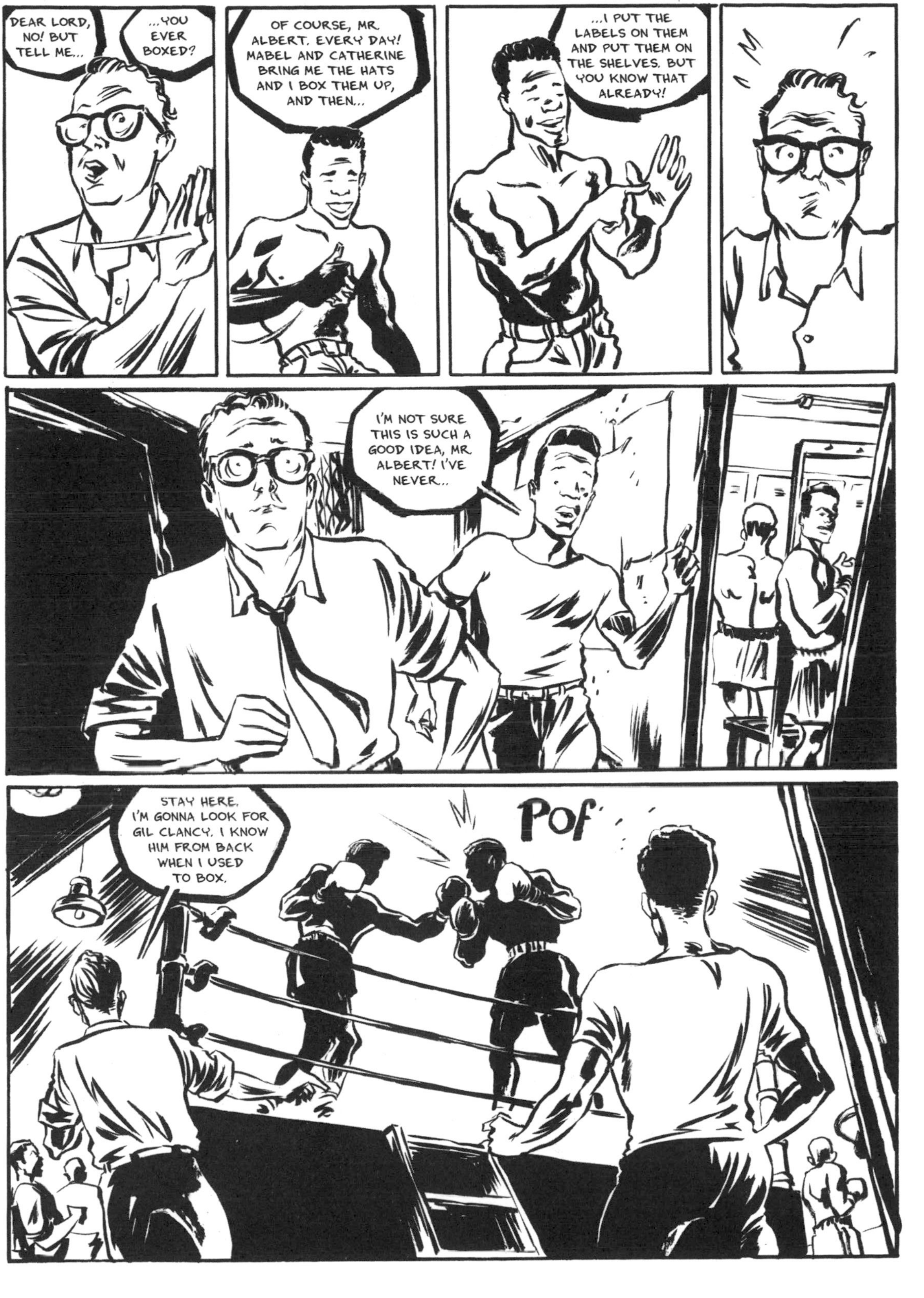
DEAR LORD, NO! BUT TELL ME...
...YOU EVER BOXED?
OF COURSE, MR. ALBERT. EVERY DAY! MABEL AND CATHERINE BRING ME THE HATS AND I BOX THEM UP, AND THEN...
...I PUT THE LABELS ON THEM AND PUT THEM ON THE SHELVES. BUT YOU KNOW THAT ALREADY!
I'M NOT SURE THIS IS SUCH A GOOD IDEA, MR. ALBERT! I'VE NEVER...
STAY HERE. I'M GONNA LOOK FOR GIL CLANCY. I KNOW HIM FROM BACK WHEN I USED TO BOX.
POF

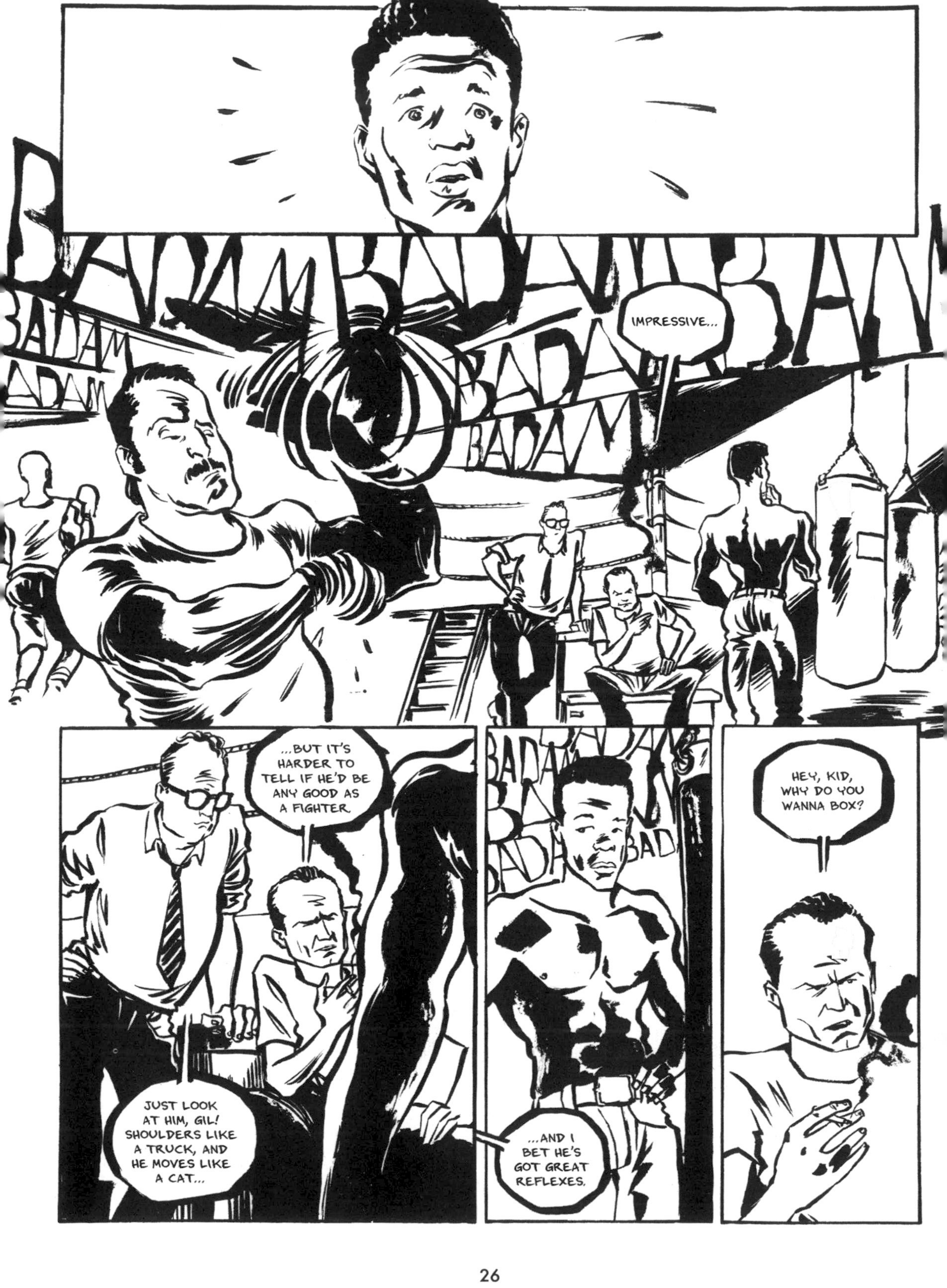
BADAM
BADAM
BADAM
BADAM
BADAM
IMPRESSIVE...
...BUT IT'S HARDER TO TELL IF HE'D BE ANY GOOD AS A FIGHTER.
JUST LOOK AT HIM, GIL! SHOULDERS LIKE A TRUCK, AND HE MOVES LIKE A CAT...
BADAM
BADAM
BAD
...AND I BET HE'S GOT GREAT REFLEXES.
HEY, KID, WHY DO YOU WANNA BOX?

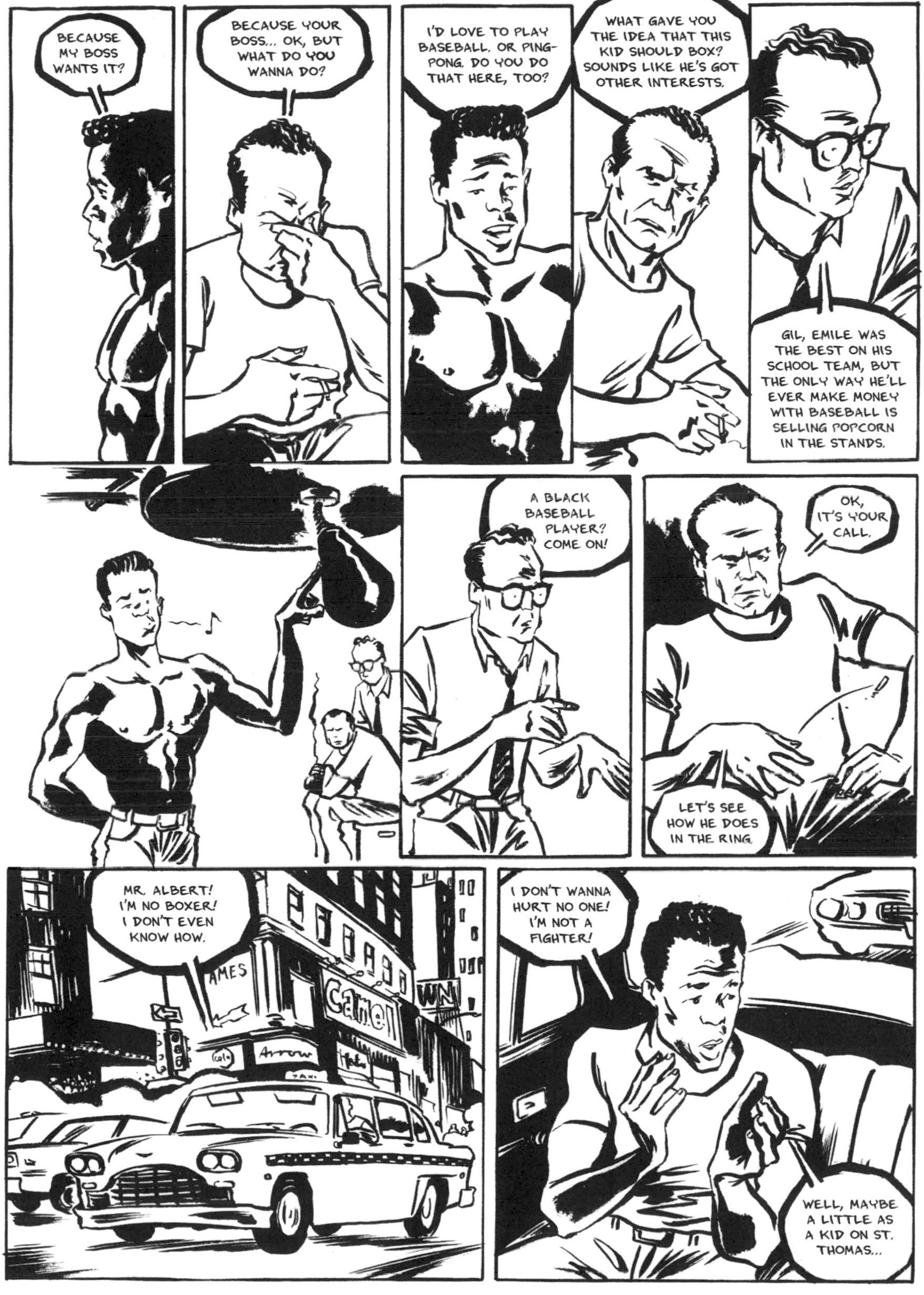

BECAUSE MY BOSS WANTS IT?
BECAUSE YOUR BOSS... OK, BUT WHAT DO YOU WANNA DO?
I'D LOVE TO PLAY BASEBALL. OR PING-PONG. DO YOU DO THAT HERE, TOO?
WHAT GAVE YOU THE IDEA THAT THIS KID SHOULD BOX? SOUNDS LIKE HE'S GOT OTHER INTERESTS.
GIL, EMILE WAS THE BEST ON HIS SCHOOL TEAM, BUT THE ONLY WAY HE'LL EVER MAKE MONEY WITH BASEBALL IS SELLING POPCORN IN THE STANDS.
A BLACK BASEBALL PLAYER? COME ON!
OK, IT'S YOUR CALL.
LET'S SEE HOW HE DOES IN THE RING.
MR. ALBERT! I'M NO BOXER! I DON'T EVEN KNOW HOW.
AMES
Camel
Arrow
I DON'T WANNA HURT NO ONE! I'M NOT A FIGHTER!
WELL, MAYBE A LITTLE AS A KID ON ST. THOMAS...

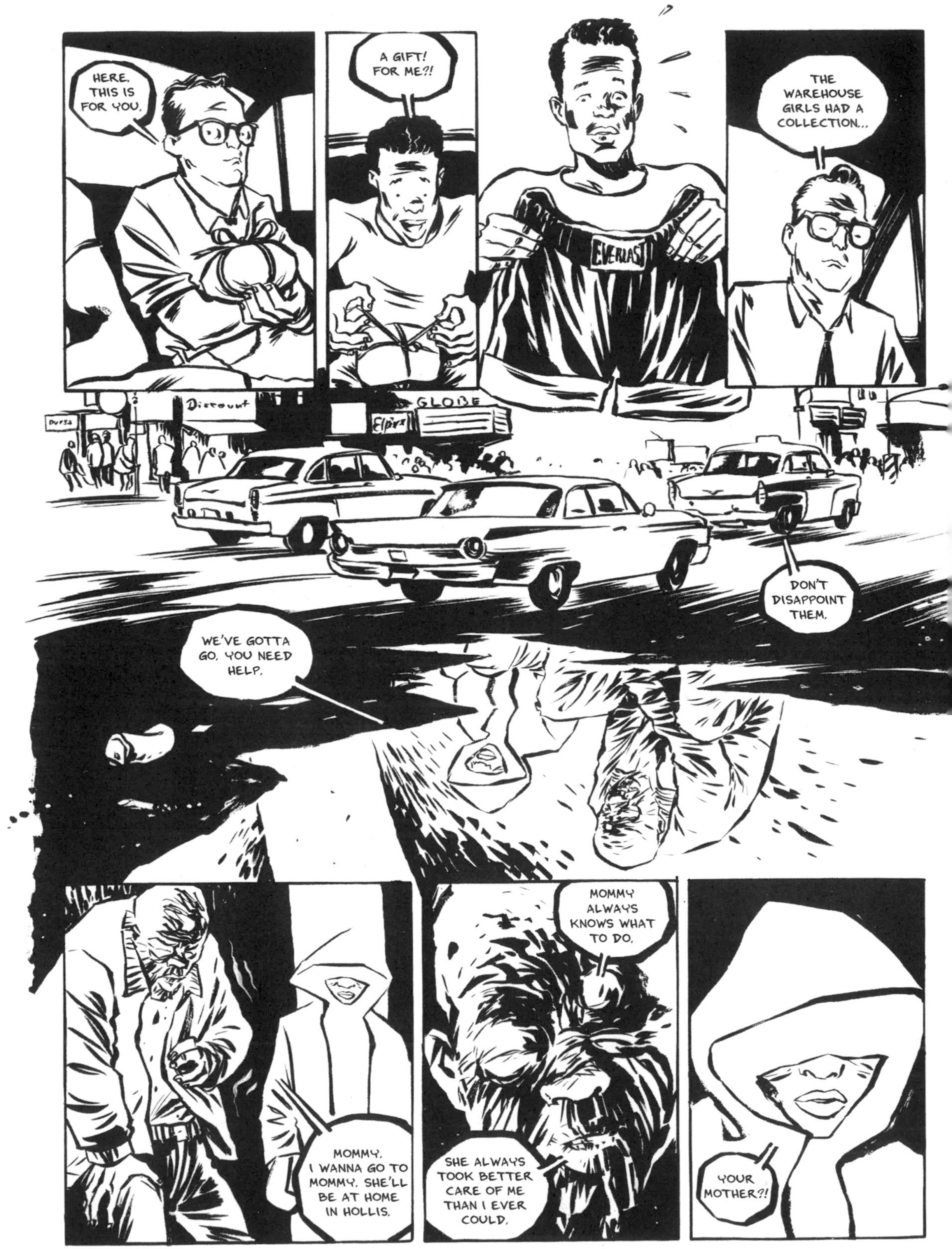
HERE, THIS IS FOR YOU.
A GIFT! FOR ME?!
EVERLAST
THE WAREHOUSE GIRLS HAD A COLLECTION...
Discount
GLOBE
DON'T DISAPPOINT THEM.
WE'VE GOTTA GO. YOU NEED HELP.
MOMMY, I WANNA GO TO MOMMY. SHE'LL BE AT HOME IN HOLLIS.
MOMMY ALWAYS KNOWS WHAT TO DO.
SHE ALWAYS TOOK BETTER CARE OF ME THAN I EVER COULD.
YOUR MOTHER?!

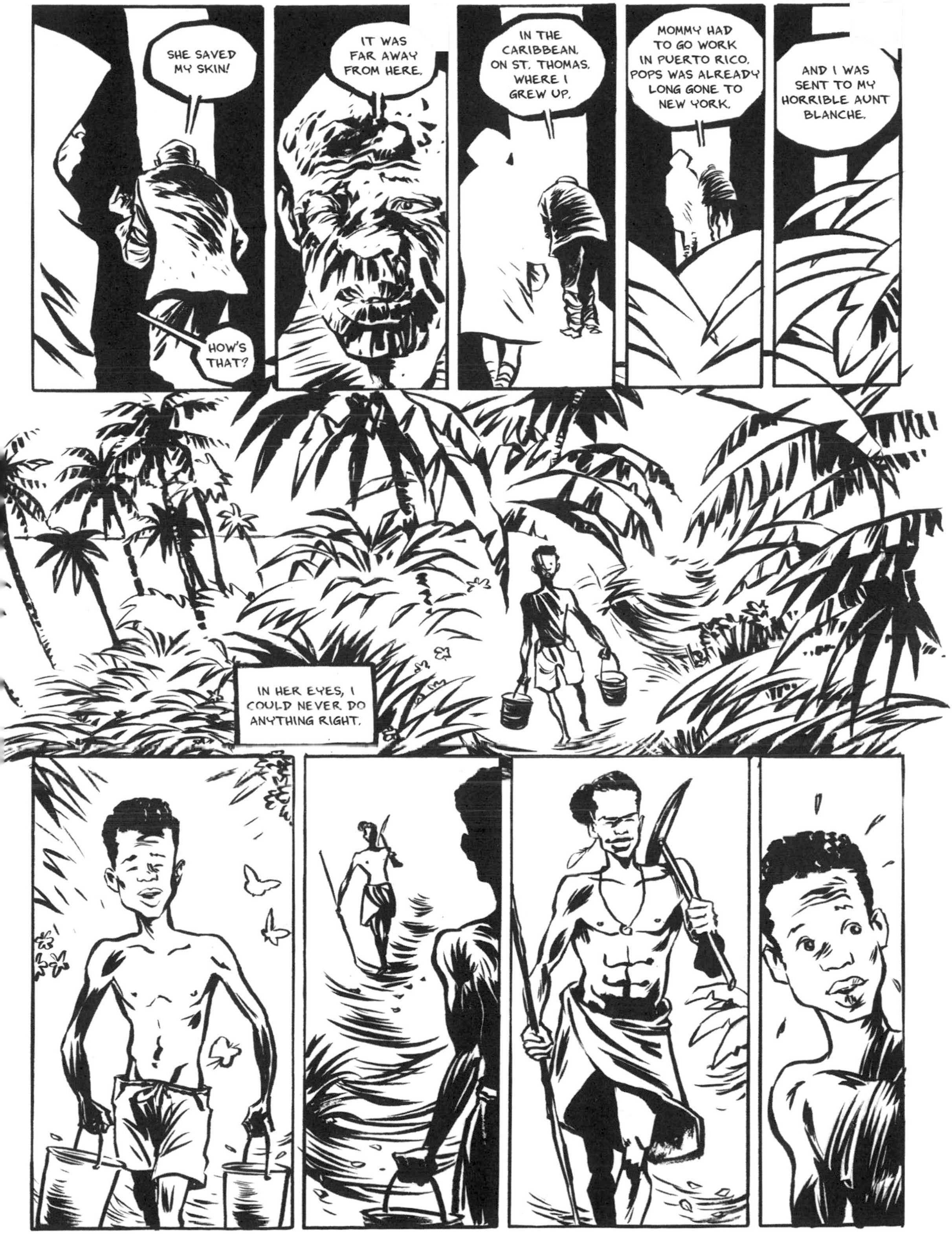
SHE SAVED MY SKIN!
HOW'S THAT?
IT WAS FAR AWAY FROM HERE.
IN THE CARIBBEAN, ON ST. THOMAS, WHERE I GREW UP.
MOMMY HAD TO GO WORK IN PUERTO RICO, POPS WAS ALREADY LONG GONE TO NEW YORK.
AND I WAS SENT TO MY HORRIBLE AUNT BLANCHE.
IN HER EYES, I COULD NEVER DO ANYTHING RIGHT.

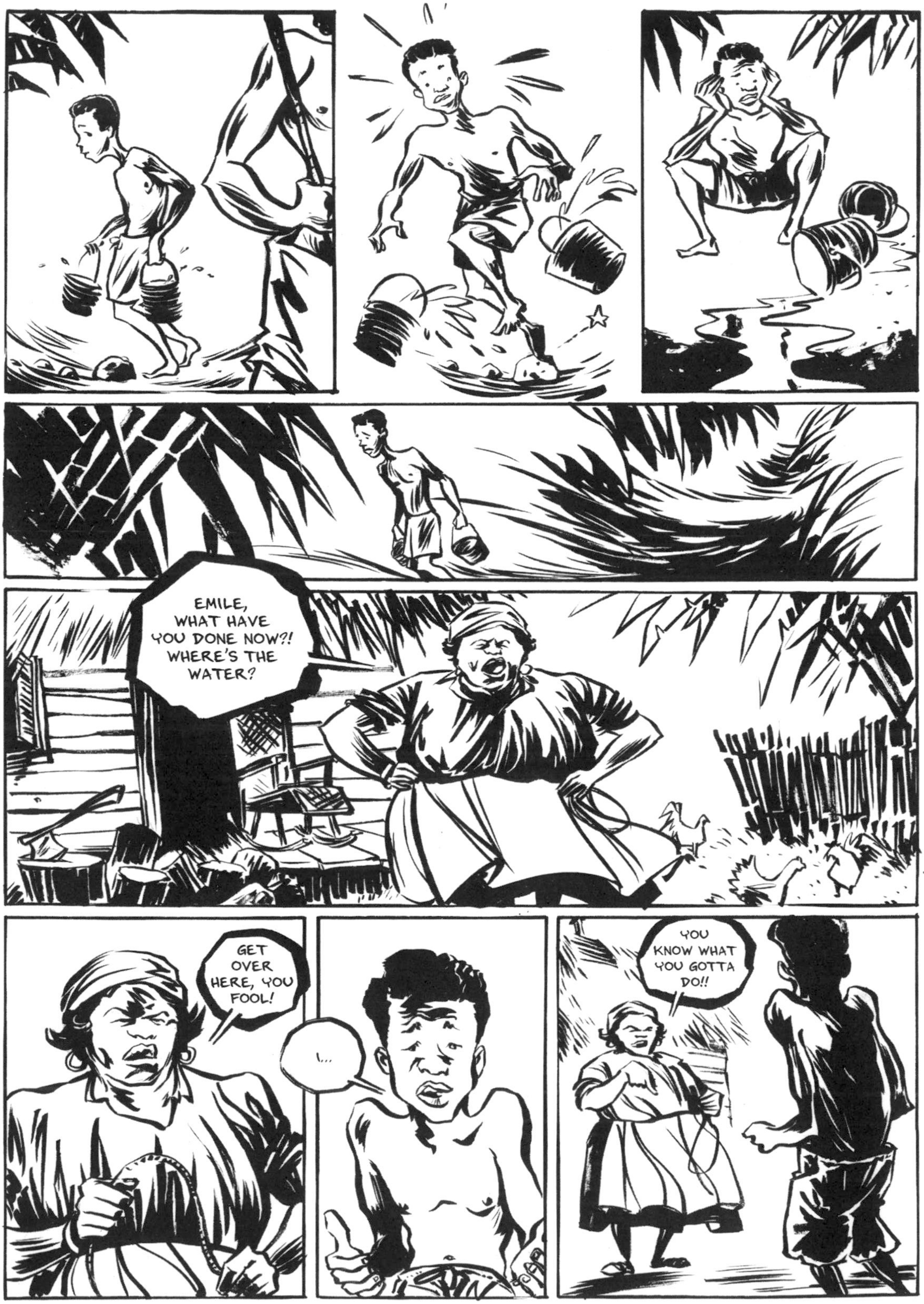
EMILE, WHAT HAVE YOU DONE NOW?! WHERE'S THE WATER?
GET OVER HERE, YOU FOOL!
I...
YOU KNOW WHAT YOU GOTTA DO!!

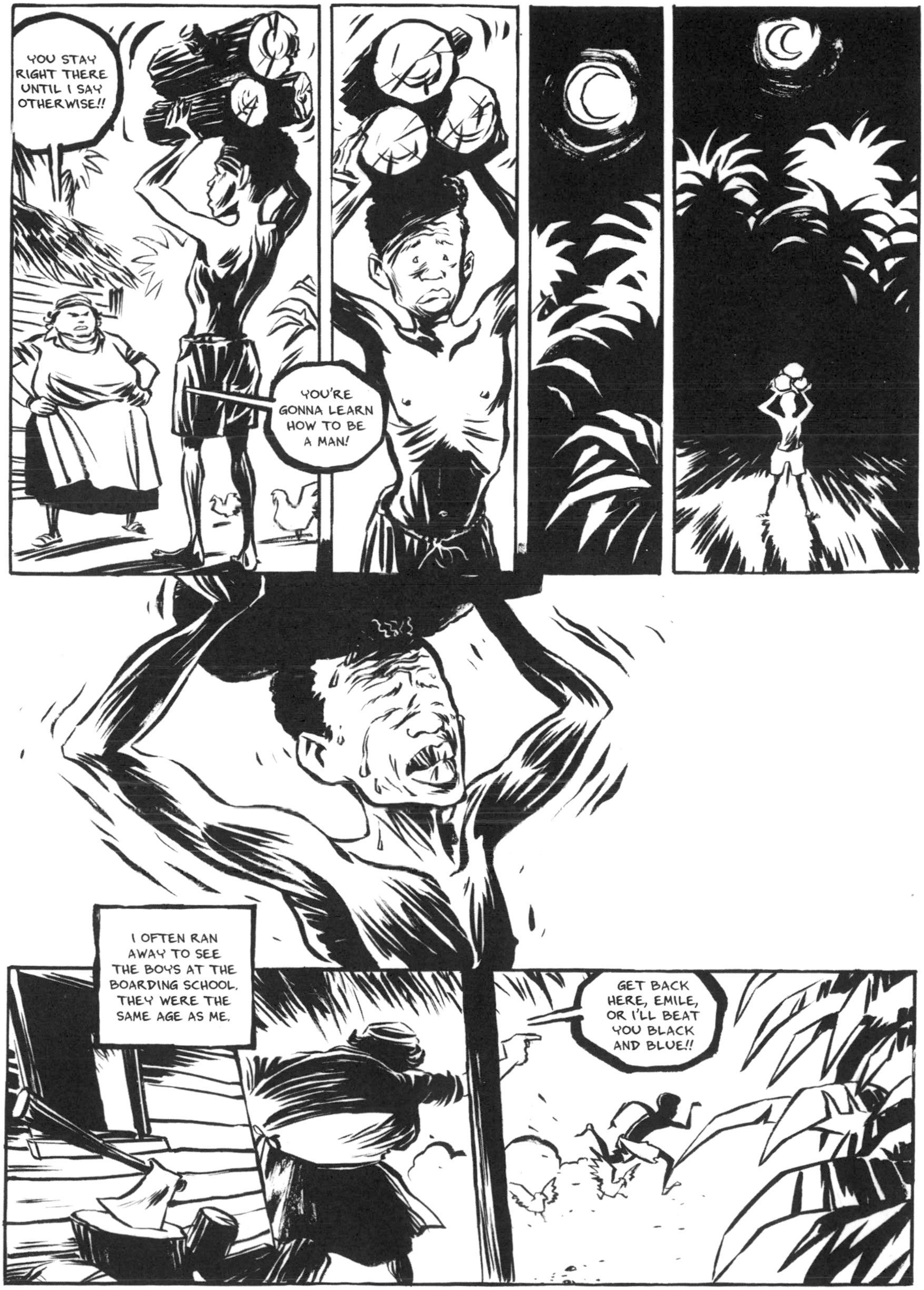
YOU STAY RIGHT THERE UNTIL I SAY OTHERWISE!!
YOU'RE GONNA LEARN HOW TO BE A MAN!
I OFTEN RAN AWAY TO SEE THE BOYS AT THE BOARDING SCHOOL. THEY WERE THE SAME AGE AS ME.
GET BACK HERE, EMILE, OR I'LL BEAT YOU BLACK AND BLUE!!

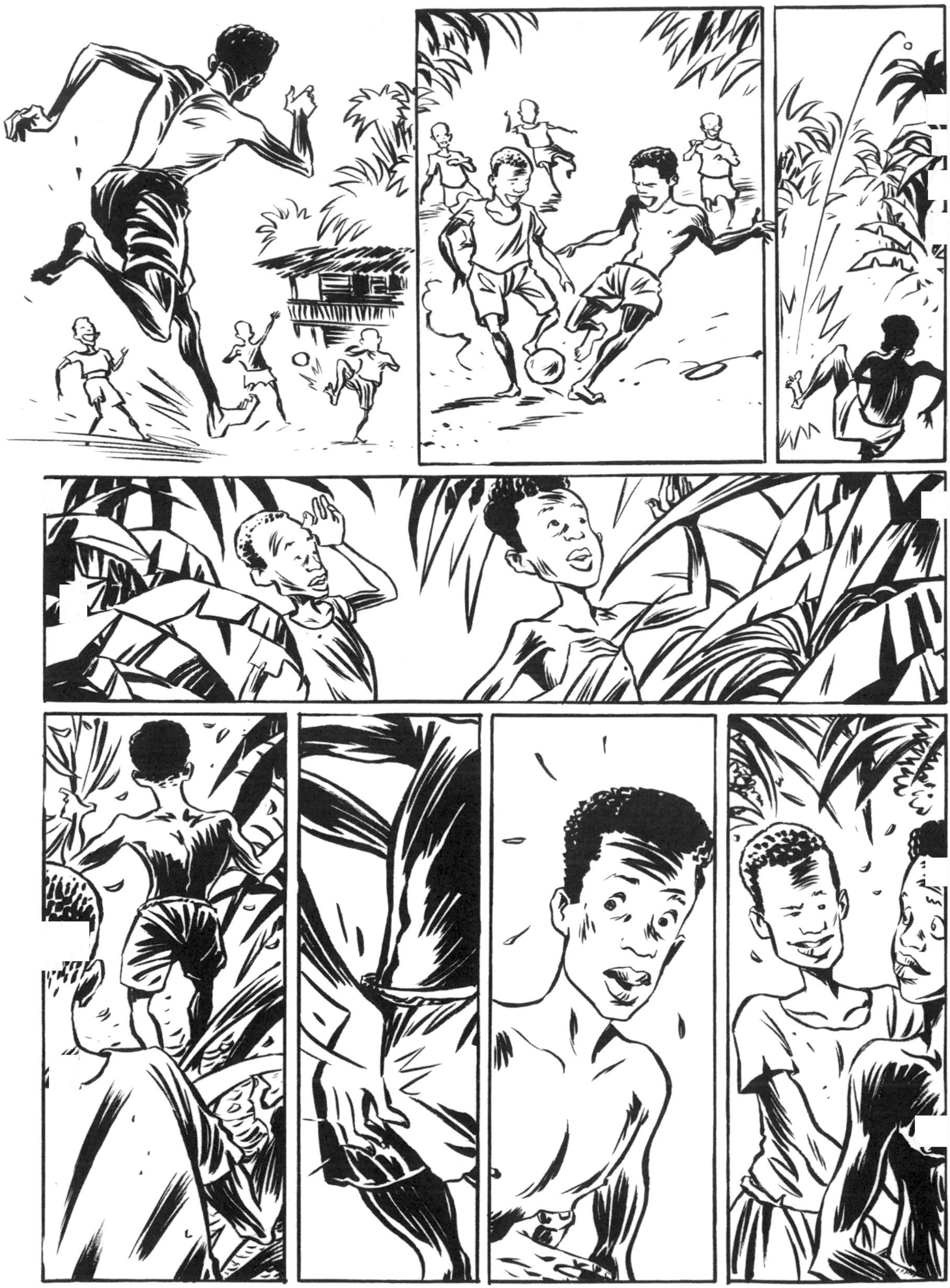

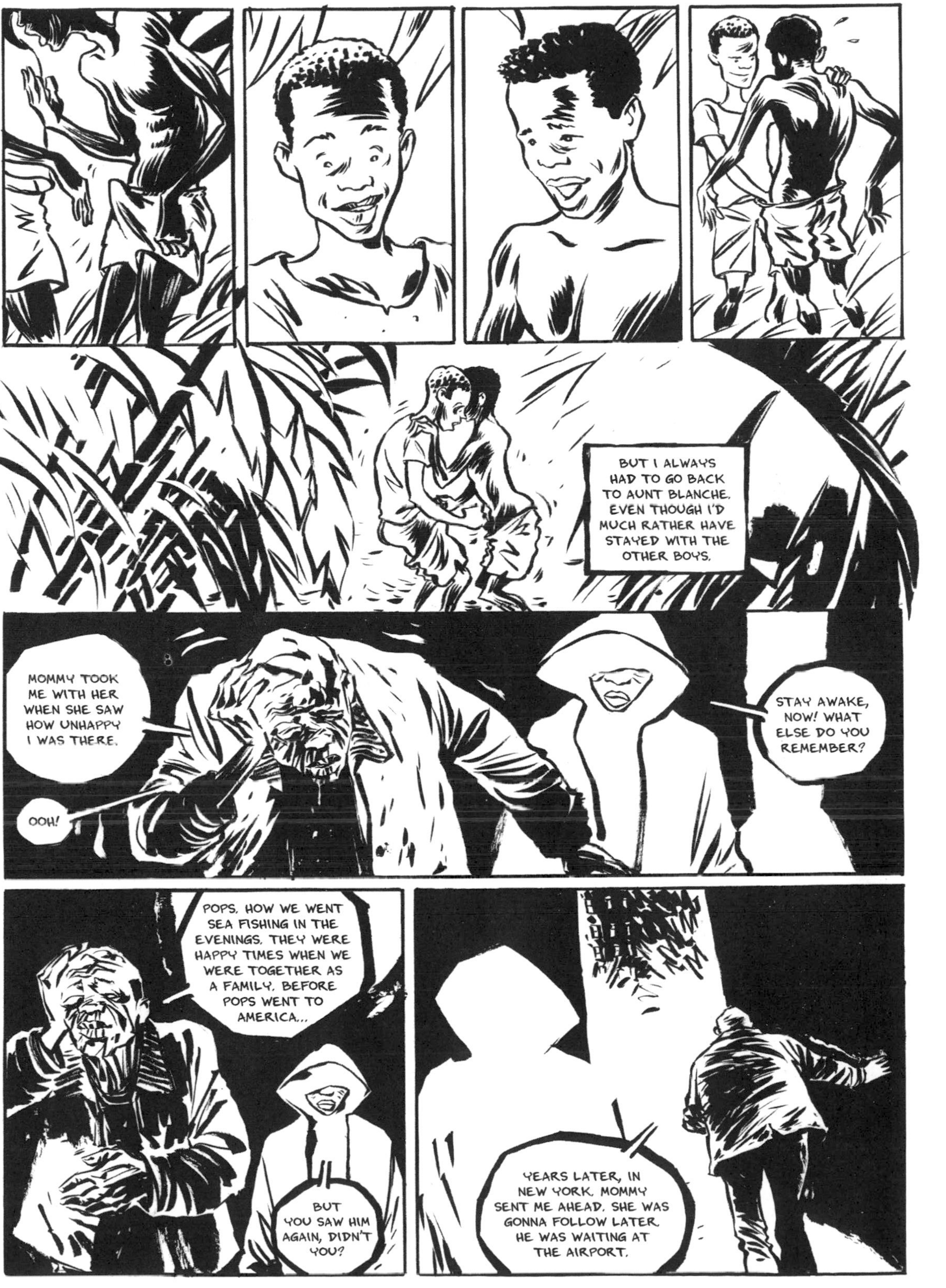
BUT I ALWAYS HAD TO GO BACK TO AUNT BLANCHE, EVEN THOUGH I'D MUCH RATHER HAVE STAYED WITH THE OTHER BOYS.
MOMMY TOOK ME WITH HER WHEN SHE SAW HOW UNHAPPY I WAS THERE.
OOH!
STAY AWAKE, NOW! WHAT ELSE DO YOU REMEMBER?
POPS, HOW WE WENT SEA FISHING IN THE EVENINGS. THEY WERE HAPPY TIMES WHEN WE WERE TOGETHER AS A FAMILY, BEFORE POPS WENT TO AMERICA...
BUT YOU SAW HIM AGAIN, DIDN'T YOU?
YEARS LATER, IN NEW YORK. MOMMY SENT ME AHEAD. SHE WAS GONNA FOLLOW LATER. HE WAS WAITING AT THE AIRPORT.

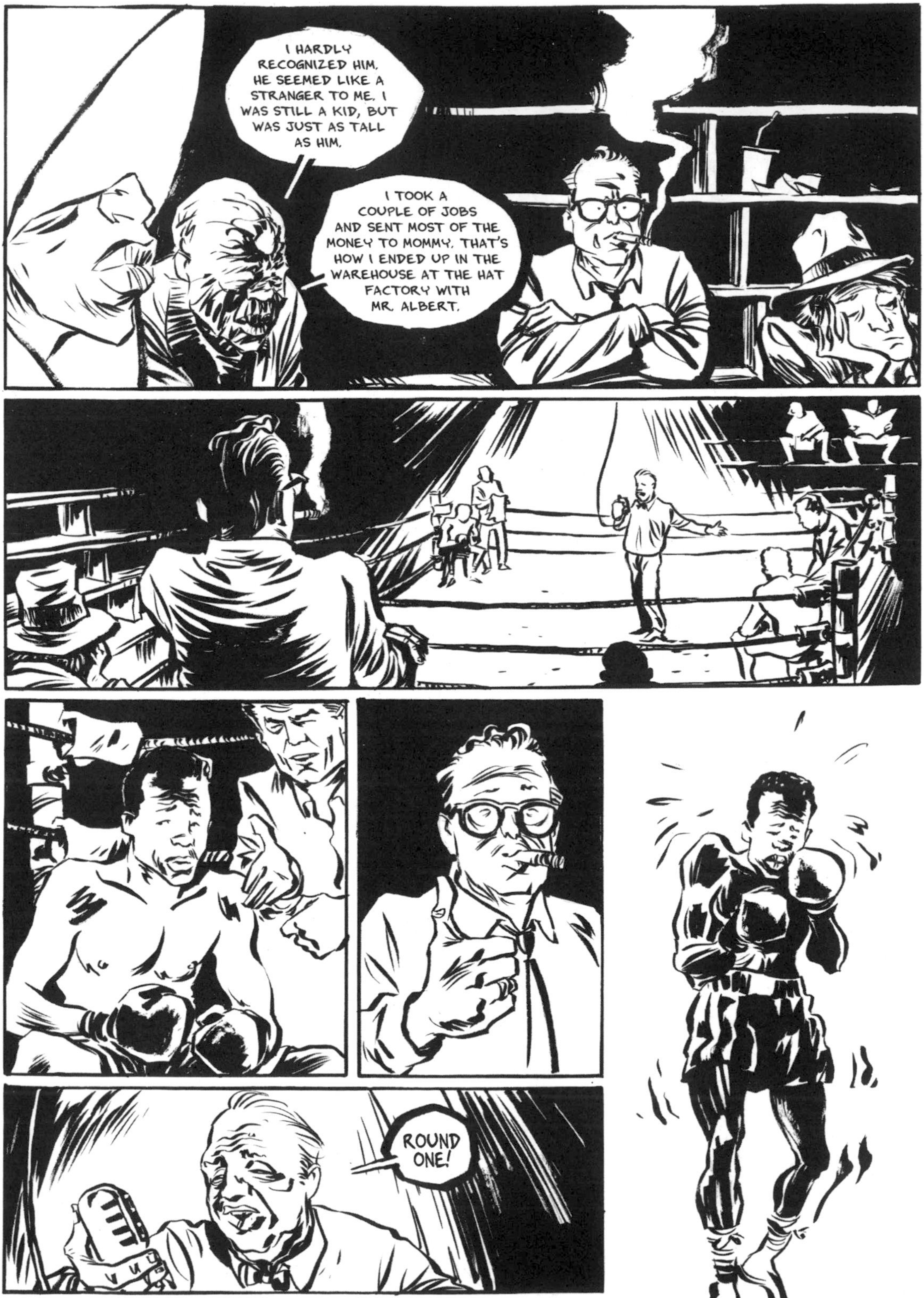
I HARDLY RECOGNIZED HIM. HE SEEMED LIKE A STRANGER TO ME. I WAS STILL A KID, BUT WAS JUST AS TALL AS HIM.
I TOOK A COUPLE OF JOBS AND SENT MOST OF THE MONEY TO MOMMY. THAT'S HOW I ENDED UP IN THE WAREHOUSE AT THE HAT FACTORY WITH MR. ALBERT.
ROUND ONE!

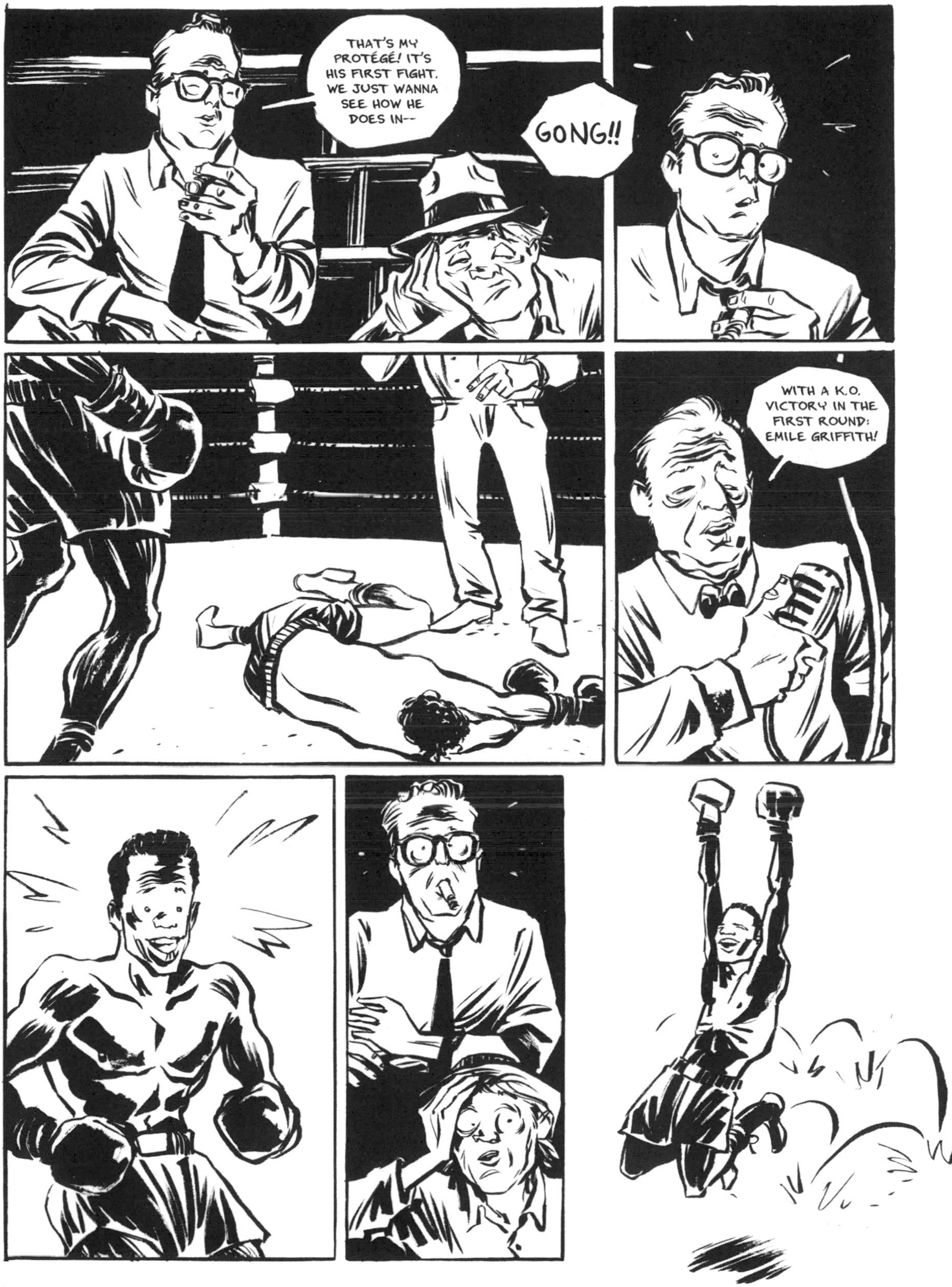
THAT'S MY PROTÉGÉ! IT'S HIS FIRST FIGHT. WE JUST WANNA SEE HOW HE DOES IN--
GONG!!
WITH A K.O. VICTORY IN THE FIRST ROUND: EMILE GRIFFITH!

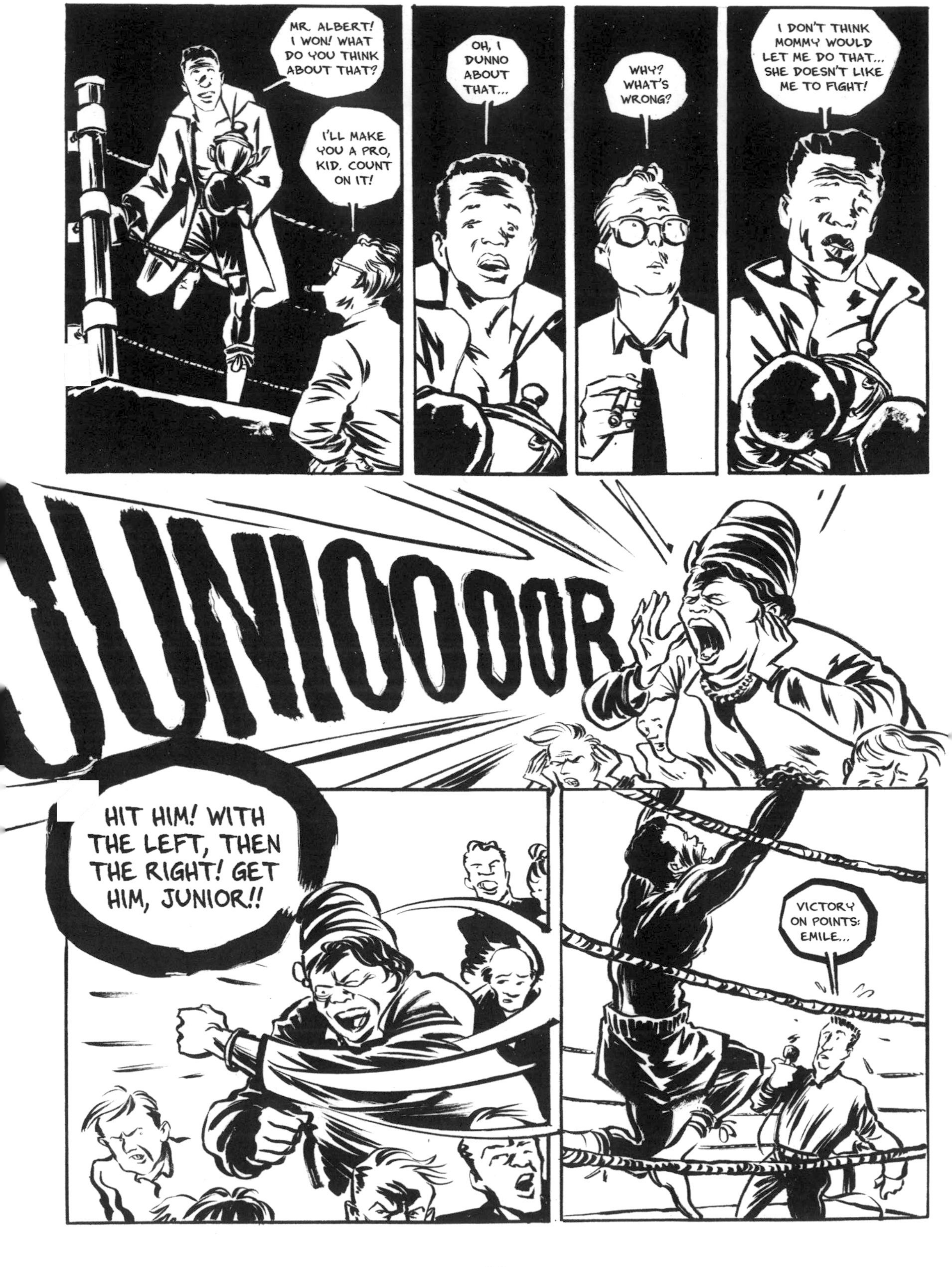
MR. ALBERT! I WON! WHAT DO YOU THINK ABOUT THAT?
I'LL MAKE YOU A PRO, KID. COUNT ON IT!
OH, I DUNNO ABOUT THAT...
WHY? WHAT'S WRONG?
I DON'T THINK MOMMY WOULD LET ME DO THAT... SHE DOESN'T LIKE ME TO FIGHT!
JUNIOOOOR
HIT HIM! WITH THE LEFT, THEN THE RIGHT! GET HIM, JUNIOR!!
VICTORY ON POINTS: EMILE...

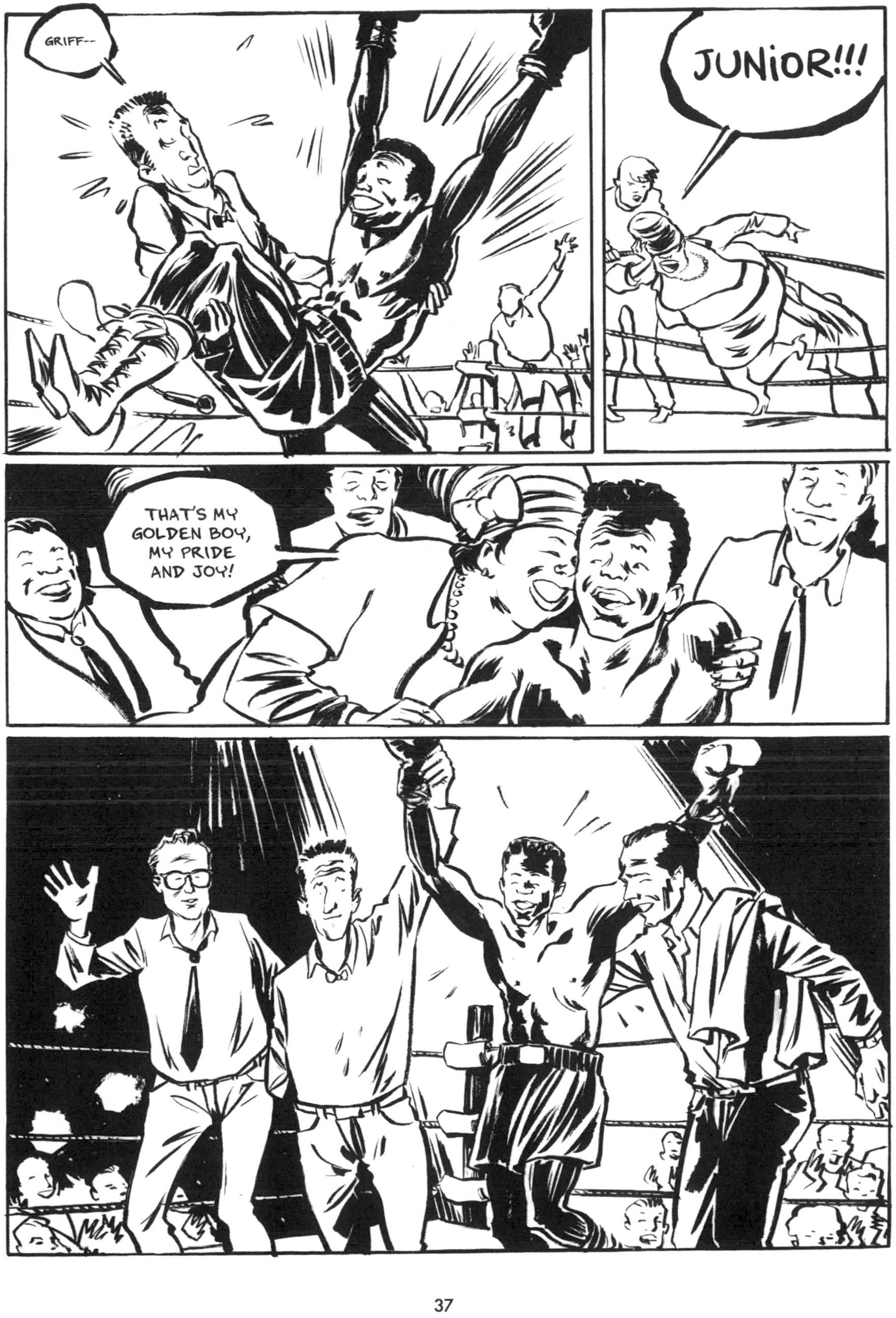
GRIFF--
JUNiOR!!!
THAT'S MY GOLDEN BOY, MY PRIDE AND JOY!

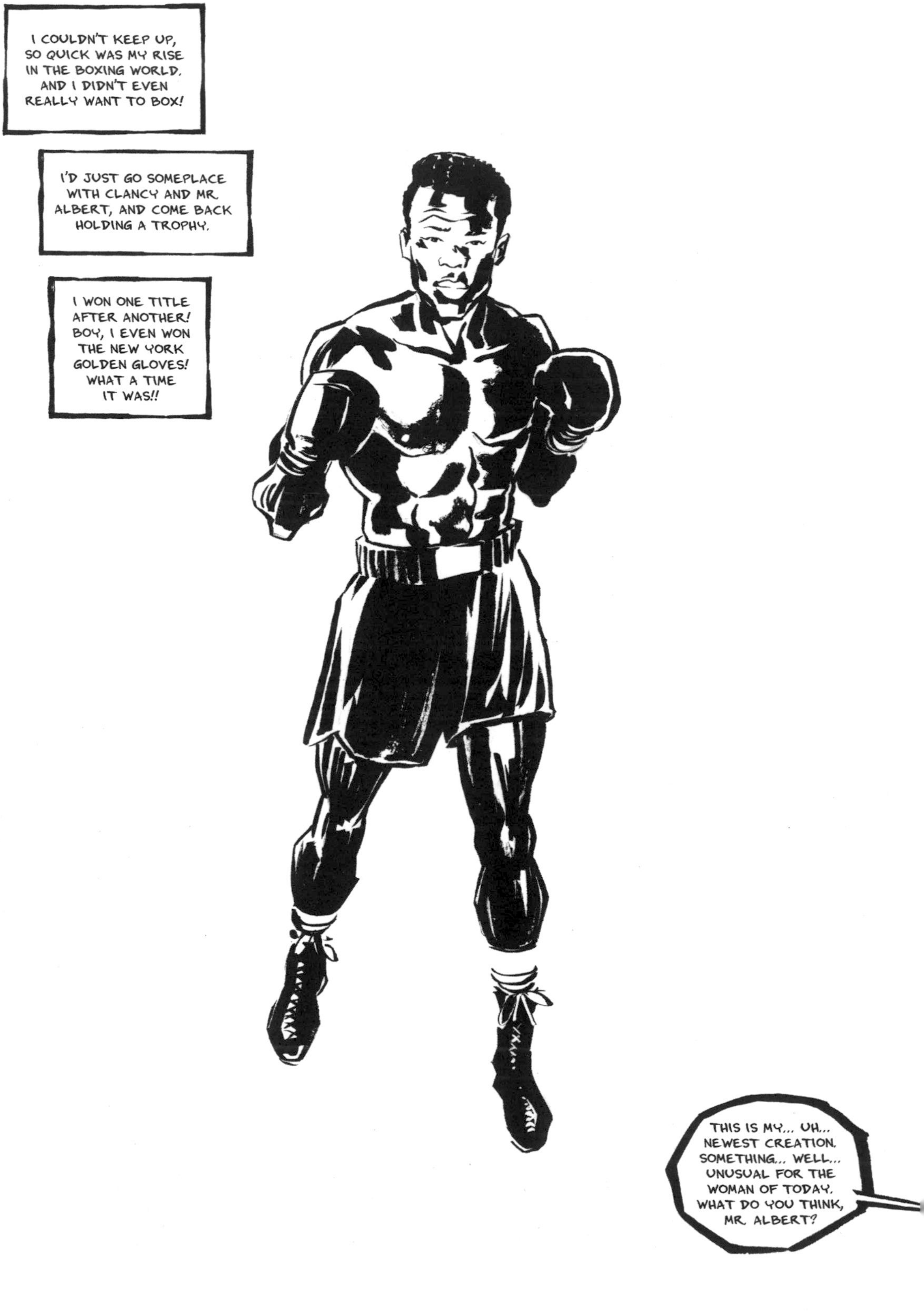
I COULDN'T KEEP UP, SO QUICK WAS MY RISE IN THE BOXING WORLD, AND I DIDN'T EVEN REALLY WANT TO BOX!
I'D JUST GO SOMEPLACE WITH CLANCY AND MR. ALBERT, AND COME BACK HOLDING A TROPHY.
I WON ONE TITLE AFTER ANOTHER! BOY, I EVEN WON THE NEW YORK GOLDEN GLOVES! WHAT A TIME IT WAS!!
THIS IS MY... UH... NEWEST CREATION. SOMETHING... WELL... UNUSUAL FOR THE WOMAN OF TODAY. WHAT DO YOU THINK, MR. ALBERT?

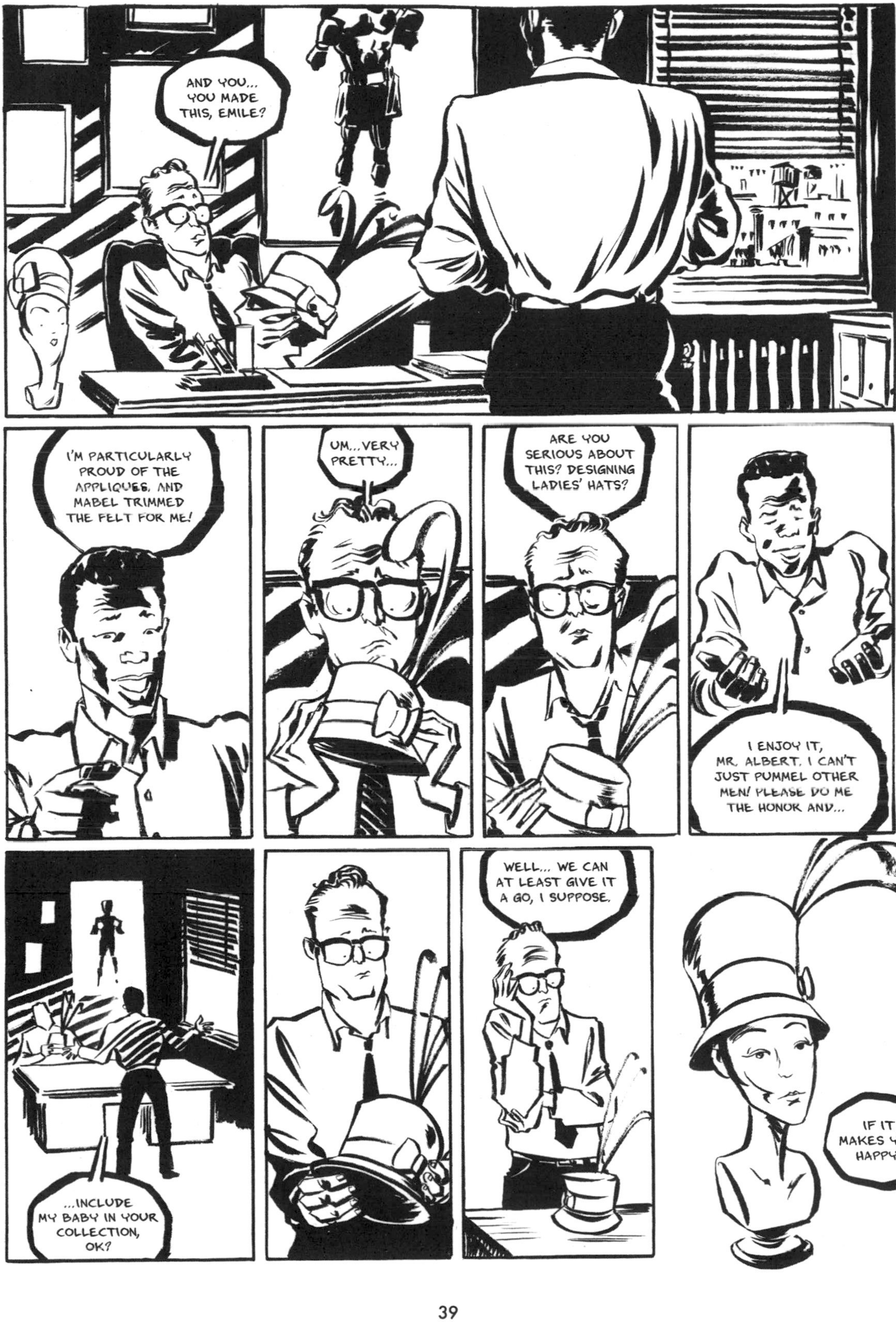
AND YOU... YOU MADE THIS, EMILE?
I'M PARTICULARLY PROUD OF THE APPLIQUES, AND MABEL TRIMMED THE FELT FOR ME!
UM... VERY PRETTY...
ARE YOU SERIOUS ABOUT THIS? DESIGNING LADIES' HATS?
I ENJOY IT, MR. ALBERT. I CAN'T JUST PUMMEL OTHER MEN! PLEASE DO ME THE HONOR AND...
...INCLUDE MY BABY IN YOUR COLLECTION, OK?
WELL... WE CAN AT LEAST GIVE IT A GO, I SUPPOSE.
IF IT MAKES YOU HAPPY.

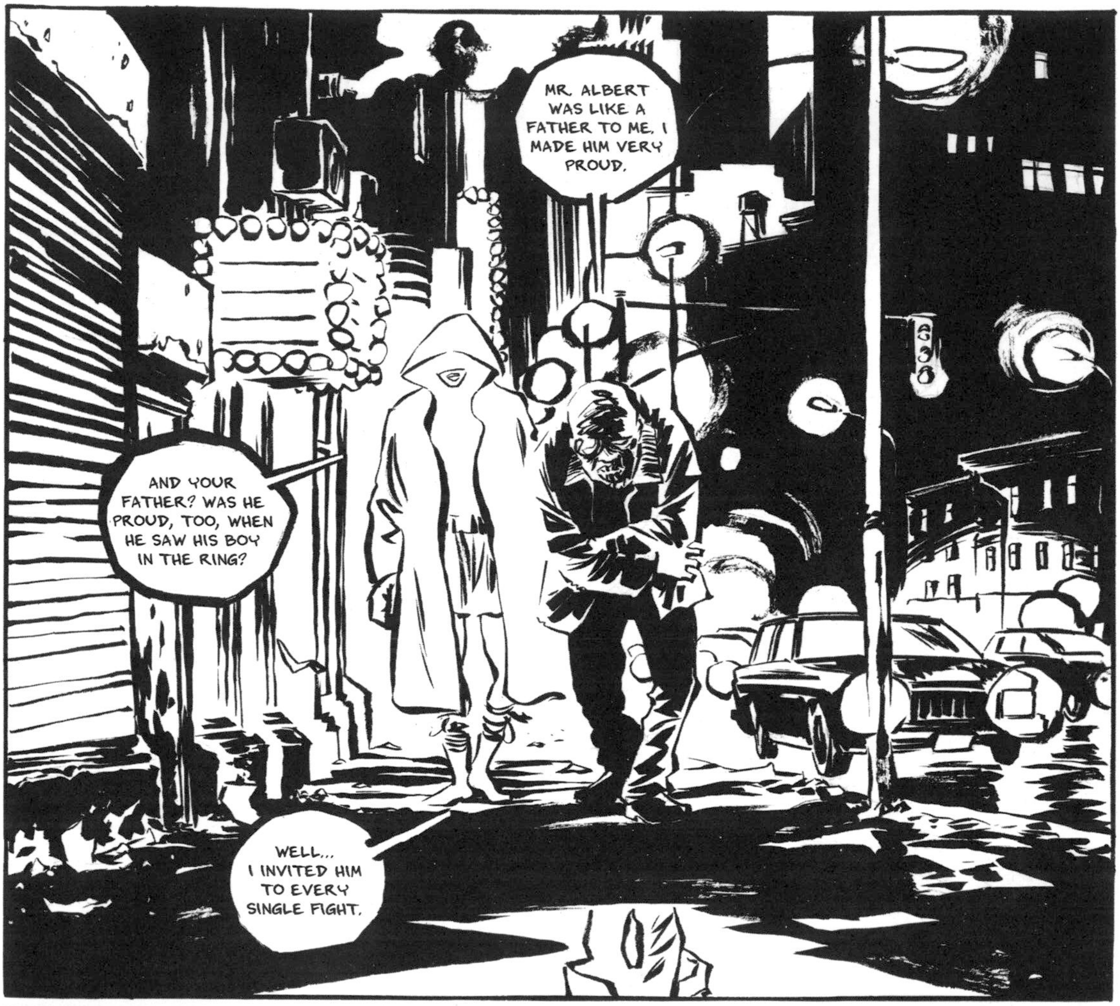
MR. ALBERT WAS LIKE A FATHER TO ME. I MADE HIM VERY PROUD.
AND YOUR FATHER? WAS HE PROUD, TOO, WHEN HE SAW HIS BOY IN THE RING?
WELL... I INVITED HIM TO EVERY SINGLE FIGHT.
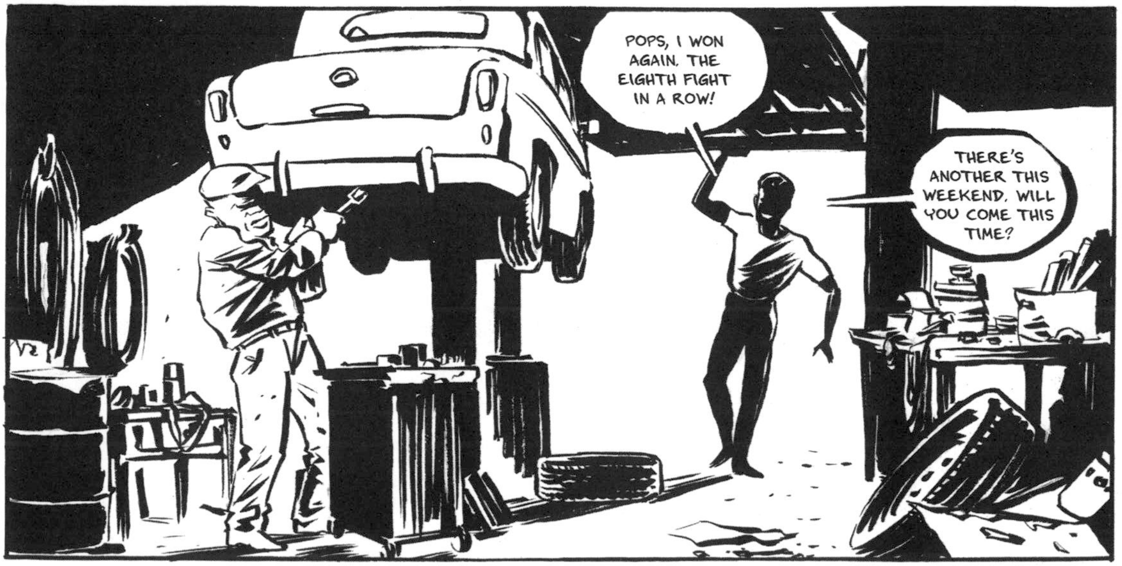
POPS, I WON AGAIN. THE EIGHTH FIGHT IN A ROW!
THERE'S ANOTHER THIS WEEKEND. WILL YOU COME THIS TIME?

SURE, SURE...

HE NEVER SAW YOU FIGHT?

I WANTED HIM TO BE PROUD OF ME.

ONE DAY, I WENT TO HIS SHOP. I THINK IT WAS BEFORE MY TWELFTH OR THIRTEENTH FIGHT.

WHERE'S MY POPS?

YOU FINALLY CAME, KID. WE DIDN'T KNOW HOW TO REACH YOU OR YOUR MOM.

YOUR DAD LEFT WORK LAST NIGHT. I FOUND HIM A FEW STREETS FROM HERE. LOOKS LIKE IT WAS A HEART ATTACK.

I'M SORRY, KID.

41

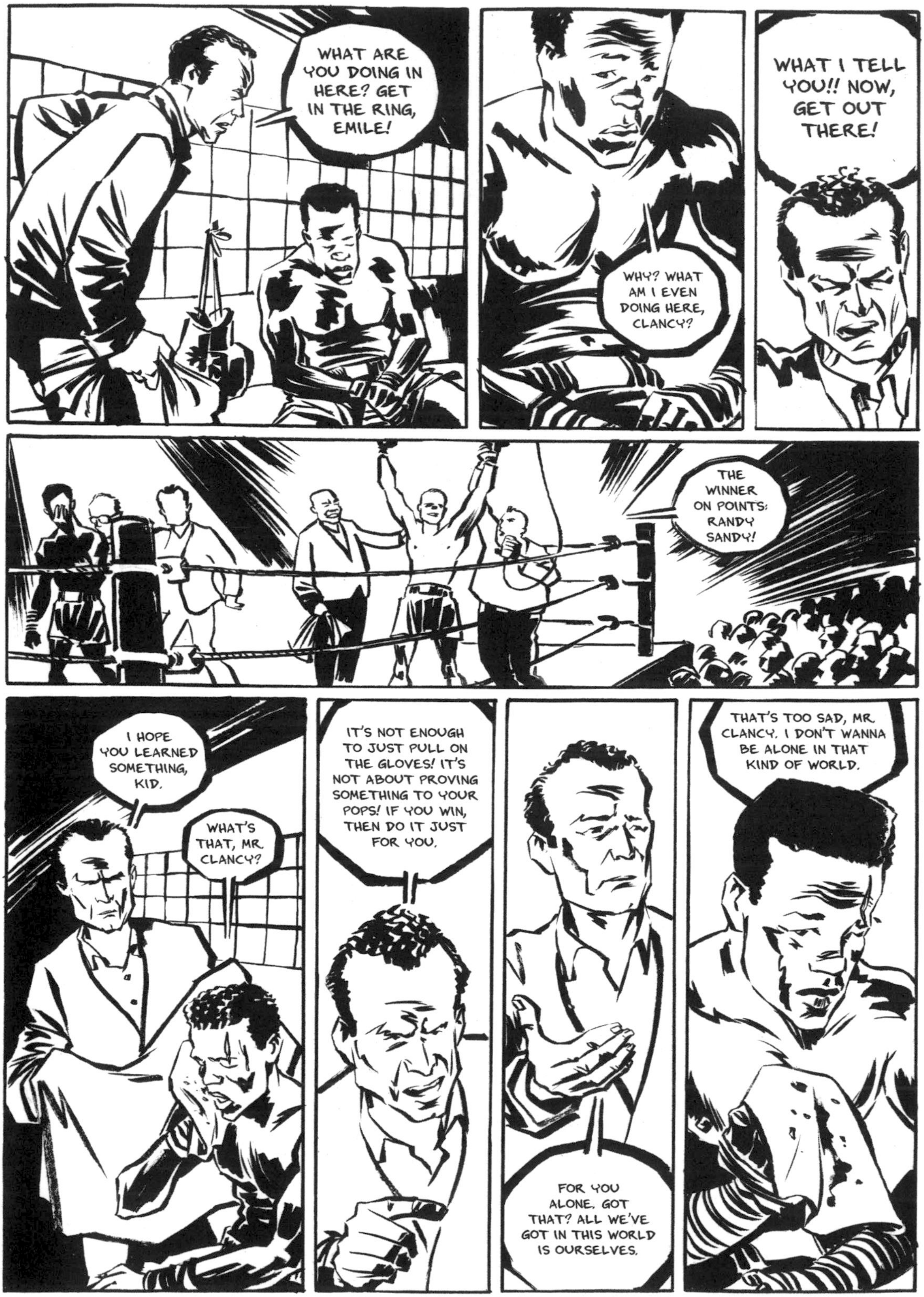

WHAT ARE YOU DOING IN HERE? GET IN THE RING, EMILE!
WHY? WHAT AM I EVEN DOING HERE, CLANCY?
WHAT I TELL YOU!! NOW, GET OUT THERE!
THE WINNER ON POINTS: RANDY SANDY!
I HOPE YOU LEARNED SOMETHING, KID.
WHAT'S THAT, MR. CLANCY?
IT'S NOT ENOUGH TO JUST PULL ON THE GLOVES! IT'S NOT ABOUT PROVING SOMETHING TO YOUR POPS! IF YOU WIN, THEN DO IT JUST FOR YOU.
FOR YOU ALONE. GOT THAT? ALL WE'VE GOT IN THIS WORLD IS OURSELVES.
THAT'S TOO SAD, MR. CLANCY. I DON'T WANNA BE ALONE IN THAT KIND OF WORLD.

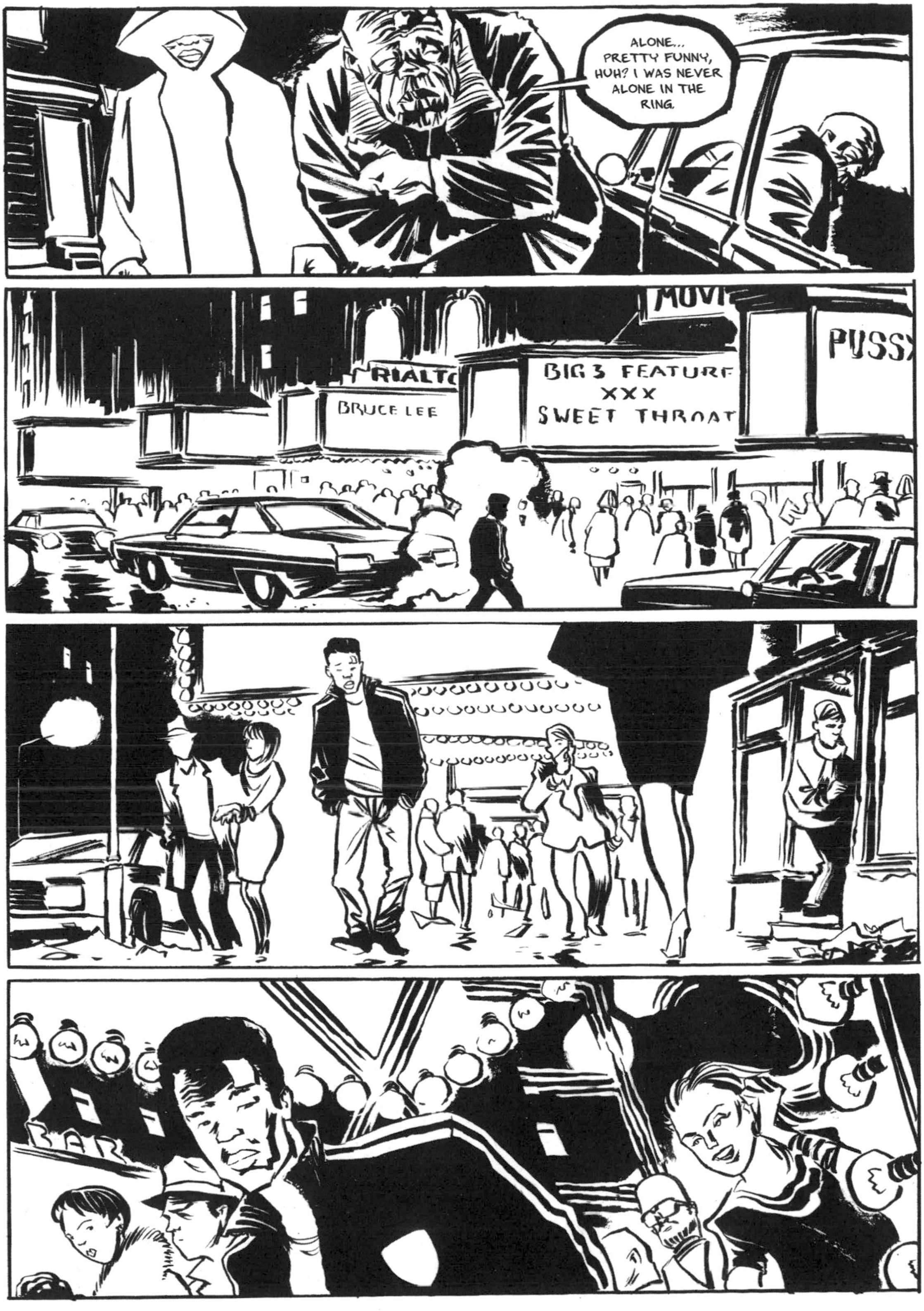
ALONE... PRETTY FUNNY, HUH? I WAS NEVER ALONE IN THE RING.
MOVI
PUSSY
RIALTO
BRUCE LEE
BIG 3 FEATURE
XXX
SWEET THROAT
BAR

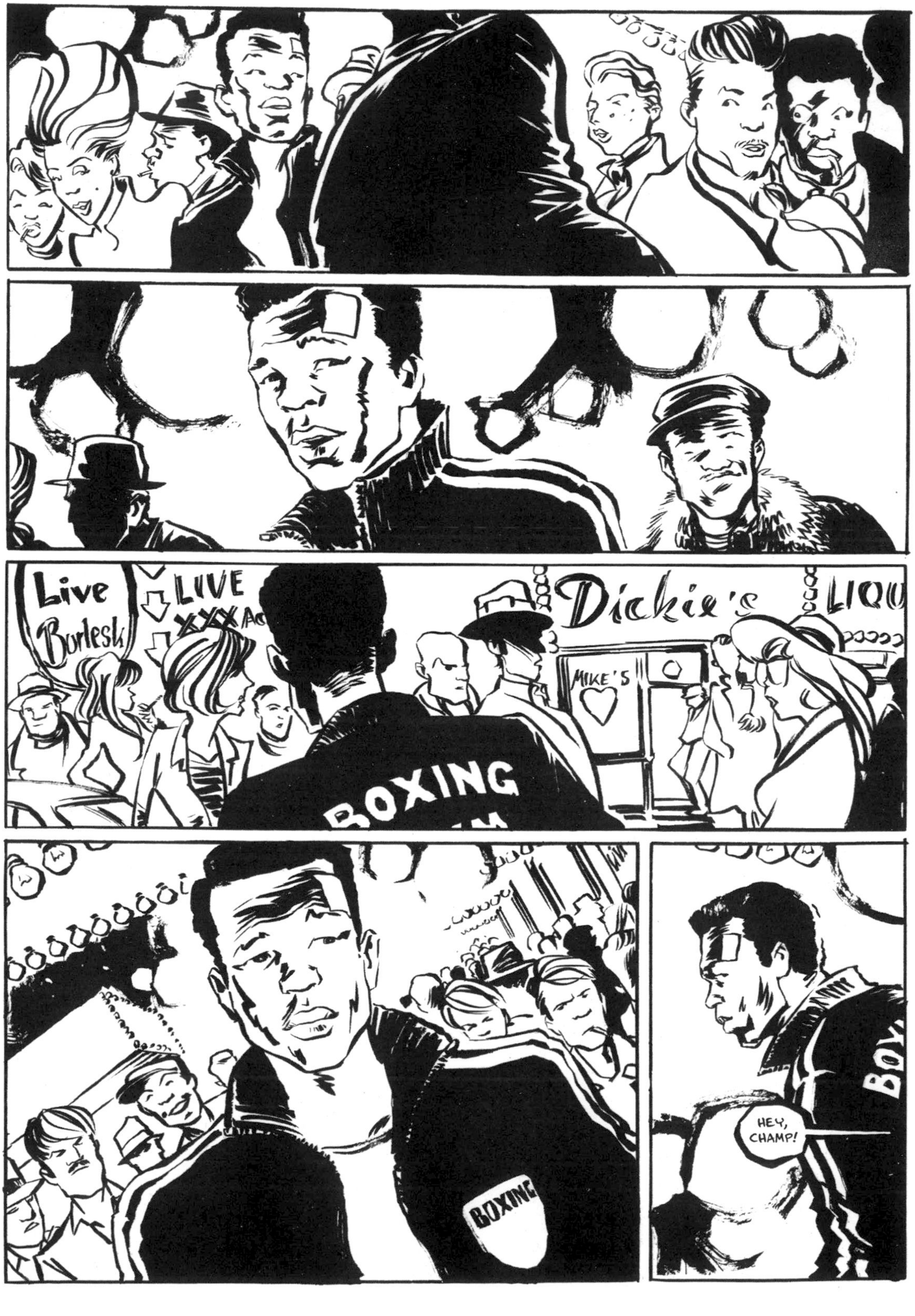
Live Burlesk
LIVE
XXX
Dickie's
MIKE'S
BOXING
BOXING
HEY, CHAMP!

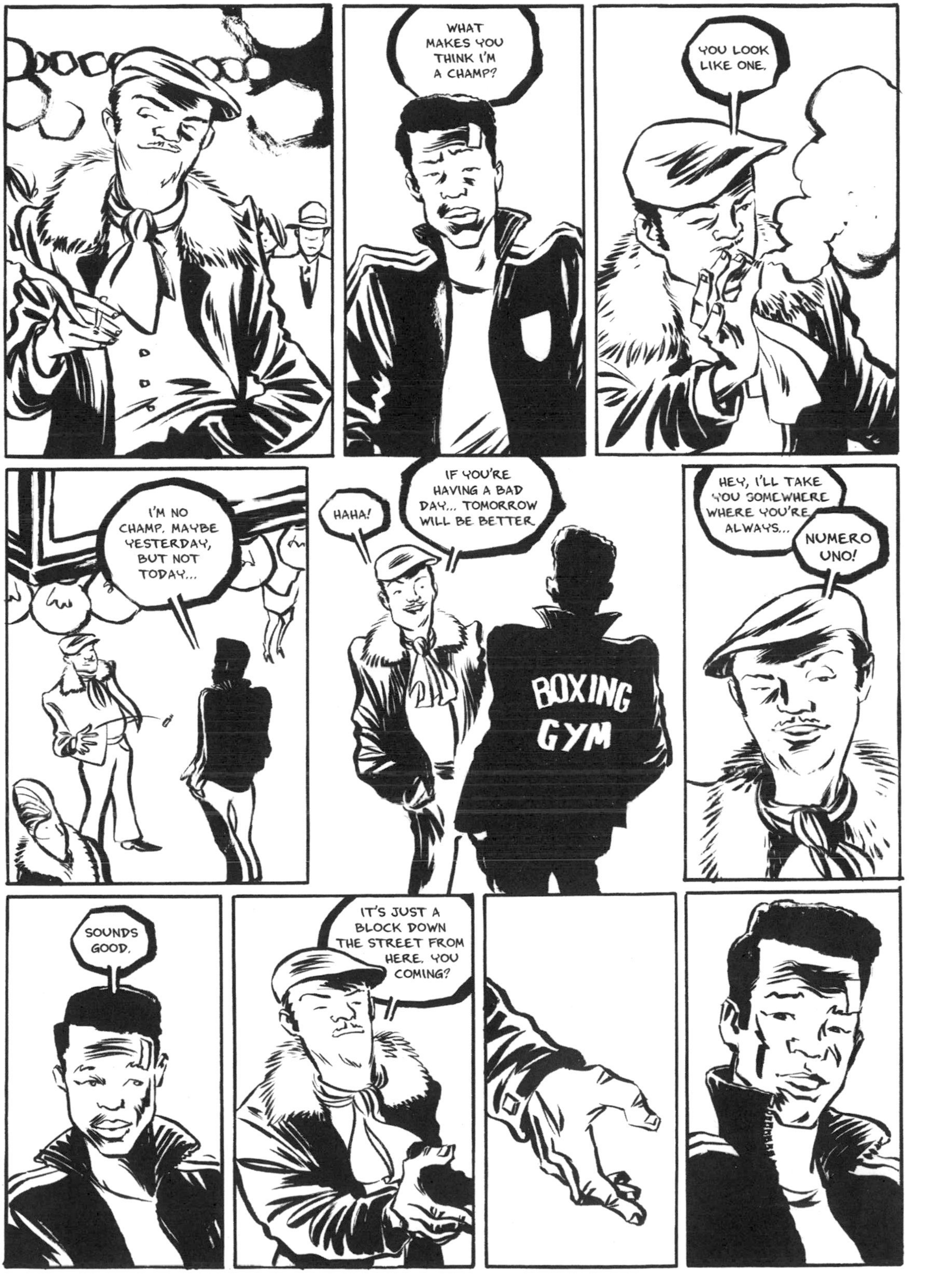
WHAT MAKES YOU THINK I'M A CHAMP?
YOU LOOK LIKE ONE.
I'M NO CHAMP. MAYBE YESTERDAY, BUT NOT TODAY...
HAHA!
IF YOU'RE HAVING A BAD DAY... TOMORROW WILL BE BETTER.
BOXING GYM
HEY, I'LL TAKE YOU SOMEWHERE WHERE YOU'RE ALWAYS...
NUMERO UNO!
SOUNDS GOOD.
IT'S JUST A BLOCK DOWN THE STREET FROM HERE. YOU COMING?

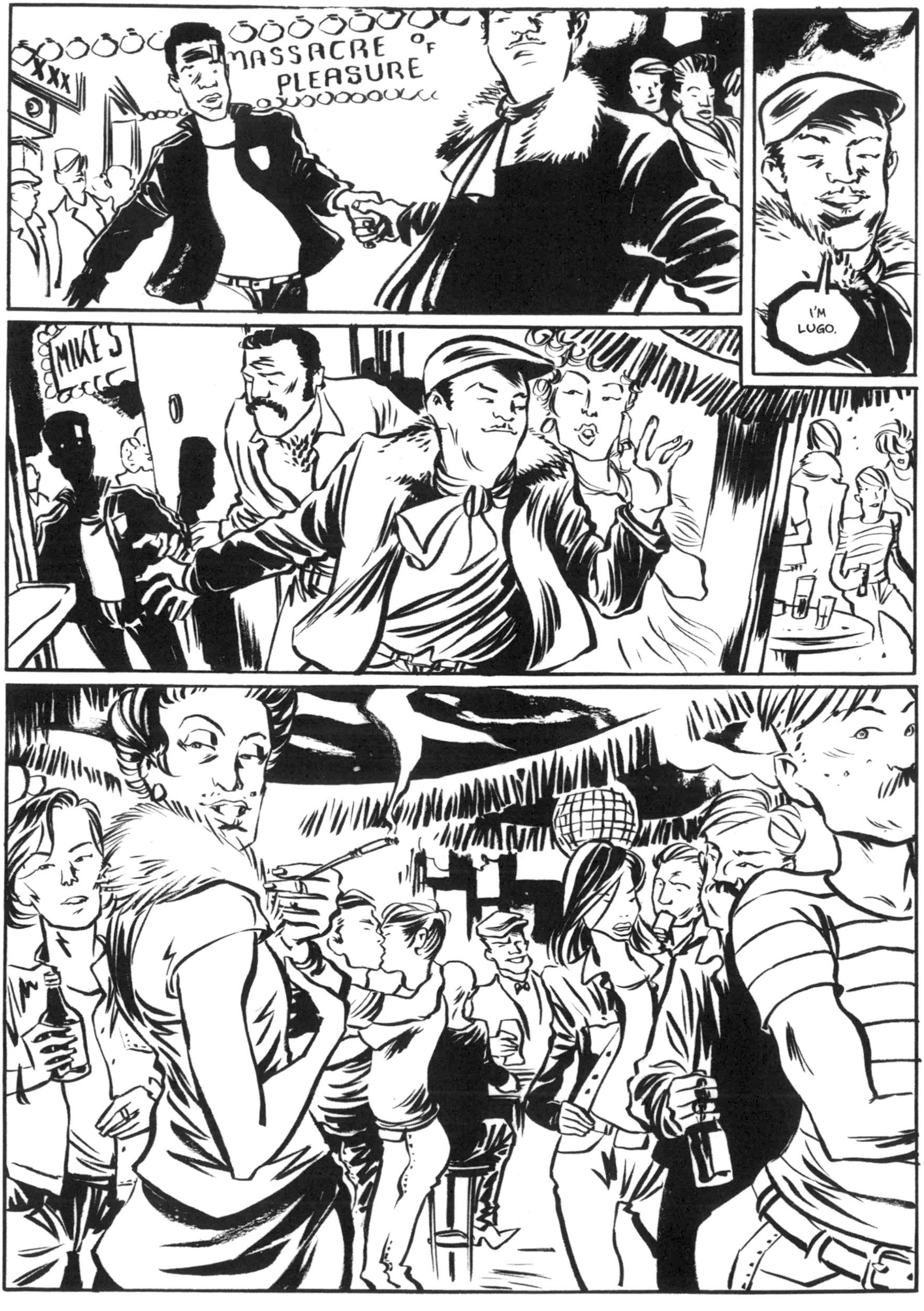
MASSACRE OF PLEASURE
XXX
I'M LUGO.
MIKE'S

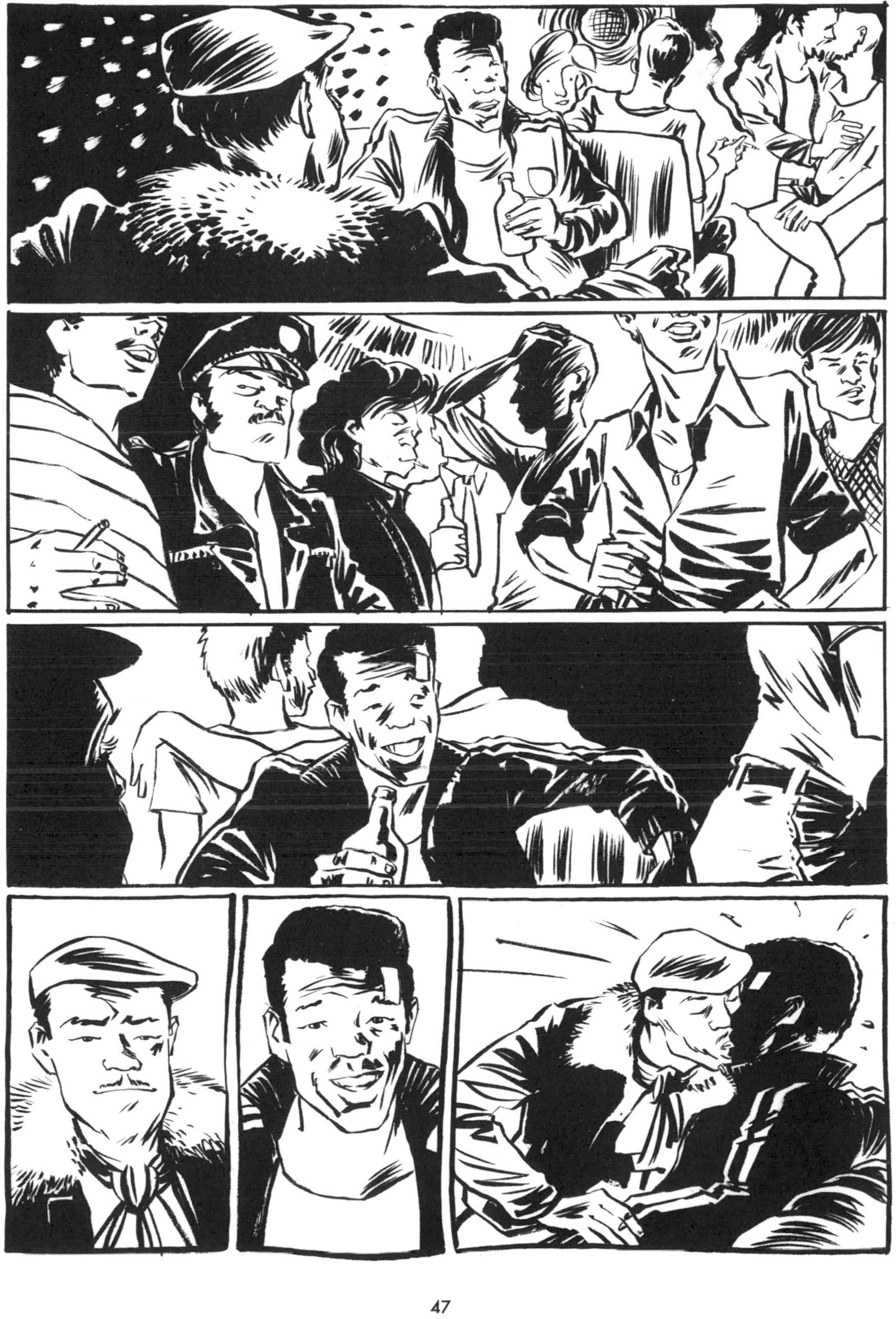

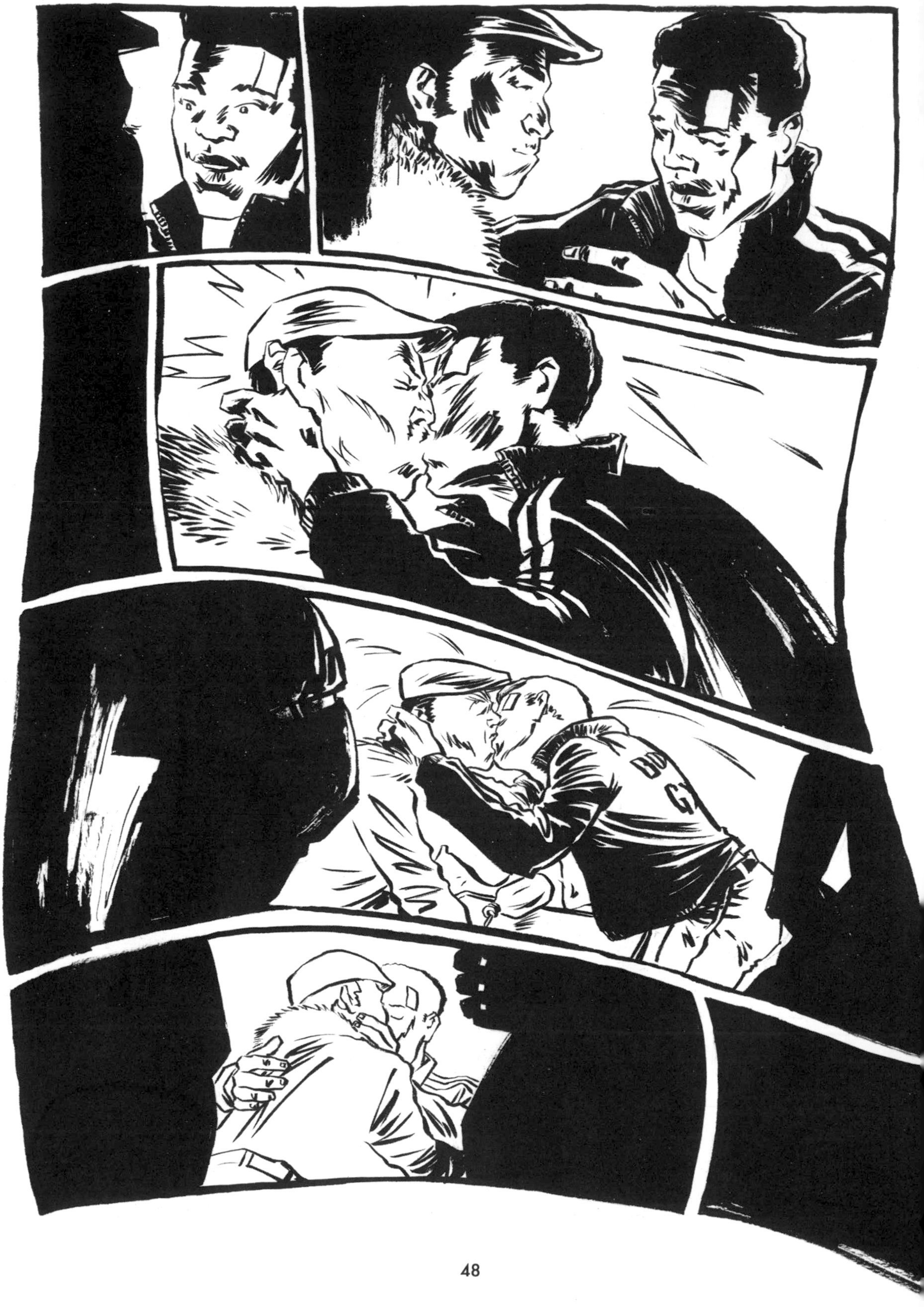

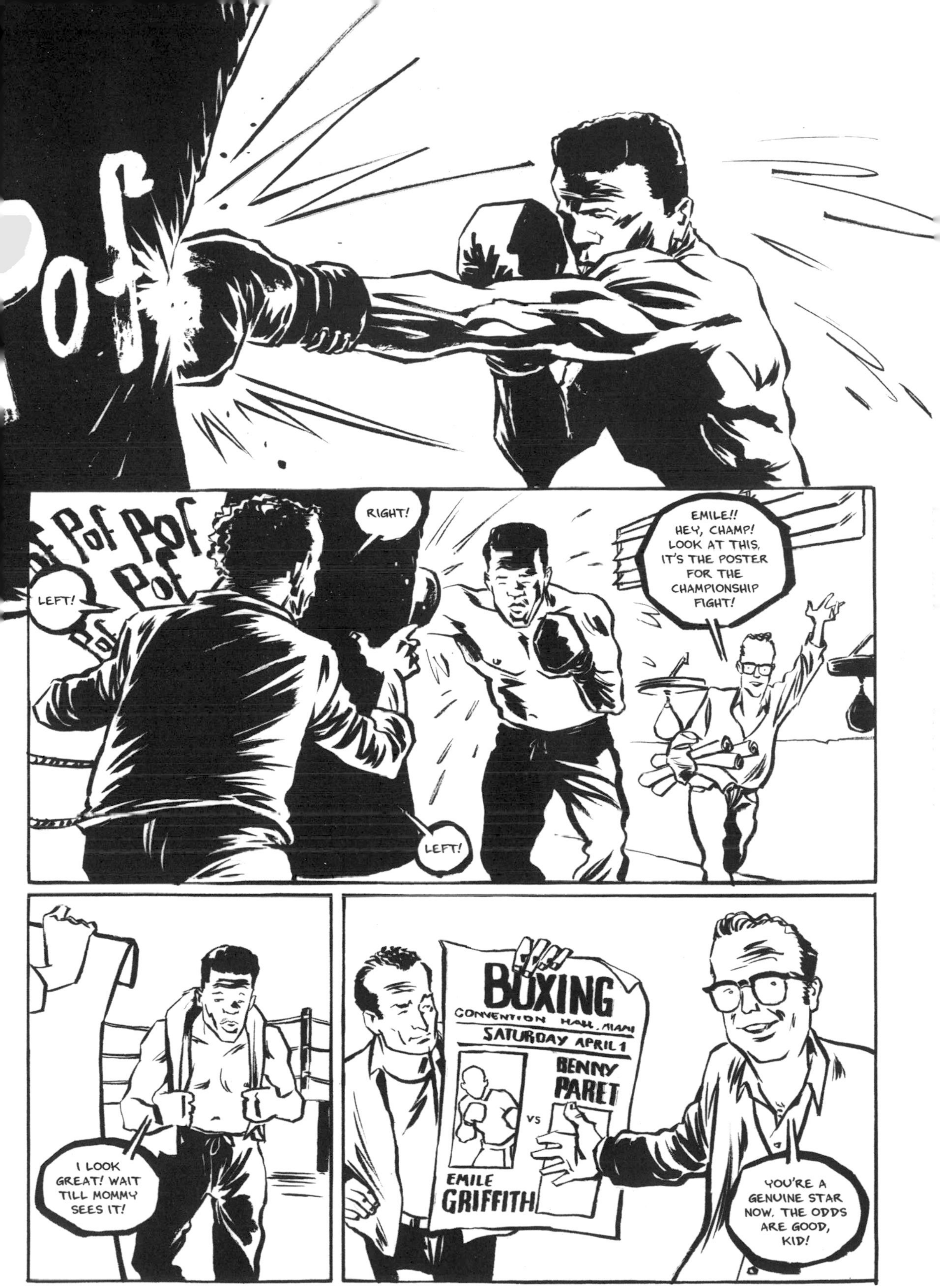
Pof
Pof Pof Pof Pof Pof
LEFT!
RIGHT!
LEFT!
EMILE!! HEY, CHAMP! LOOK AT THIS, IT'S THE POSTER FOR THE CHAMPIONSHIP FIGHT!
I LOOK GREAT! WAIT TILL MOMMY SEES IT!
BOXING
CONVENTION HALL, MIAMI
SATURDAY APRIL 1
BENNY PARET
VS
EMILE GRIFFITH
YOU'RE A GENUINE STAR NOW. THE ODDS ARE GOOD, KID!

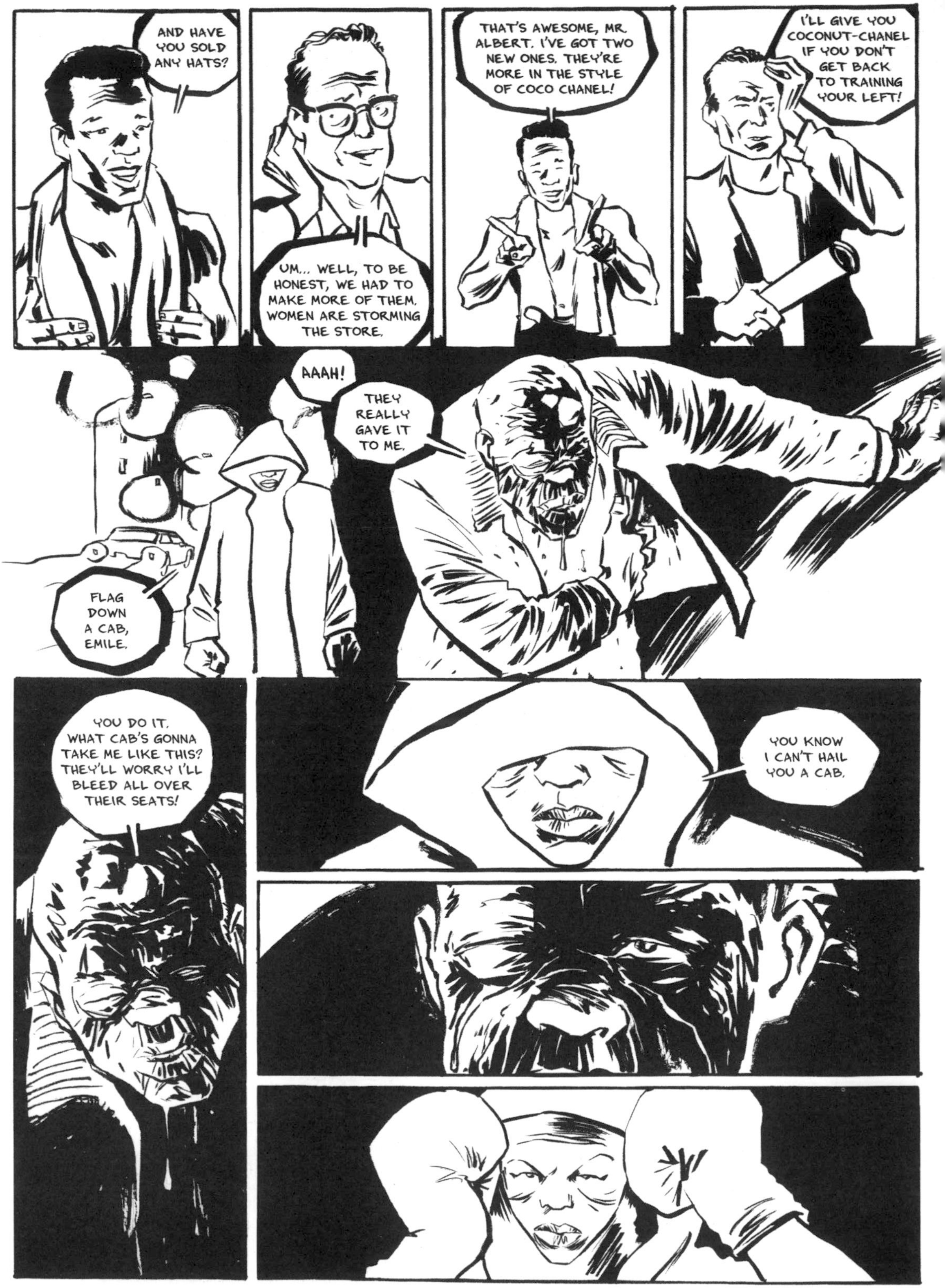
AND HAVE YOU SOLD ANY HATS?
UM... WELL, TO BE HONEST, WE HAD TO MAKE MORE OF THEM. WOMEN ARE STORMING THE STORE.
THAT'S AWESOME, MR. ALBERT. I'VE GOT TWO NEW ONES. THEY'RE MORE IN THE STYLE OF COCO CHANEL!
I'LL GIVE YOU COCONUT-CHANEL IF YOU DON'T GET BACK TO TRAINING YOUR LEFT!
AAAH!
THEY REALLY GAVE IT TO ME.
FLAG DOWN A CAB, EMILE.
YOU DO IT. WHAT CAB'S GONNA TAKE ME LIKE THIS? THEY'LL WORRY I'LL BLEED ALL OVER THEIR SEATS!
YOU KNOW I CAN'T HAIL YOU A CAB.

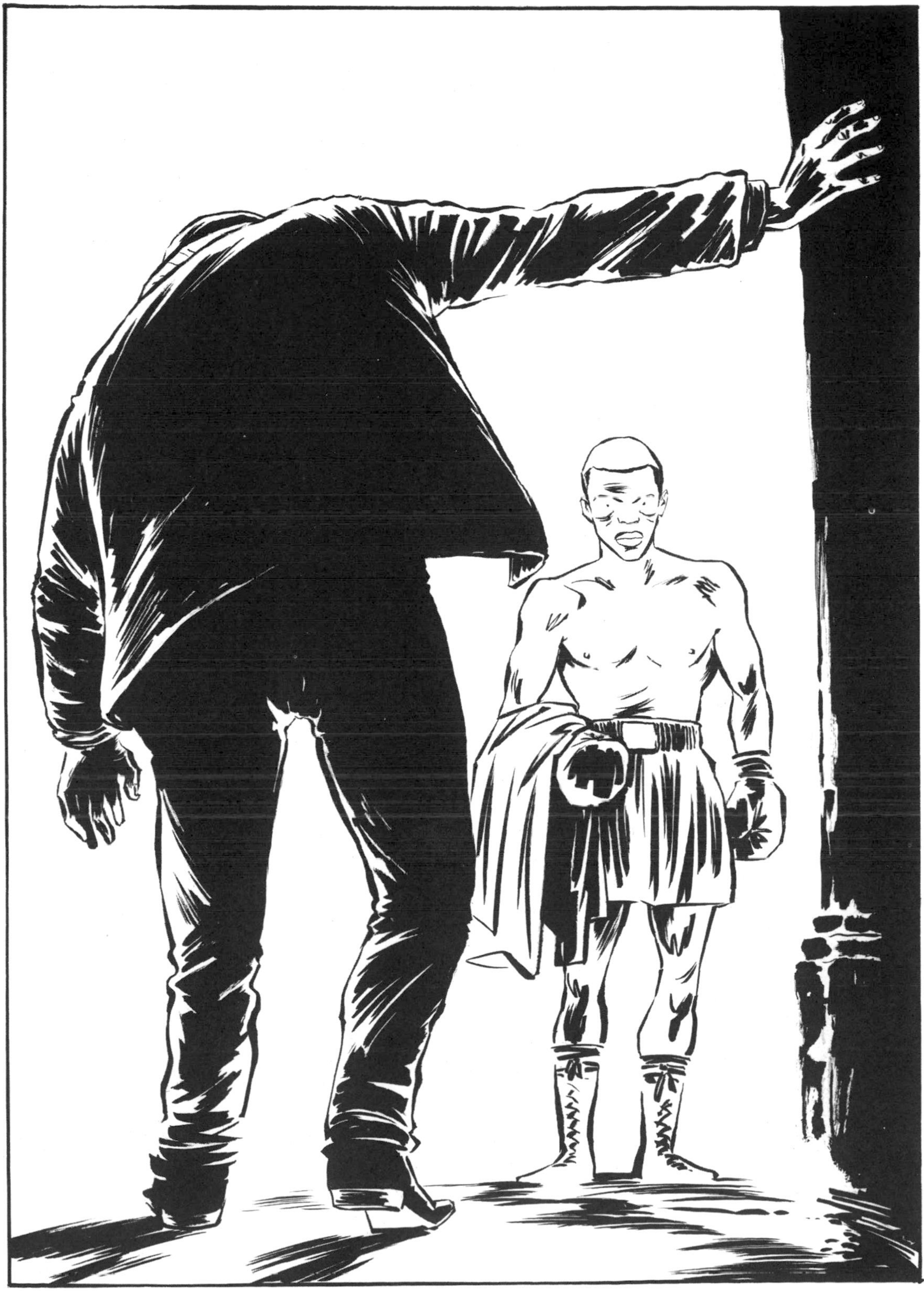

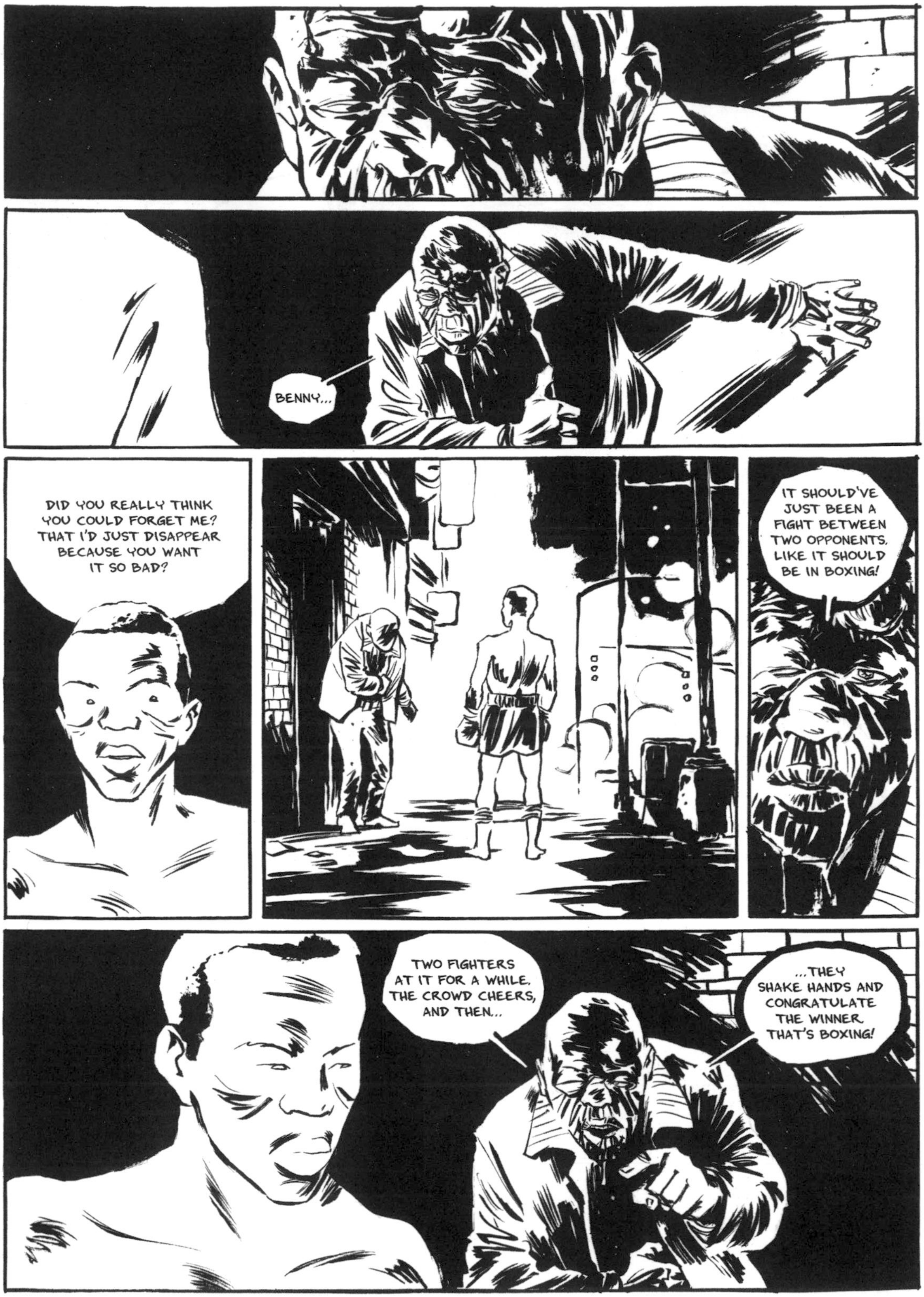
BENNY...
DID YOU REALLY THINK YOU COULD FORGET ME? THAT I'D JUST DISAPPEAR BECAUSE YOU WANT IT SO BAD?
IT SHOULD'VE JUST BEEN A FIGHT BETWEEN TWO OPPONENTS, LIKE IT SHOULD BE IN BOXING!
TWO FIGHTERS AT IT FOR A WHILE. THE CROWD CHEERS, AND THEN...
...THEY SHAKE HANDS AND CONGRATULATE THE WINNER. THAT'S BOXING!

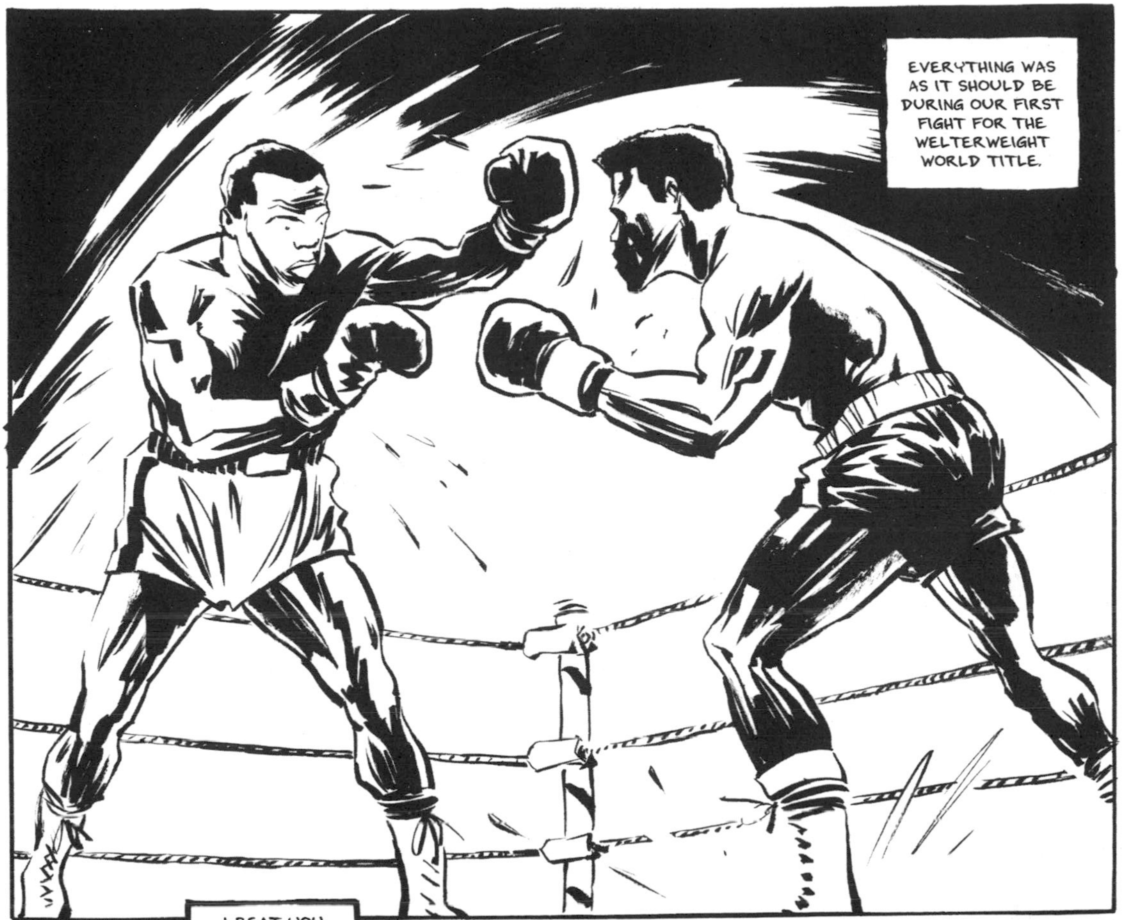
EVERYTHING WAS AS IT SHOULD BE DURING OUR FIRST FIGHT FOR THE WELTERWEIGHT WORLD TITLE.

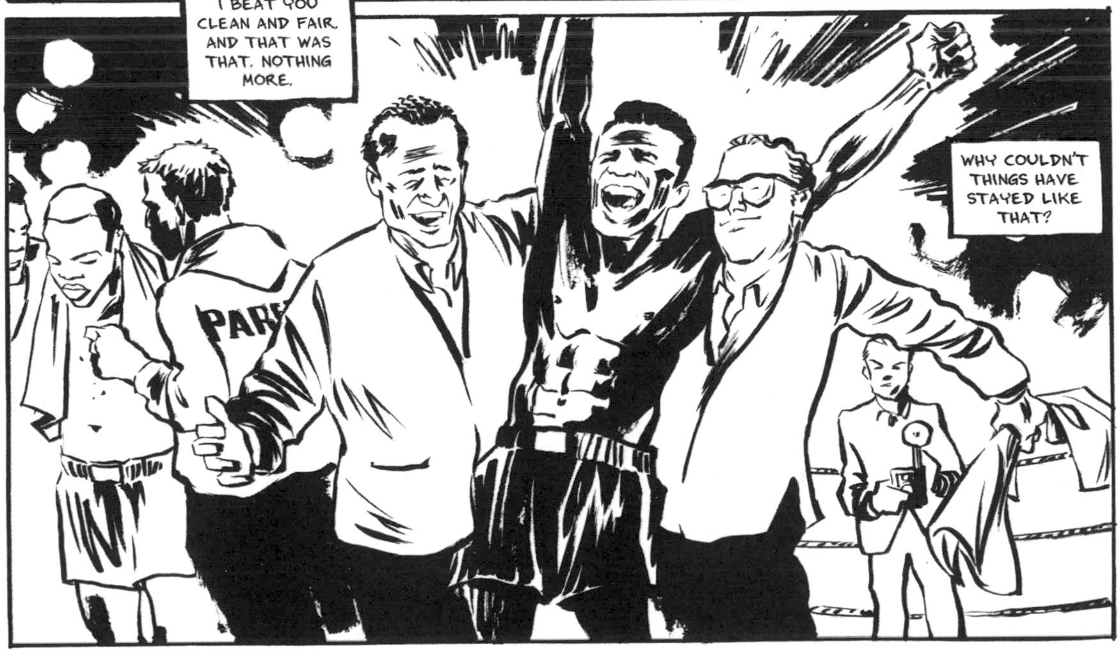
I BEAT YOU CLEAN AND FAIR. AND THAT WAS THAT. NOTHING MORE.
PARE
WHY COULDN'T THINGS HAVE STAYED LIKE THAT?

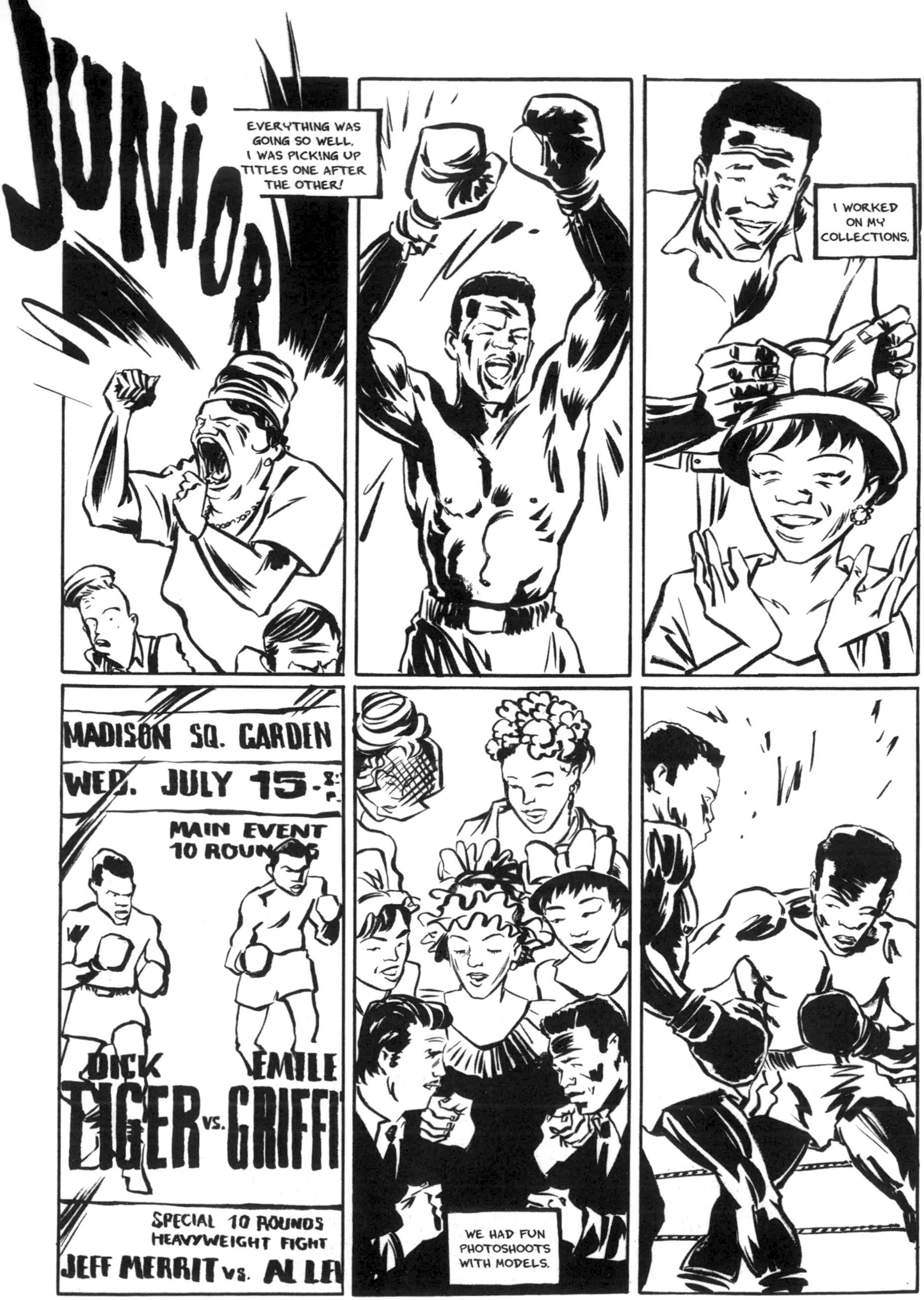
JUNIOR
EVERYTHING WAS GOING SO WELL, I WAS PICKING UP TITLES ONE AFTER THE OTHER!
I WORKED ON MY COLLECTIONS.
MADISON SQ. GARDEN
WED. JULY 15
MAIN EVENT
10 ROUN
DICK
TIGER
VS.
EMILE
GRIFFI
SPECIAL 10 ROUNDS
HEAVYWEIGHT FIGHT
JEFF MERRIT VS. AL LE
WE HAD FUN PHOTOSHOOTS WITH MODELS.

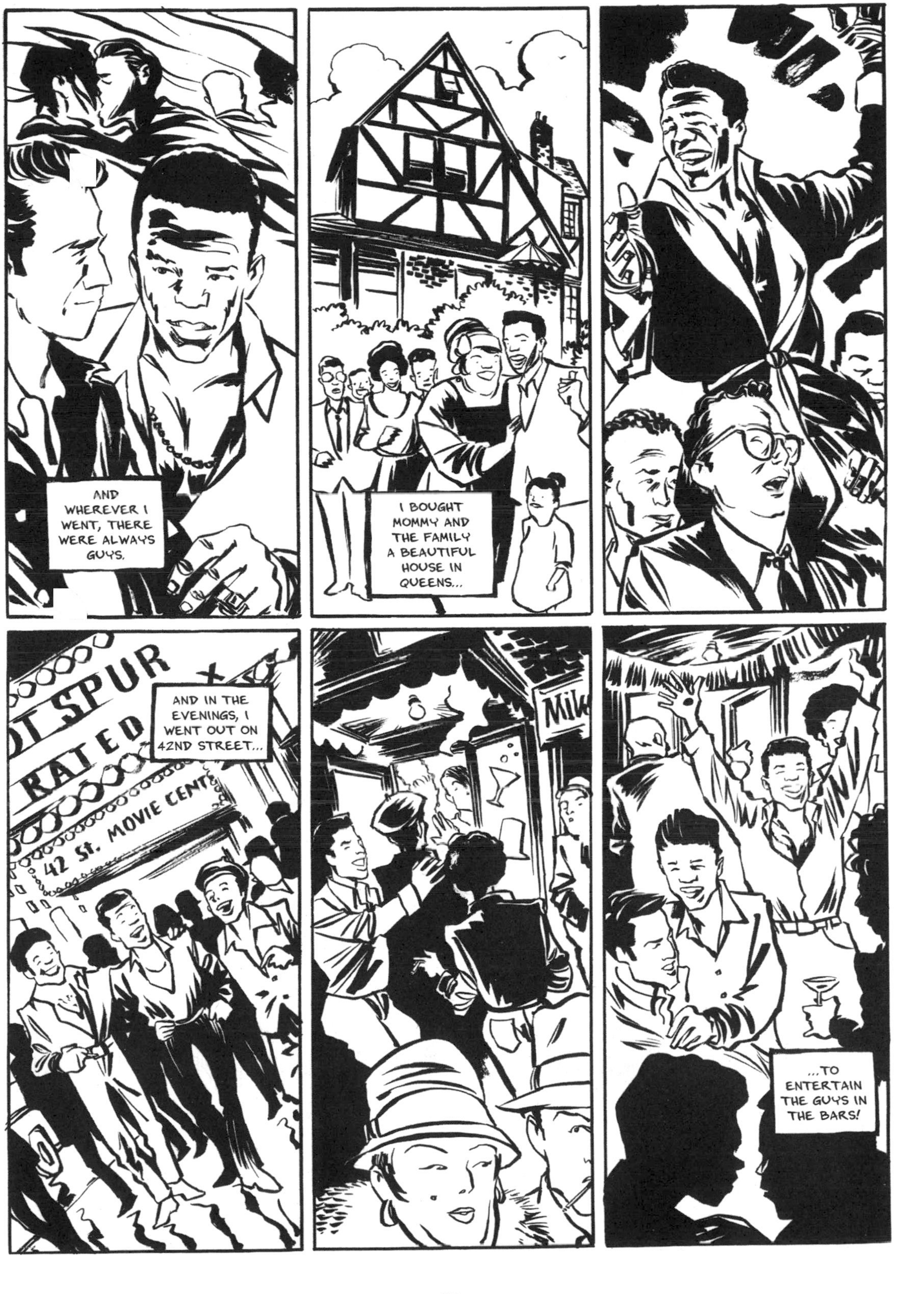
AND WHEREVER I WENT, THERE WERE ALWAYS GUYS.
I BOUGHT MOMMY AND THE FAMILY A BEAUTIFUL HOUSE IN QUEENS...
OT SPUR
RATED
42 St. MOVIE CENT
AND IN THE EVENINGS, I WENT OUT ON 42ND STREET...
Mik
...TO ENTERTAIN THE GUYS IN THE BARS!

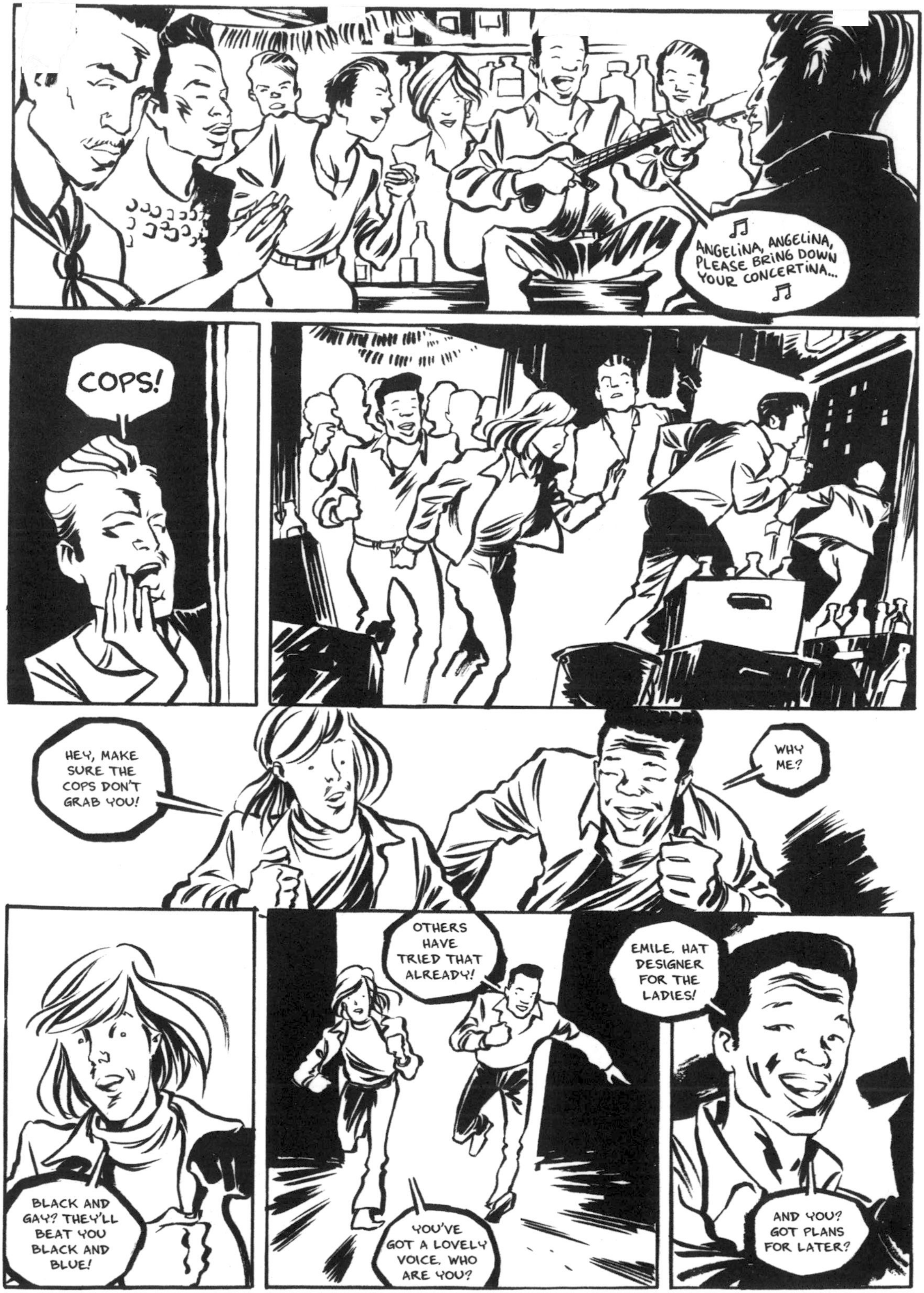
♫ ANGELINA, ANGELINA, PLEASE BRING DOWN YOUR CONCERTINA... ♫
COPS!
HEY, MAKE SURE THE COPS DON'T GRAB YOU!
WHY ME?
BLACK AND GAY? THEY'LL BEAT YOU BLACK AND BLUE!
OTHERS HAVE TRIED THAT ALREADY!
YOU'VE GOT A LOVELY VOICE. WHO ARE YOU?
EMILE. HAT DESIGNER FOR THE LADIES!
AND YOU? GOT PLANS FOR LATER?

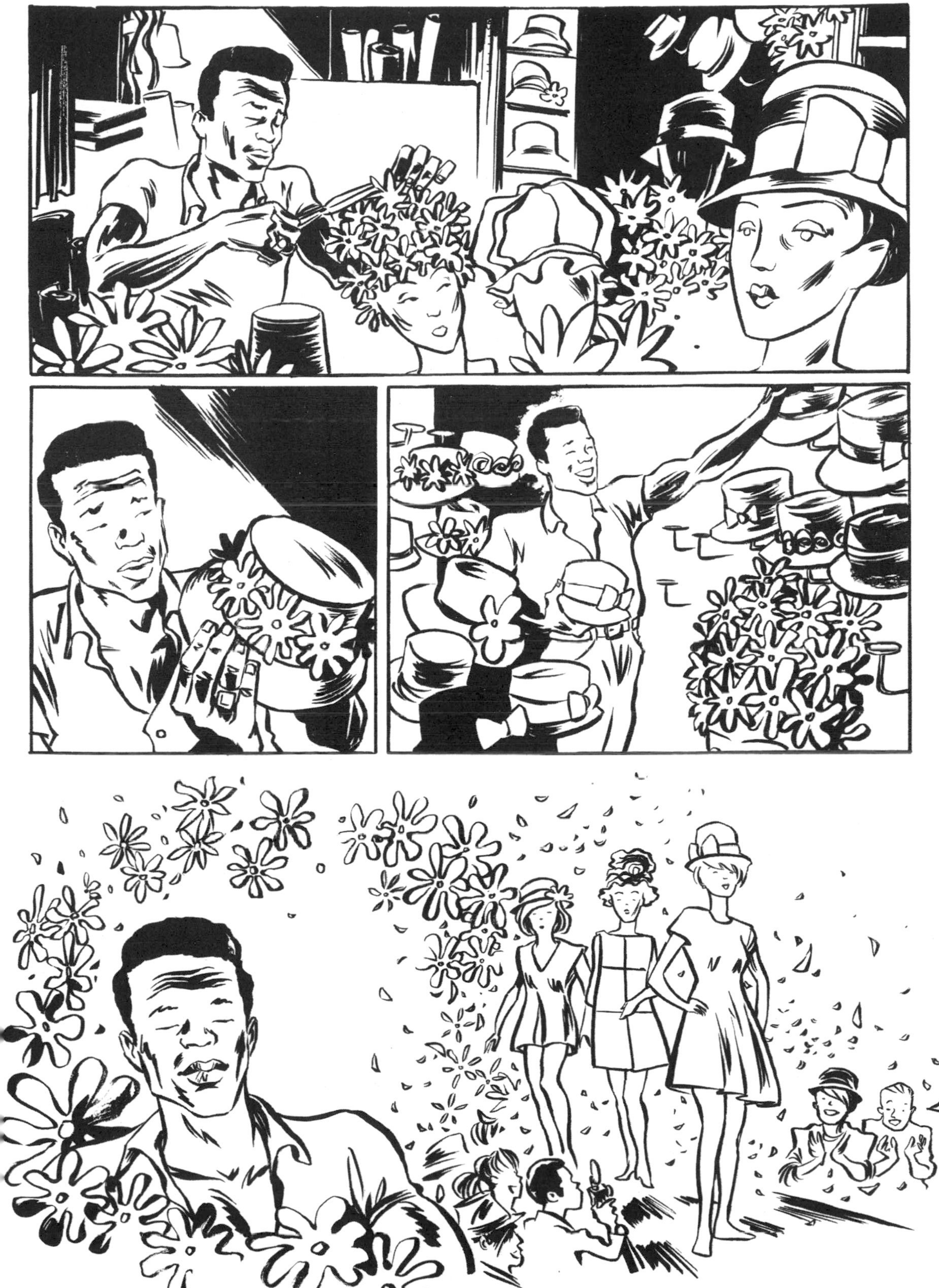

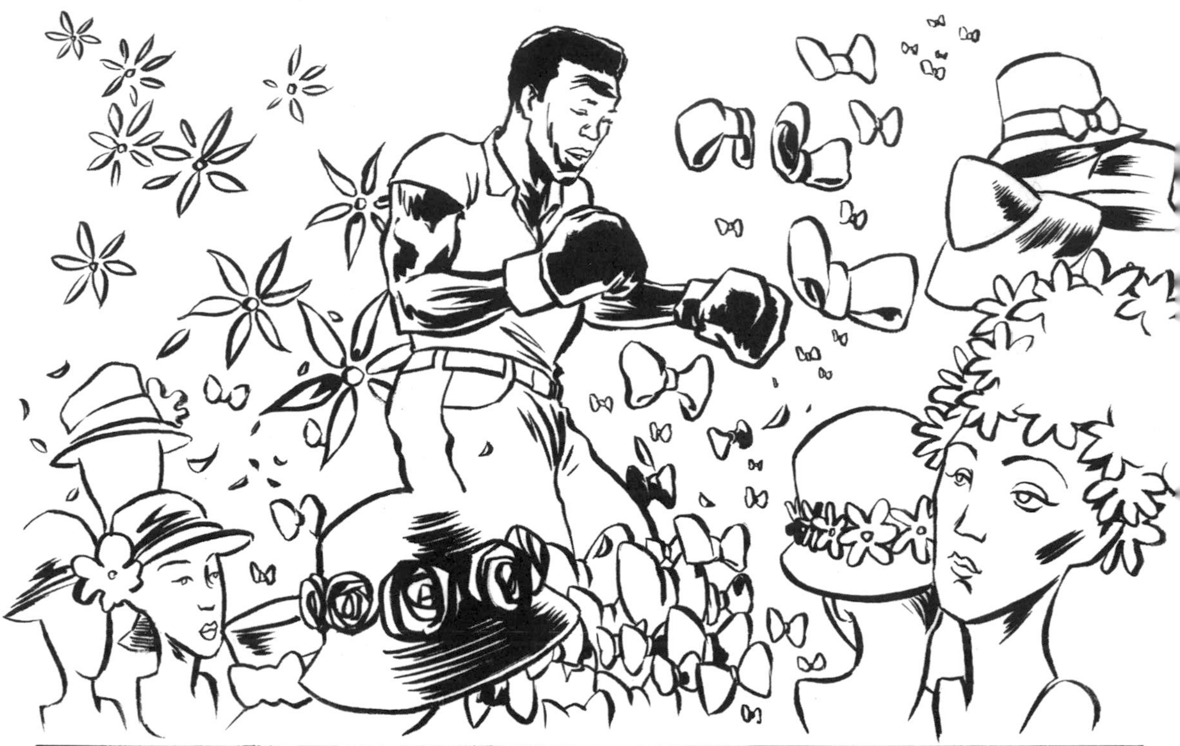

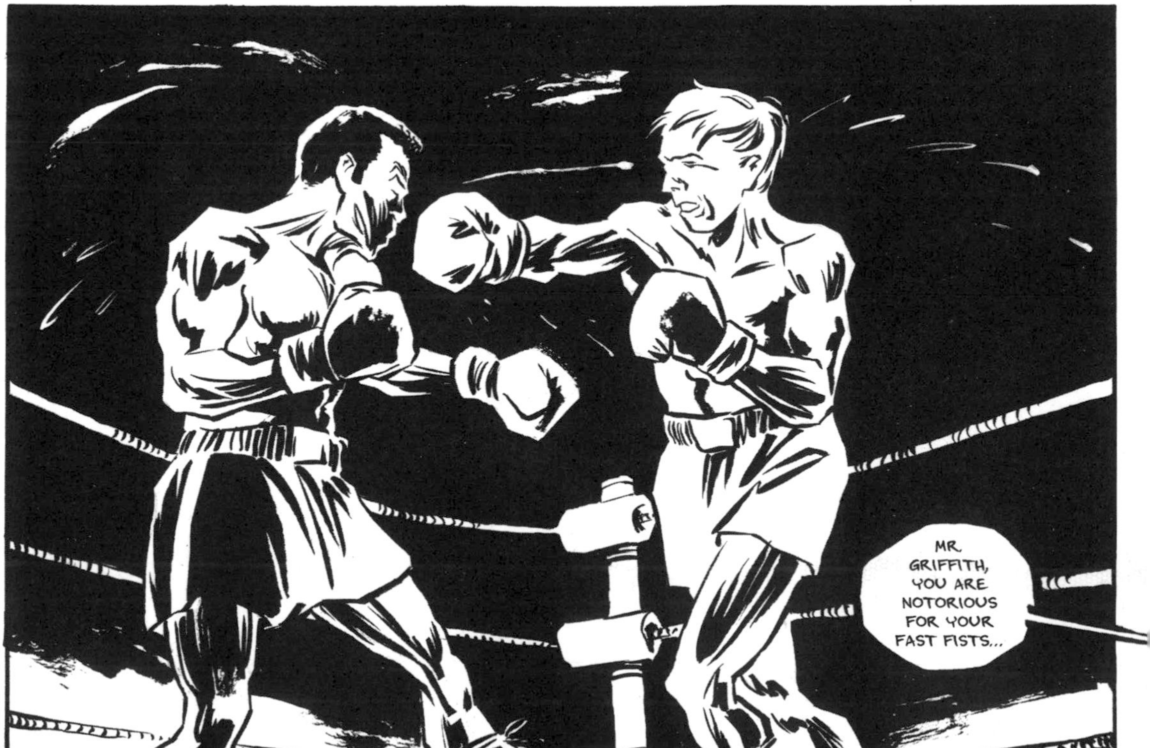
MR. GRIFFITH, YOU ARE NOTORIOUS FOR YOUR FAST FISTS...

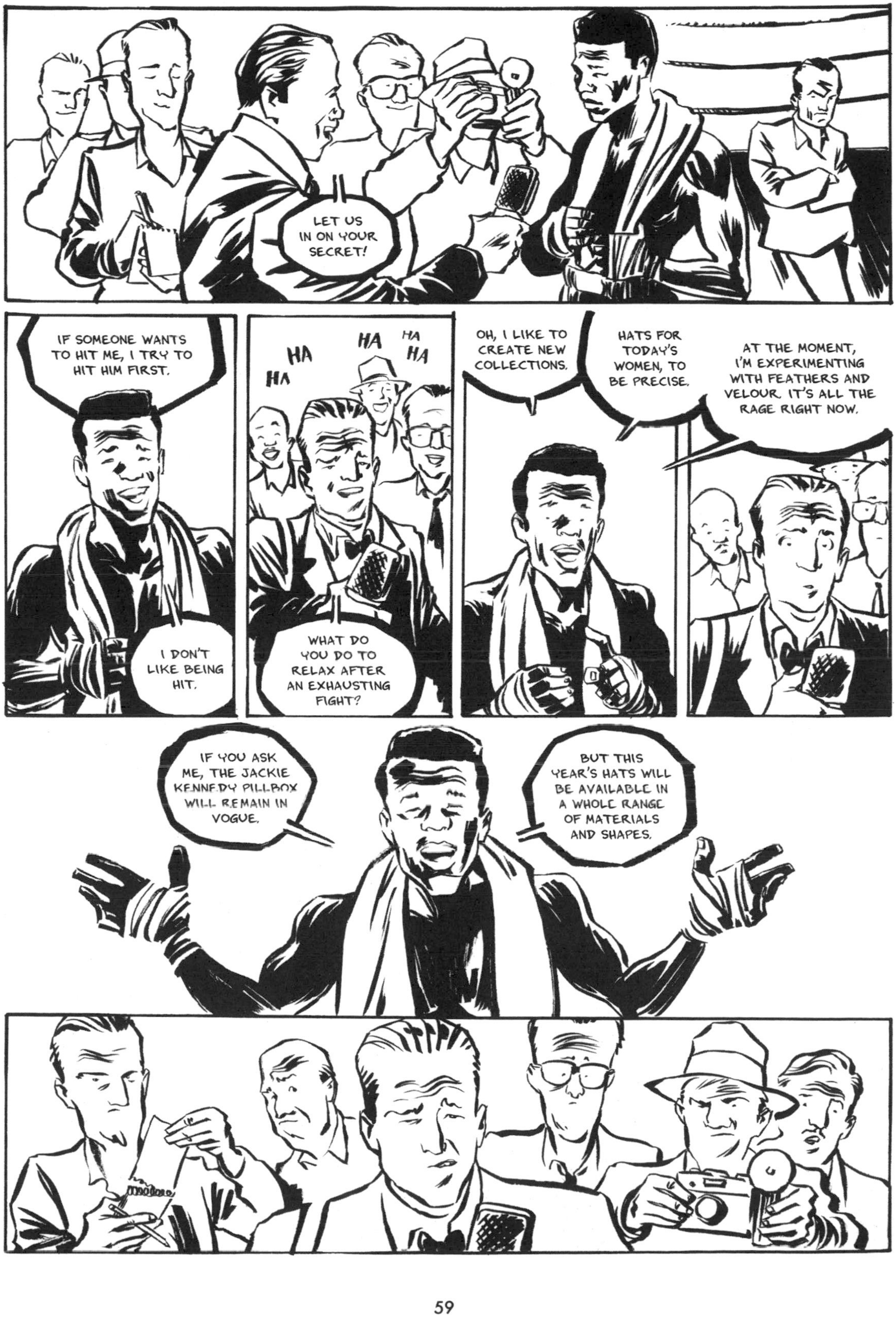
LET US IN ON YOUR SECRET!
IF SOMEONE WANTS TO HIT ME, I TRY TO HIT HIM FIRST.
I DON'T LIKE BEING HIT.
HA HA HA HA HA
WHAT DO YOU DO TO RELAX AFTER AN EXHAUSTING FIGHT?
OH, I LIKE TO CREATE NEW COLLECTIONS.
HATS FOR TODAY'S WOMEN, TO BE PRECISE.
AT THE MOMENT, I'M EXPERIMENTING WITH FEATHERS AND VELOUR. IT'S ALL THE RAGE RIGHT NOW.
IF YOU ASK ME, THE JACKIE KENNEDY PILLBOX WILL REMAIN IN VOGUE.
BUT THIS YEAR'S HATS WILL BE AVAILABLE IN A WHOLE RANGE OF MATERIALS AND SHAPES.

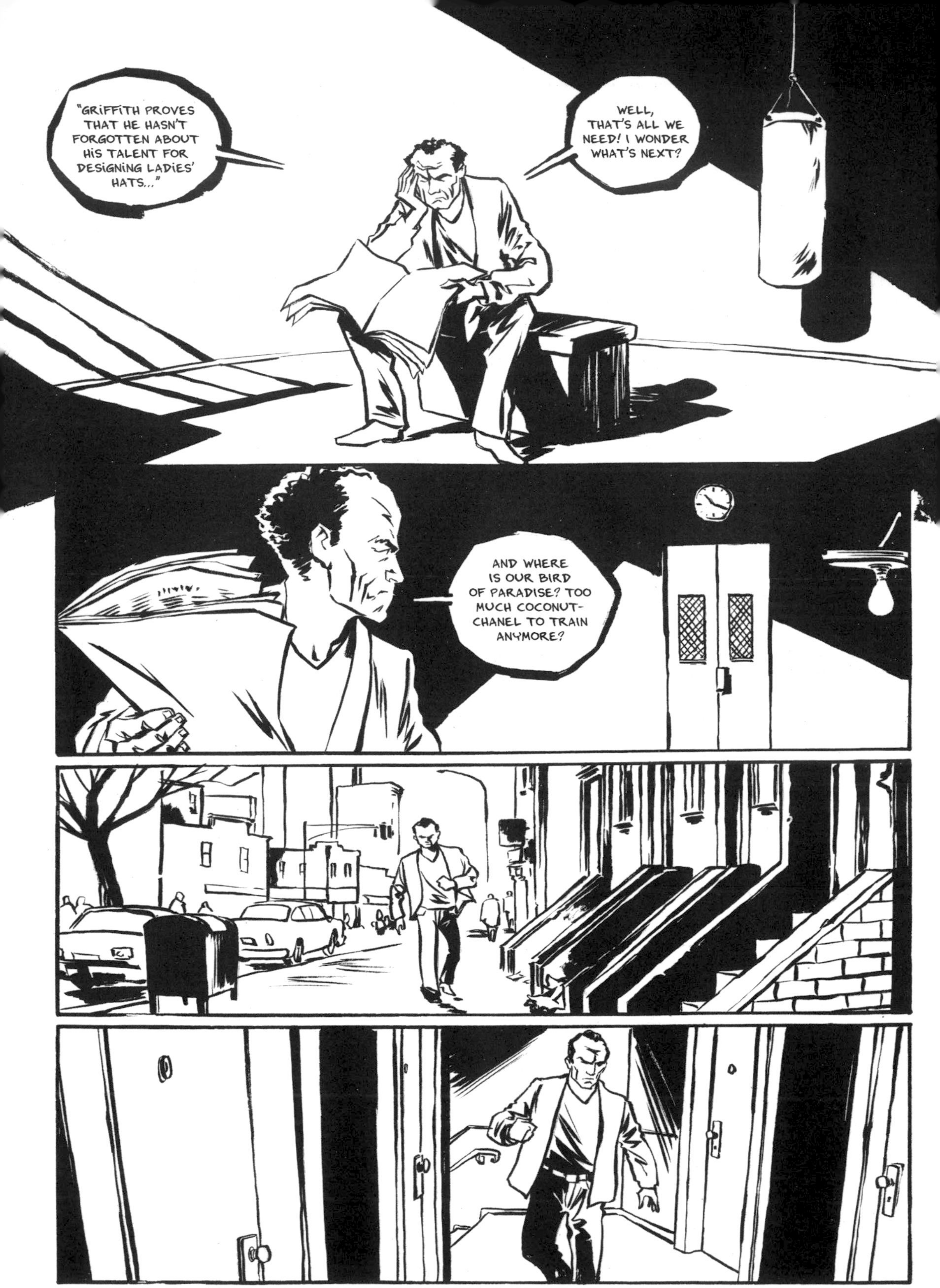
"GRIFFITH PROVES THAT HE HASN'T FORGOTTEN ABOUT HIS TALENT FOR DESIGNING LADIES' HATS..."
WELL, THAT'S ALL WE NEED! I WONDER WHAT'S NEXT?
AND WHERE IS OUR BIRD OF PARADISE? TOO MUCH COCONUT-CHANEL TO TRAIN ANYMORE?

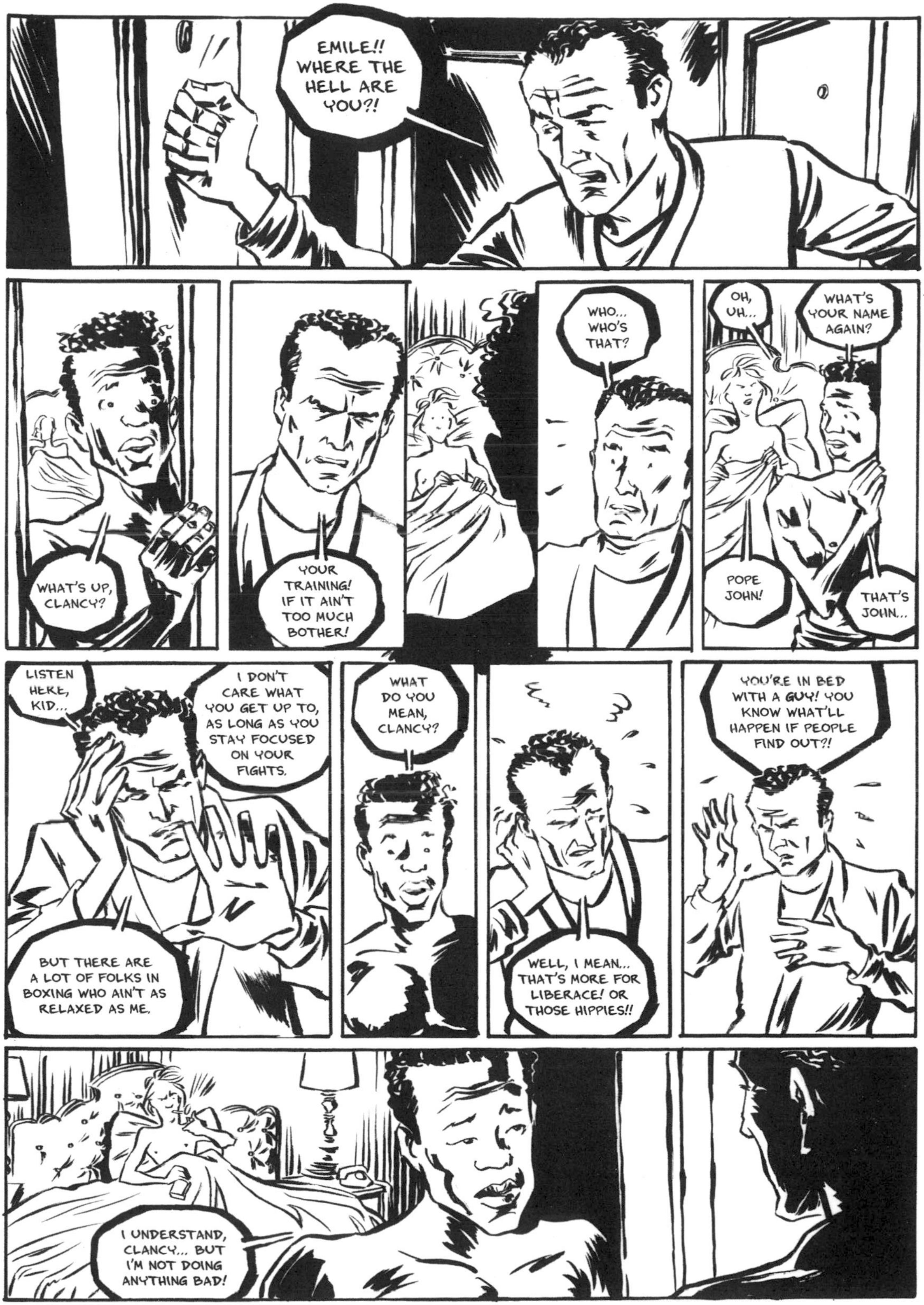
EMILE!! WHERE THE HELL ARE YOU?!
WHAT'S UP, CLANCY?
YOUR TRAINING! IF IT AIN'T TOO MUCH BOTHER!
WHO... WHO'S THAT?
OH, UH...
WHAT'S YOUR NAME AGAIN?
POPE JOHN!
THAT'S JOHN...
LISTEN HERE, KID...
I DON'T CARE WHAT YOU GET UP TO, AS LONG AS YOU STAY FOCUSED ON YOUR FIGHTS.
BUT THERE ARE A LOT OF FOLKS IN BOXING WHO AIN'T AS RELAXED AS ME.
WHAT DO YOU MEAN, CLANCY?
WELL, I MEAN... THAT'S MORE FOR LIBERACE! OR THOSE HIPPIES!!
YOU'RE IN BED WITH A GUY! YOU KNOW WHAT'LL HAPPEN IF PEOPLE FIND OUT?!
I UNDERSTAND, CLANCY... BUT I'M NOT DOING ANYTHING BAD!

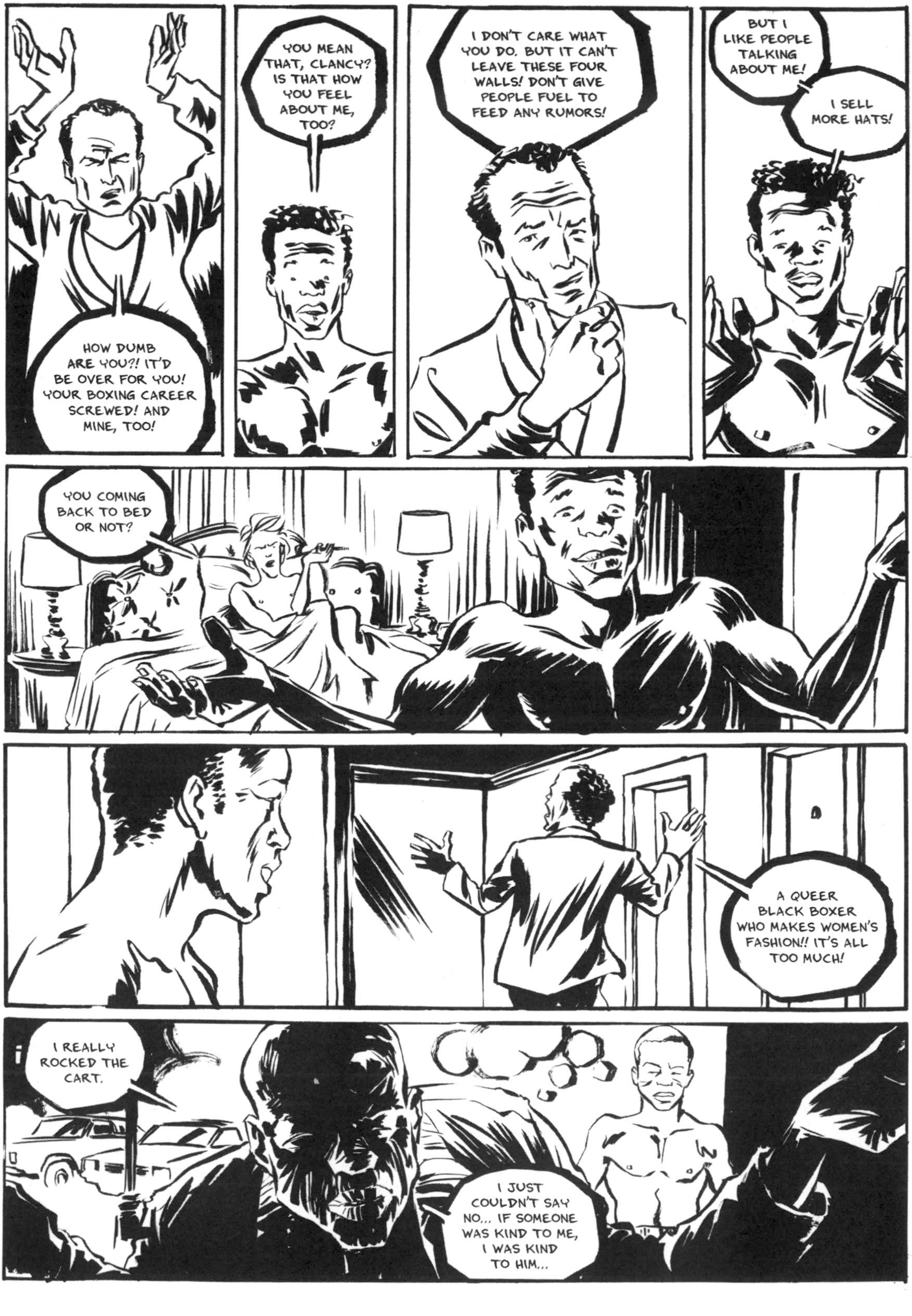
HOW DUMB ARE YOU?! IT'D BE OVER FOR YOU! YOUR BOXING CAREER SCREWED! AND MINE, TOO!
YOU MEAN THAT, CLANCY? IS THAT HOW YOU FEEL ABOUT ME, TOO?
I DON'T CARE WHAT YOU DO. BUT IT CAN'T LEAVE THESE FOUR WALLS! DON'T GIVE PEOPLE FUEL TO FEED ANY RUMORS!
BUT I LIKE PEOPLE TALKING ABOUT ME!
I SELL MORE HATS!
YOU COMING BACK TO BED OR NOT?
A QUEER BLACK BOXER WHO MAKES WOMEN'S FASHION!! IT'S ALL TOO MUCH!
I REALLY ROCKED THE CART.
I JUST COULDN'T SAY NO... IF SOMEONE WAS KIND TO ME, I WAS KIND TO HIM...

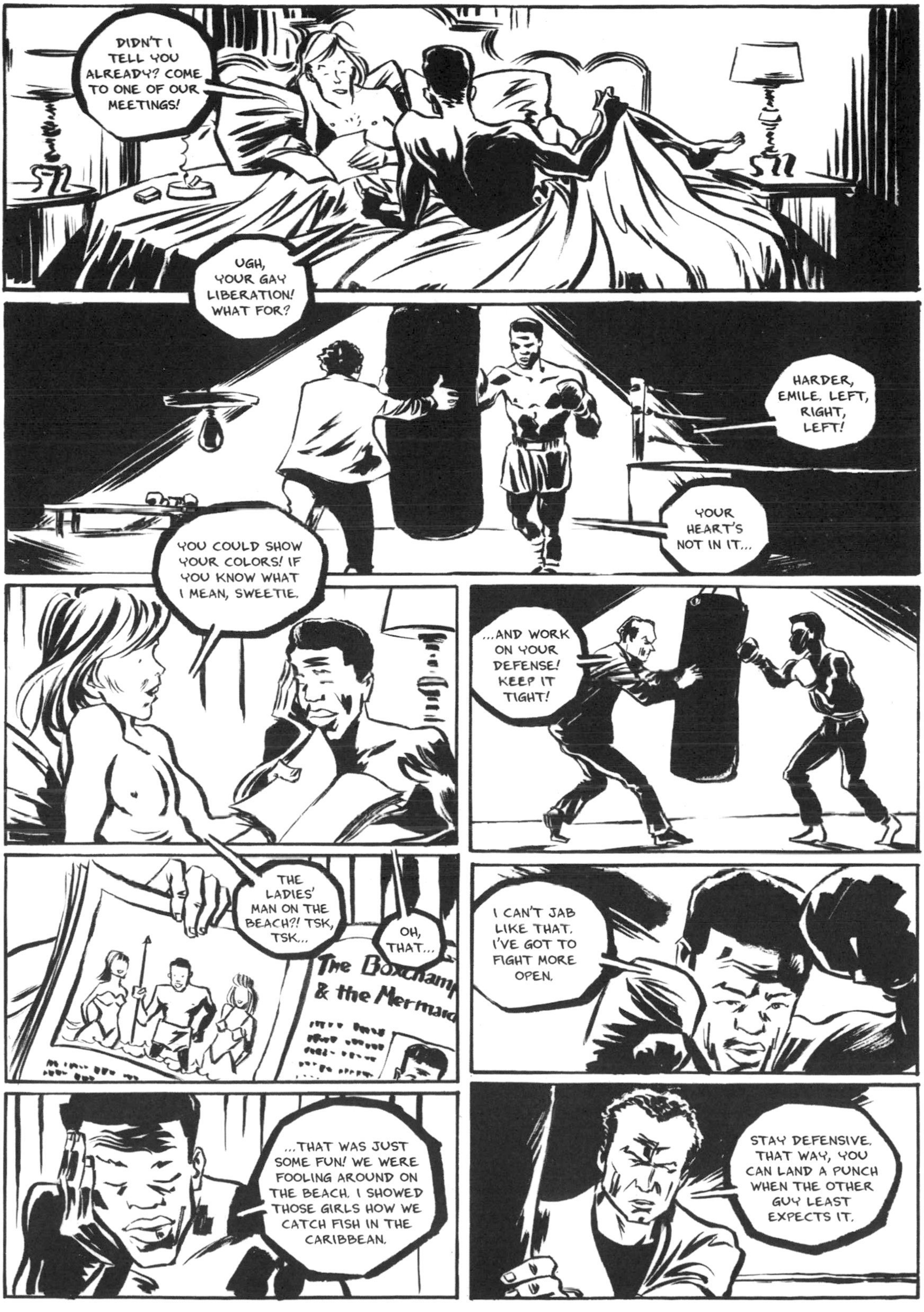
DIDN'T I TELL YOU ALREADY? COME TO ONE OF OUR MEETINGS!
UGH, YOUR GAY LIBERATION! WHAT FOR?
HARDER, EMILE. LEFT, RIGHT, LEFT!
YOUR HEART'S NOT IN IT...
YOU COULD SHOW YOUR COLORS! IF YOU KNOW WHAT I MEAN, SWEETIE.
...AND WORK ON YOUR DEFENSE! KEEP IT TIGHT!
THE LADIES' MAN ON THE BEACH?! TSK, TSK...
OH, THAT...
The Boxchamp & the Mermaid
I CAN'T JAB LIKE THAT. I'VE GOT TO FIGHT MORE OPEN.
...THAT WAS JUST SOME FUN! WE WERE FOOLING AROUND ON THE BEACH. I SHOWED THOSE GIRLS HOW WE CATCH FISH IN THE CARIBBEAN.
STAY DEFENSIVE. THAT WAY, YOU CAN LAND A PUNCH WHEN THE OTHER GUY LEAST EXPECTS IT.

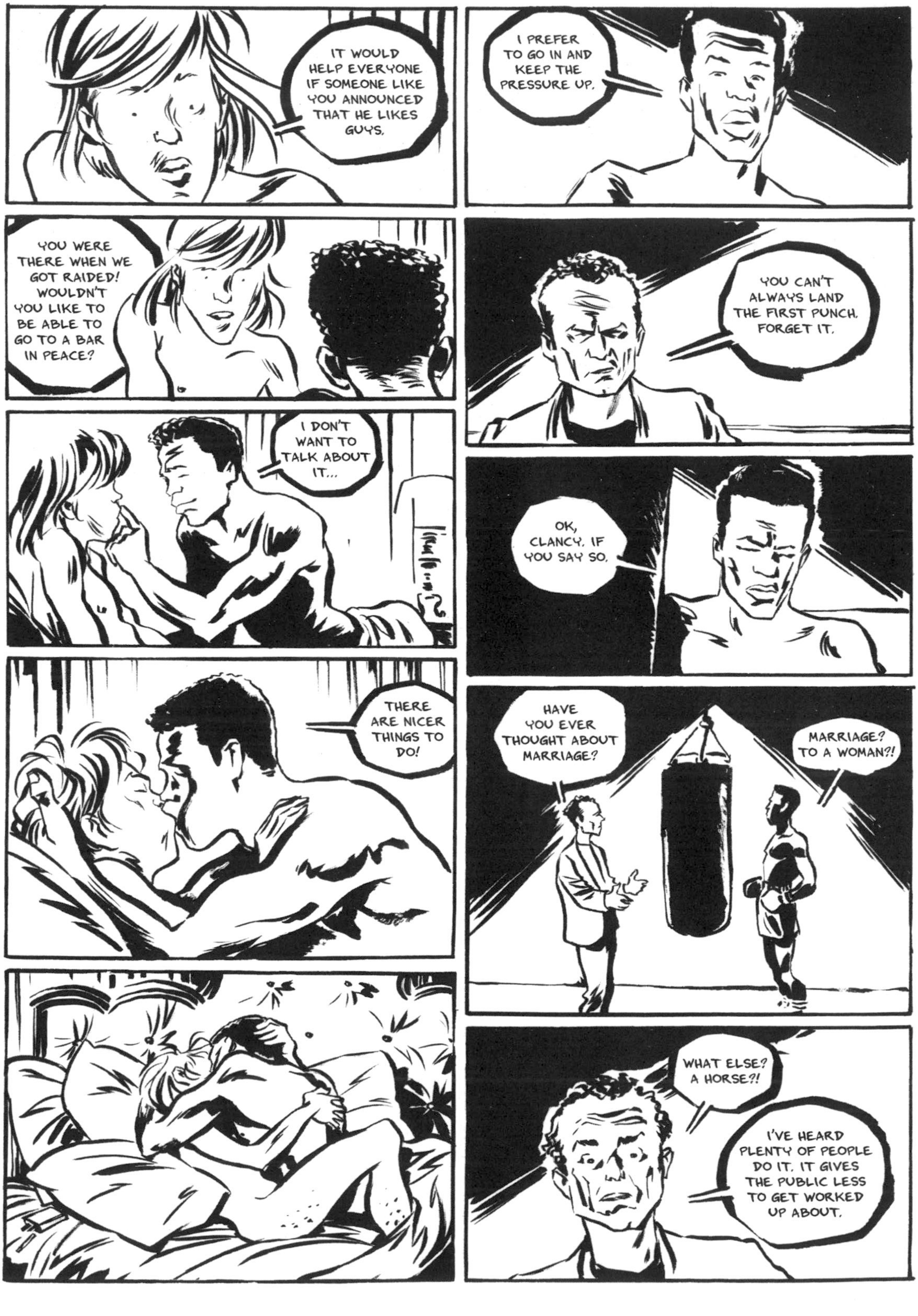
IT WOULD HELP EVERYONE IF SOMEONE LIKE YOU ANNOUNCED THAT HE LIKES GUYS.
I PREFER TO GO IN AND KEEP THE PRESSURE UP.
YOU WERE THERE WHEN WE GOT RAIDED! WOULDN'T YOU LIKE TO BE ABLE TO GO TO A BAR IN PEACE?
YOU CAN'T ALWAYS LAND THE FIRST PUNCH. FORGET IT.
I DON'T WANT TO TALK ABOUT IT...
OK, CLANCY. IF YOU SAY SO.
THERE ARE NICER THINGS TO DO!
HAVE YOU EVER THOUGHT ABOUT MARRIAGE?
MARRIAGE? TO A WOMAN?!
WHAT ELSE? A HORSE?!
I'VE HEARD PLENTY OF PEOPLE DO IT. IT GIVES THE PUBLIC LESS TO GET WORKED UP ABOUT.

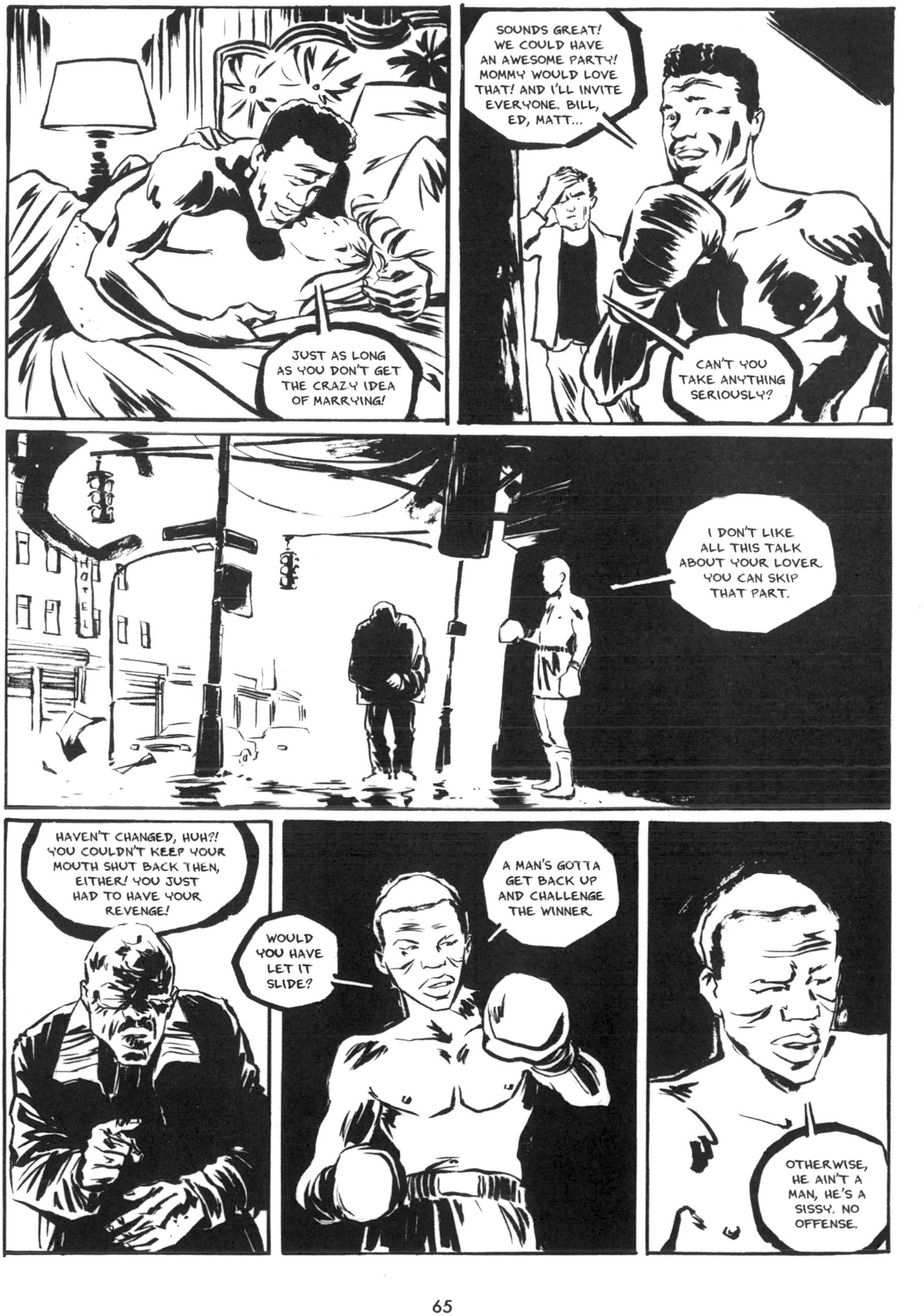
JUST AS LONG AS YOU DON'T GET THE CRAZY IDEA OF MARRYING!
SOUNDS GREAT! WE COULD HAVE AN AWESOME PARTY! MOMMY WOULD LOVE THAT! AND I'LL INVITE EVERYONE. BILL, ED, MATT...
CAN'T YOU TAKE ANYTHING SERIOUSLY?
HOTEL
I DON'T LIKE ALL THIS TALK ABOUT YOUR LOVER. YOU CAN SKIP THAT PART.
HAVEN'T CHANGED, HUH?! YOU COULDN'T KEEP YOUR MOUTH SHUT BACK THEN, EITHER! YOU JUST HAD TO HAVE YOUR REVENGE!
WOULD YOU HAVE LET IT SLIDE?
A MAN'S GOTTA GET BACK UP AND CHALLENGE THE WINNER.
OTHERWISE, HE AIN'T A MAN, HE'S A SISSY. NO OFFENSE.

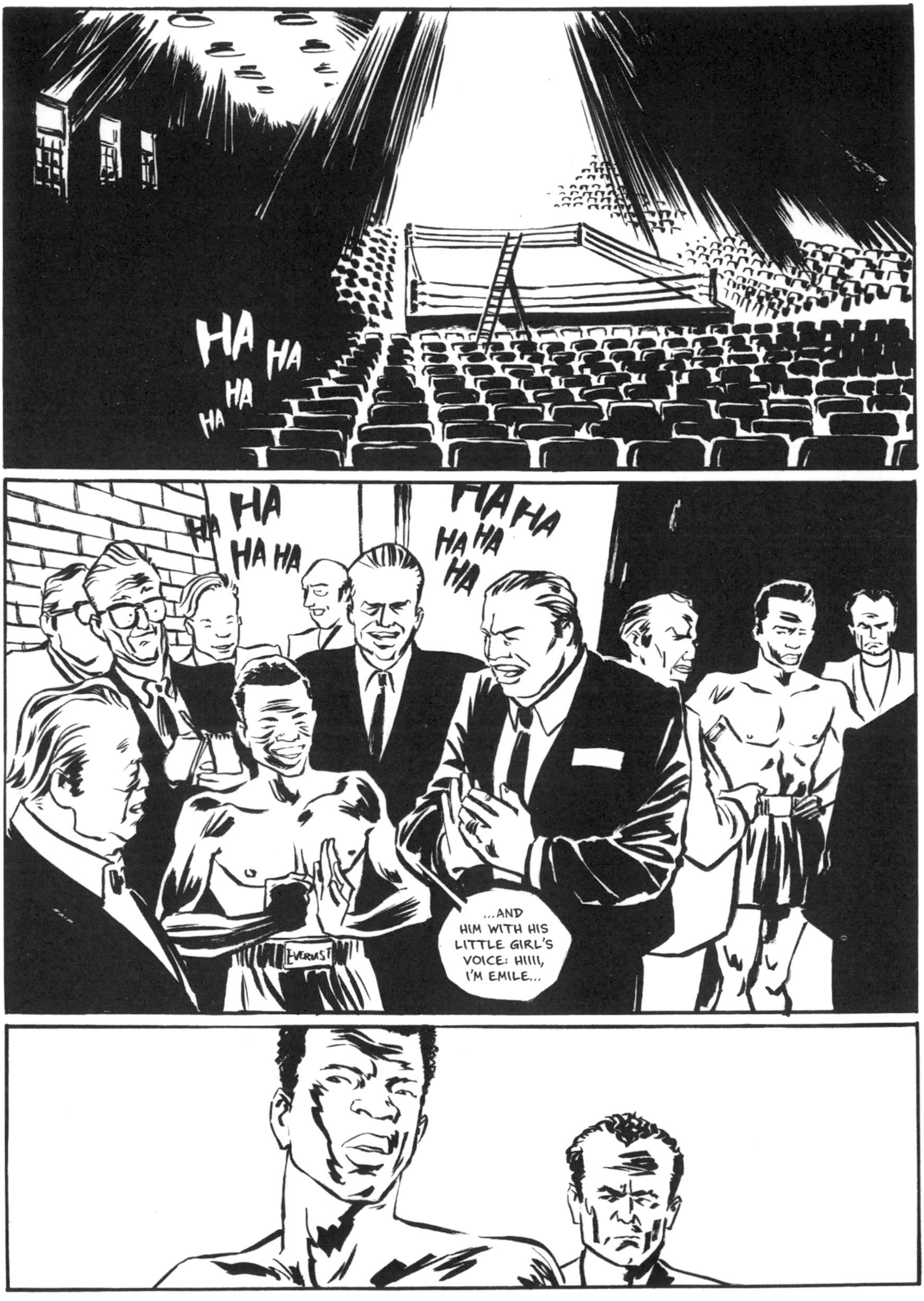
HA HA HA HA
HA HA HA HA
HA HA HA HA HA
EVERLAST
...AND HIM WITH HIS LITTLE GIRL'S VOICE: HIIII, I'M EMILE...

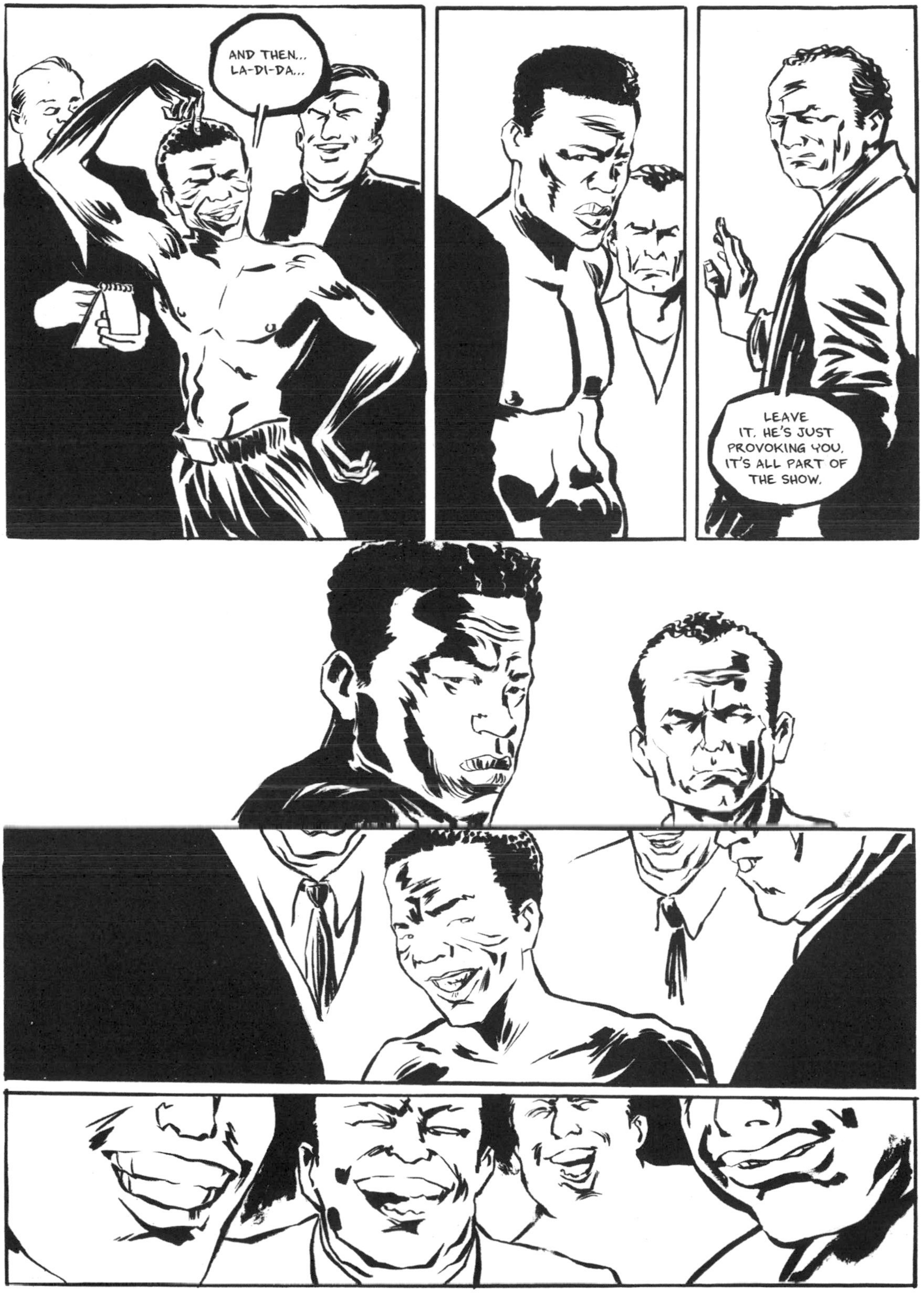
AND THEN... LA-DI-DA...
LEAVE IT. HE'S JUST PROVOKING YOU, IT'S ALL PART OF THE SHOW.

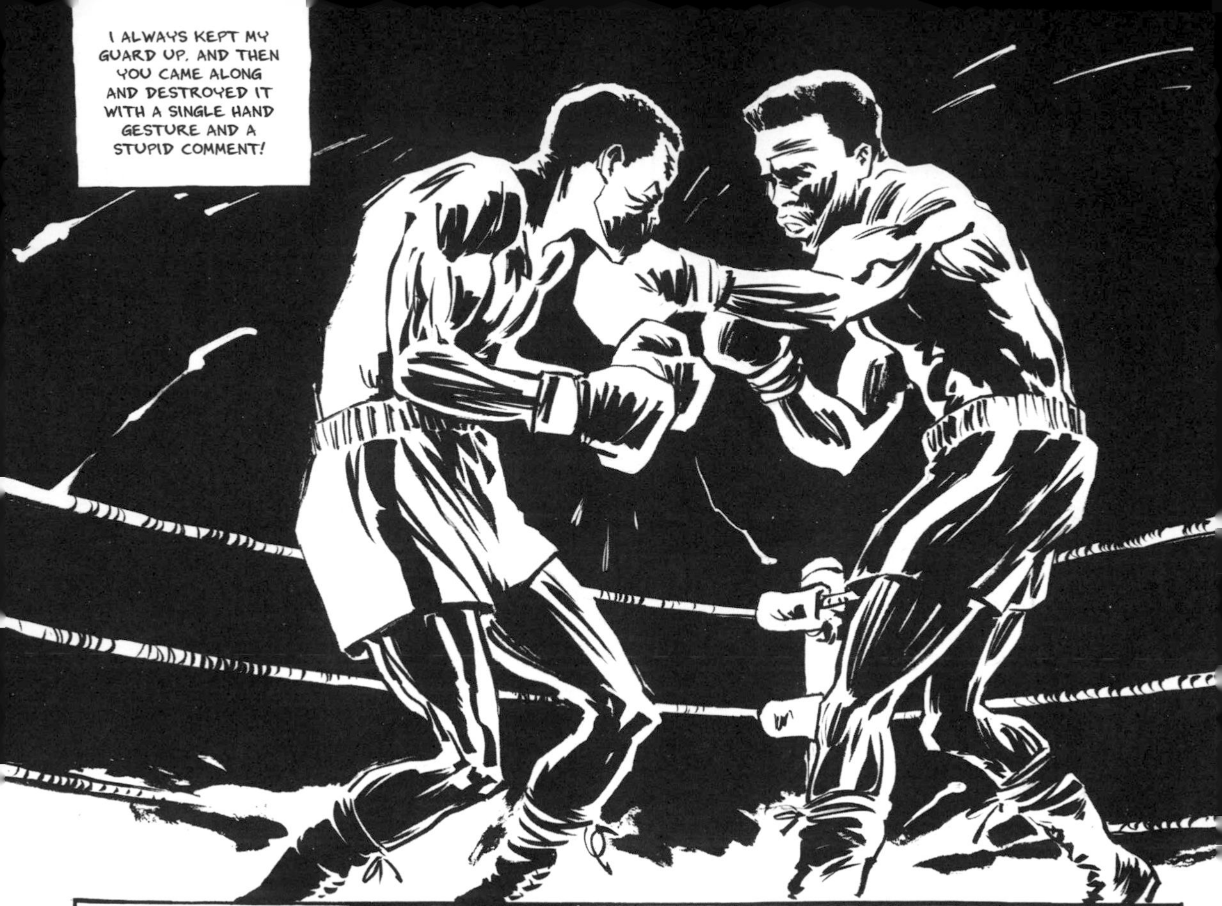
I ALWAYS KEPT MY GUARD UP, AND THEN YOU CAME ALONG AND DESTROYED IT WITH A SINGLE HAND GESTURE AND A STUPID COMMENT!

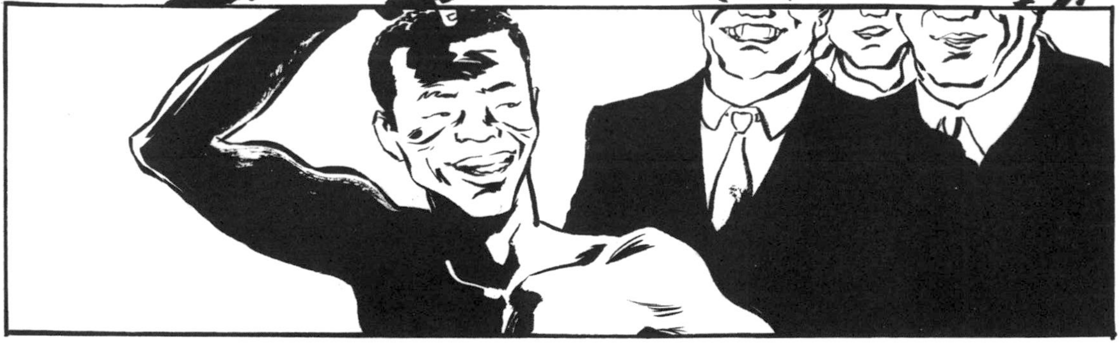

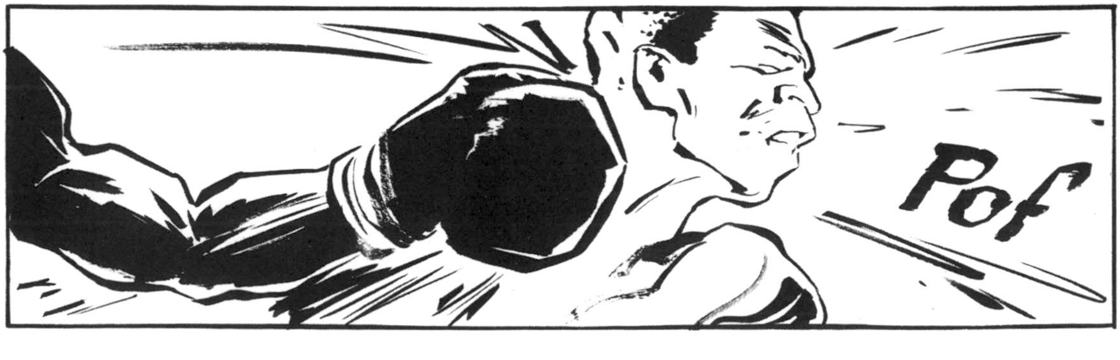
Pof

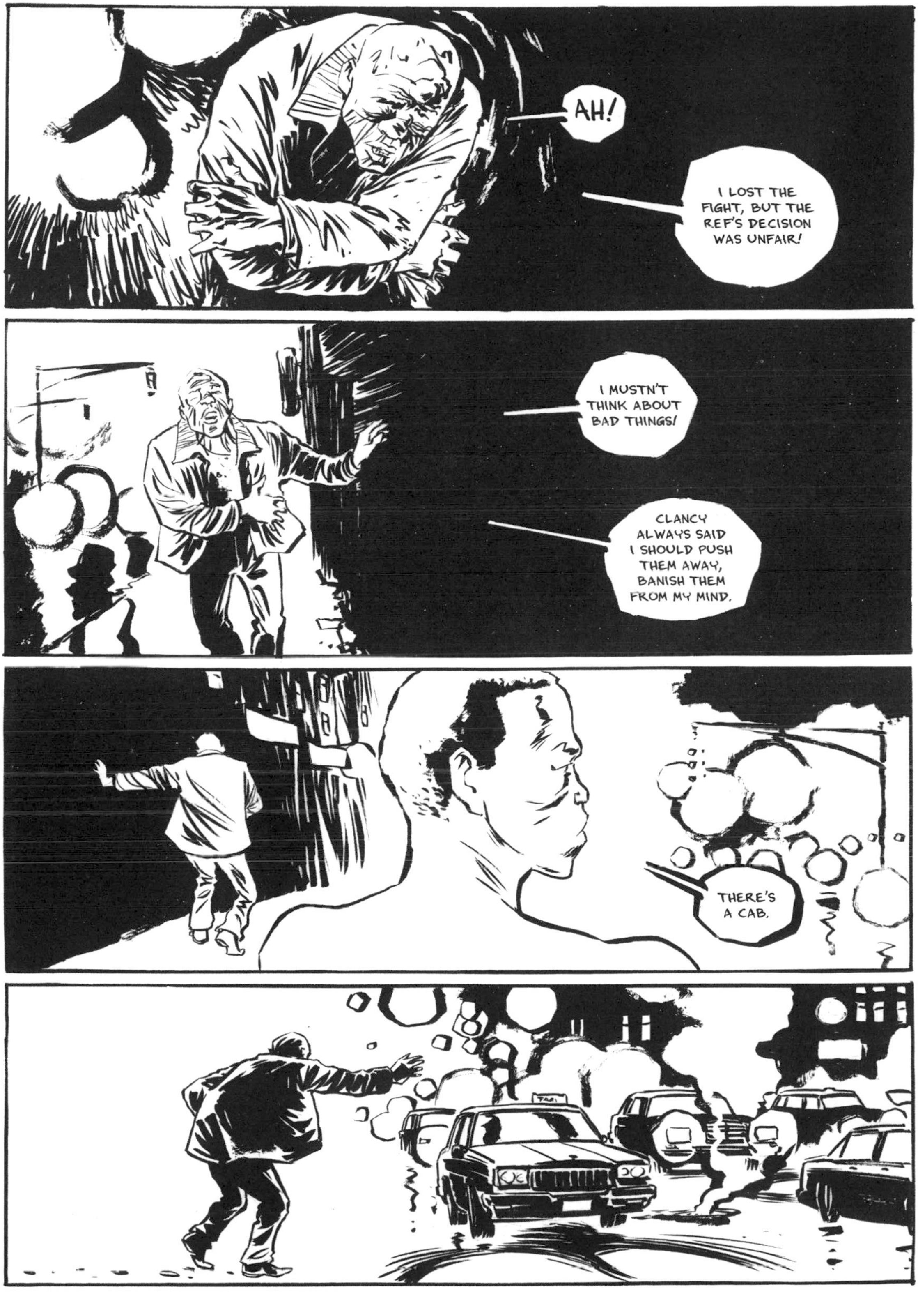
AH!
I LOST THE FIGHT, BUT THE REF'S DECISION WAS UNFAIR!
I MUSTN'T THINK ABOUT BAD THINGS!
CLANCY ALWAYS SAID I SHOULD PUSH THEM AWAY, BANISH THEM FROM MY MIND.
THERE'S A CAB.

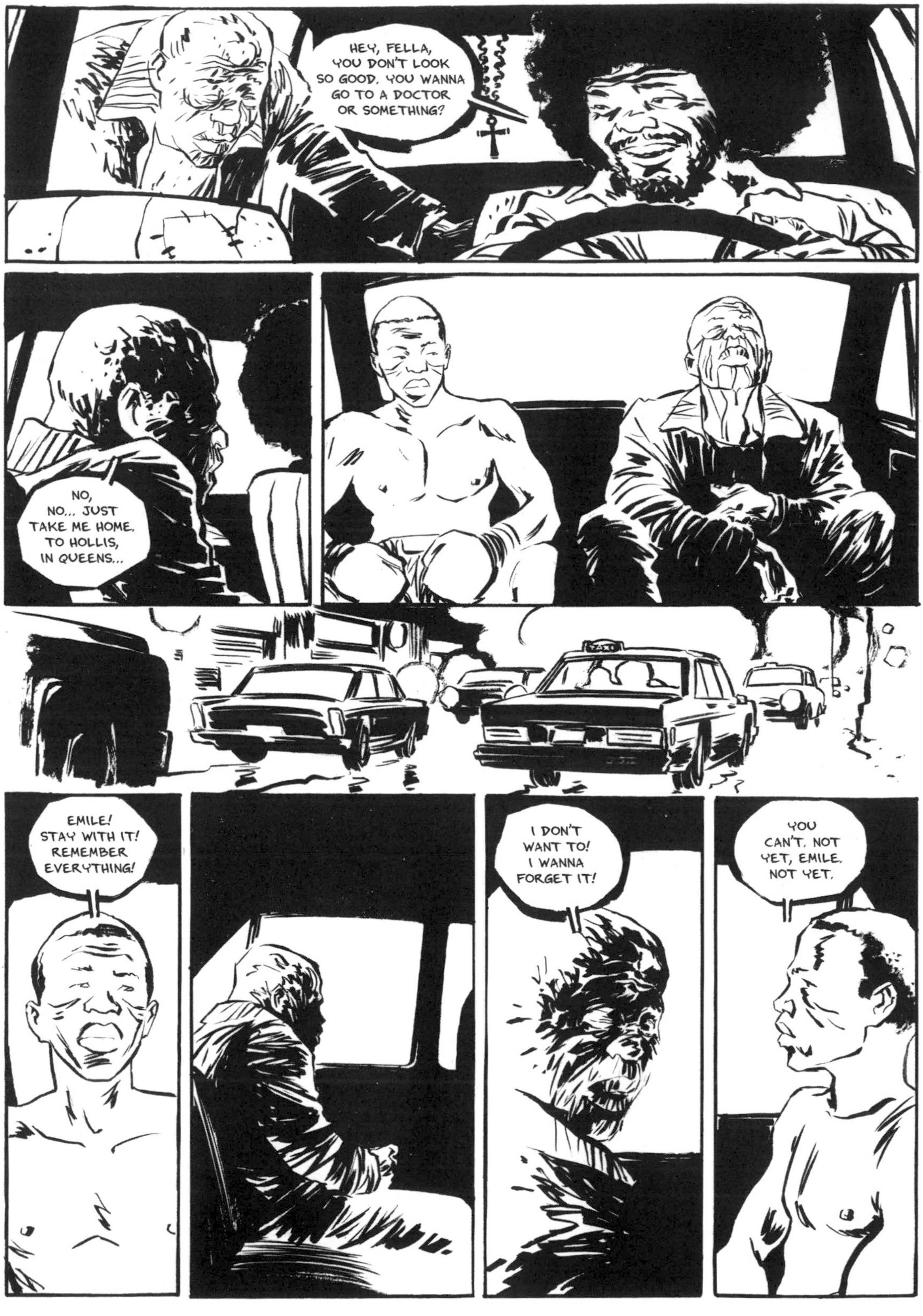
HEY, FELLA, YOU DON'T LOOK SO GOOD. YOU WANNA GO TO A DOCTOR OR SOMETHING?
NO, NO... JUST TAKE ME HOME. TO HOLLIS, IN QUEENS...
EMILE! STAY WITH IT! REMEMBER EVERYTHING!
I DON'T WANT TO! I WANNA FORGET IT!
YOU CAN'T. NOT YET, EMILE. NOT YET.

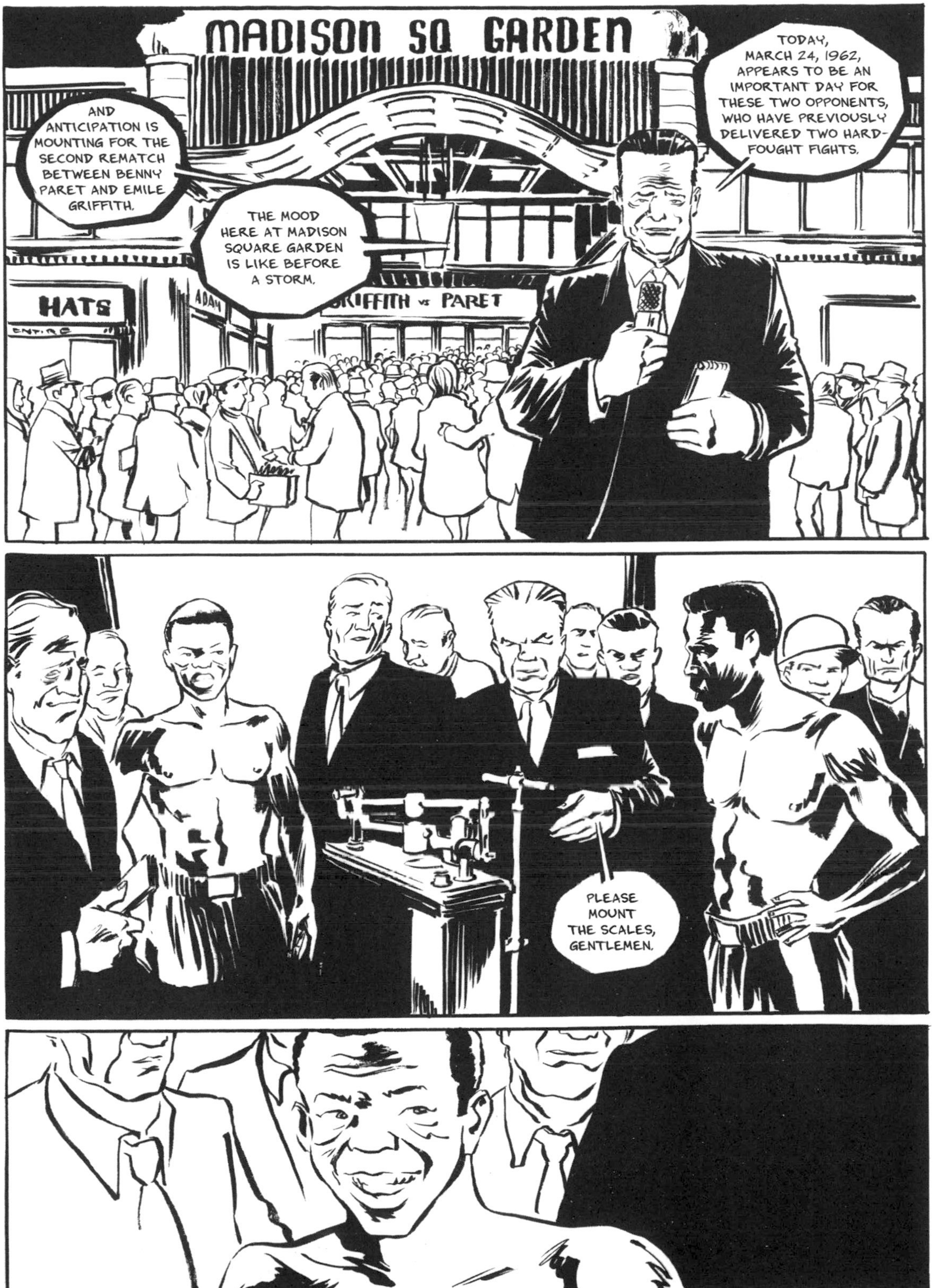
MADISON SQ GARDEN
AND ANTICIPATION IS MOUNTING FOR THE SECOND REMATCH BETWEEN BENNY PARET AND EMILE GRIFFITH.
THE MOOD HERE AT MADISON SQUARE GARDEN IS LIKE BEFORE A STORM.
TODAY, MARCH 24, 1962, APPEARS TO BE AN IMPORTANT DAY FOR THESE TWO OPPONENTS, WHO HAVE PREVIOUSLY DELIVERED TWO HARD-FOUGHT FIGHTS.
HATS
GRIFFITH vs PARET
PLEASE MOUNT THE SCALES, GENTLEMEN.

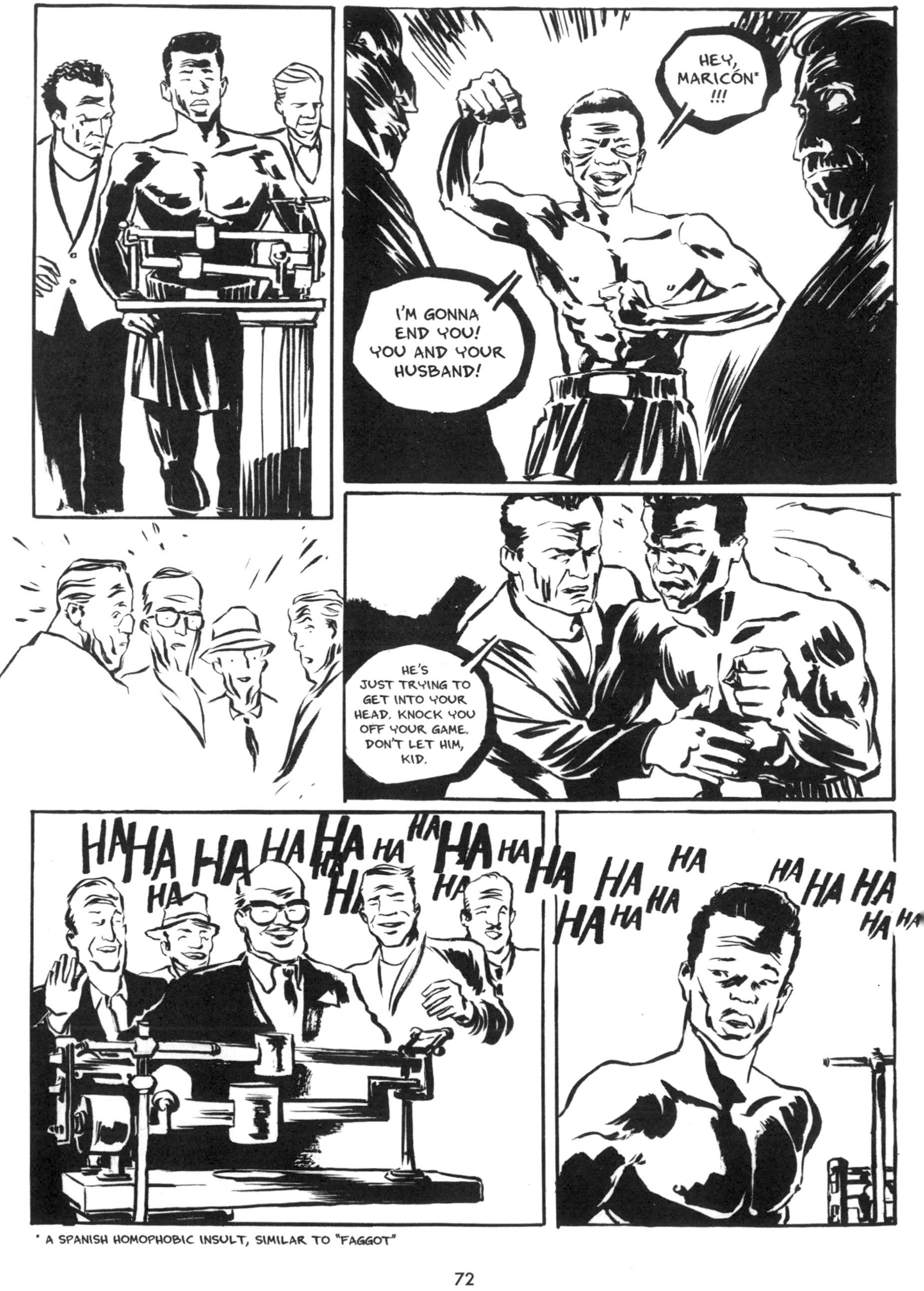
HEY, MARICÓN* !!!
I'M GONNA END YOU! YOU AND YOUR HUSBAND!
HE'S JUST TRYING TO GET INTO YOUR HEAD. KNOCK YOU OFF YOUR GAME. DON'T LET HIM, KID.
HA HA HA HA HA HA HA HA HA HA HA HA HA HA HA HA
HA HA HA HA HA HA HA HA HA HA HA HA

* A SPANISH HOMOPHOBIC INSULT, SIMILAR TO "FAGGOT"

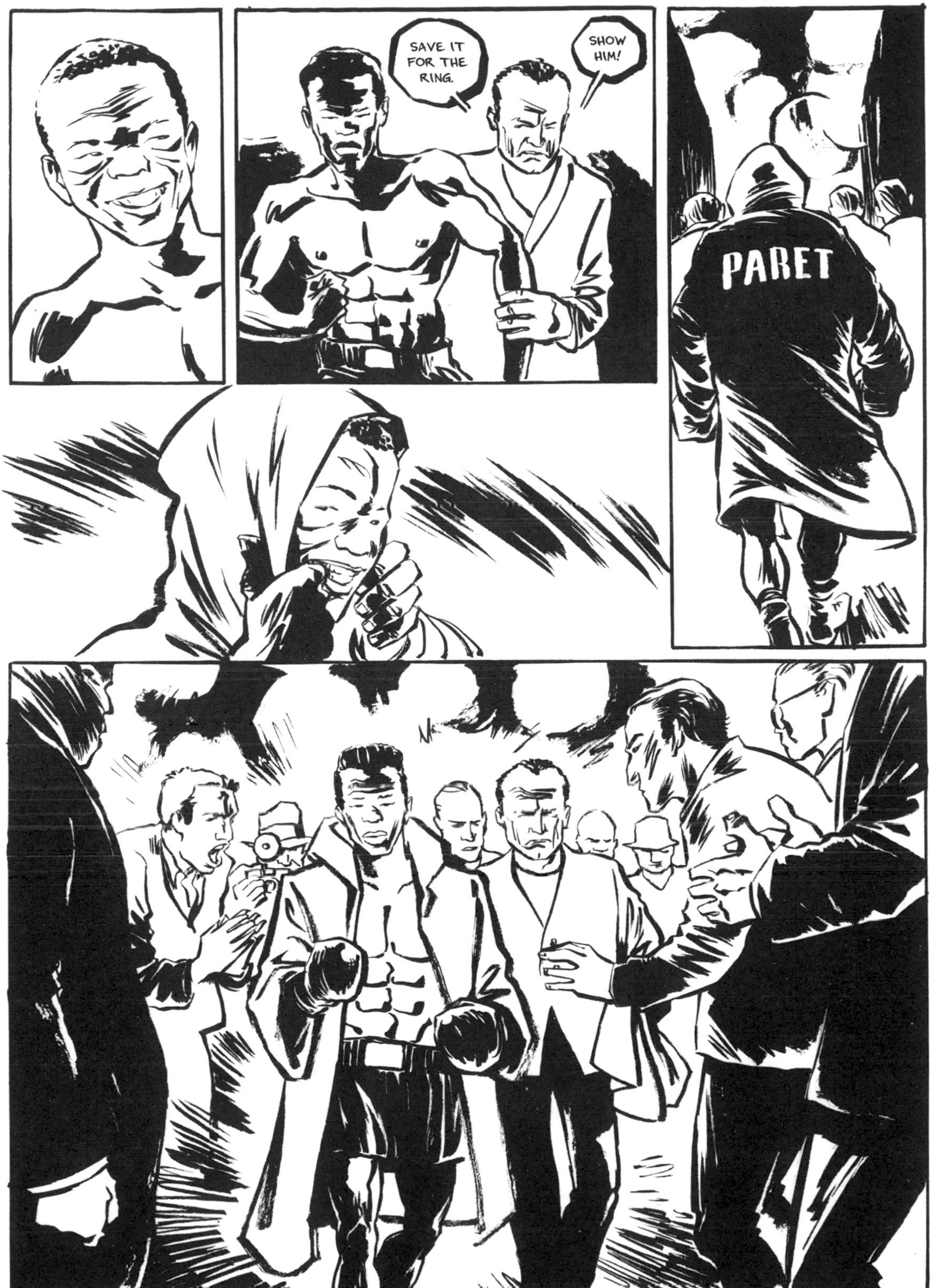
SAVE IT FOR THE RING.
SHOW HIM!
PARET

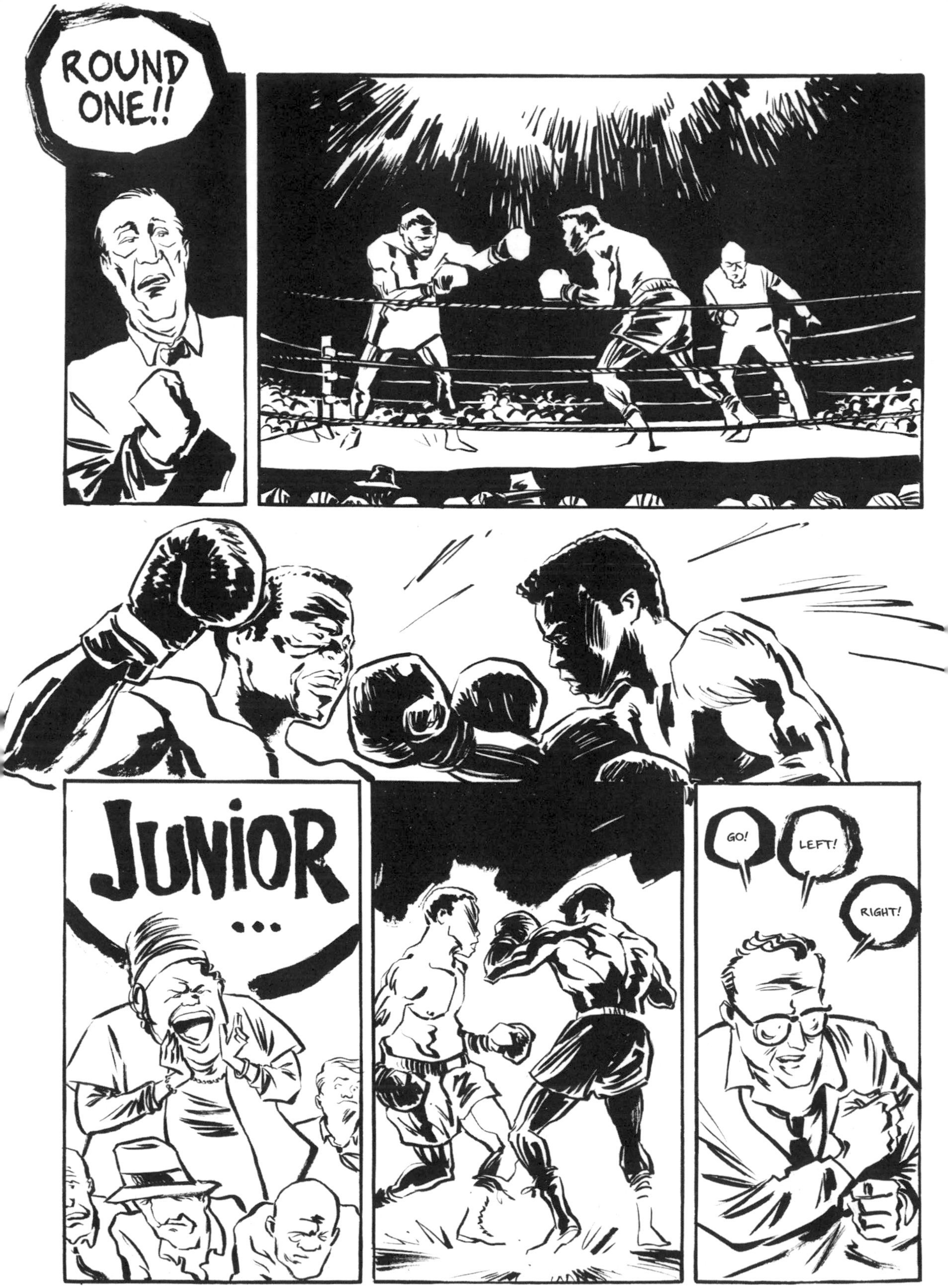
ROUND ONE!!
JUNIOR
...
GO!
LEFT!
RIGHT!

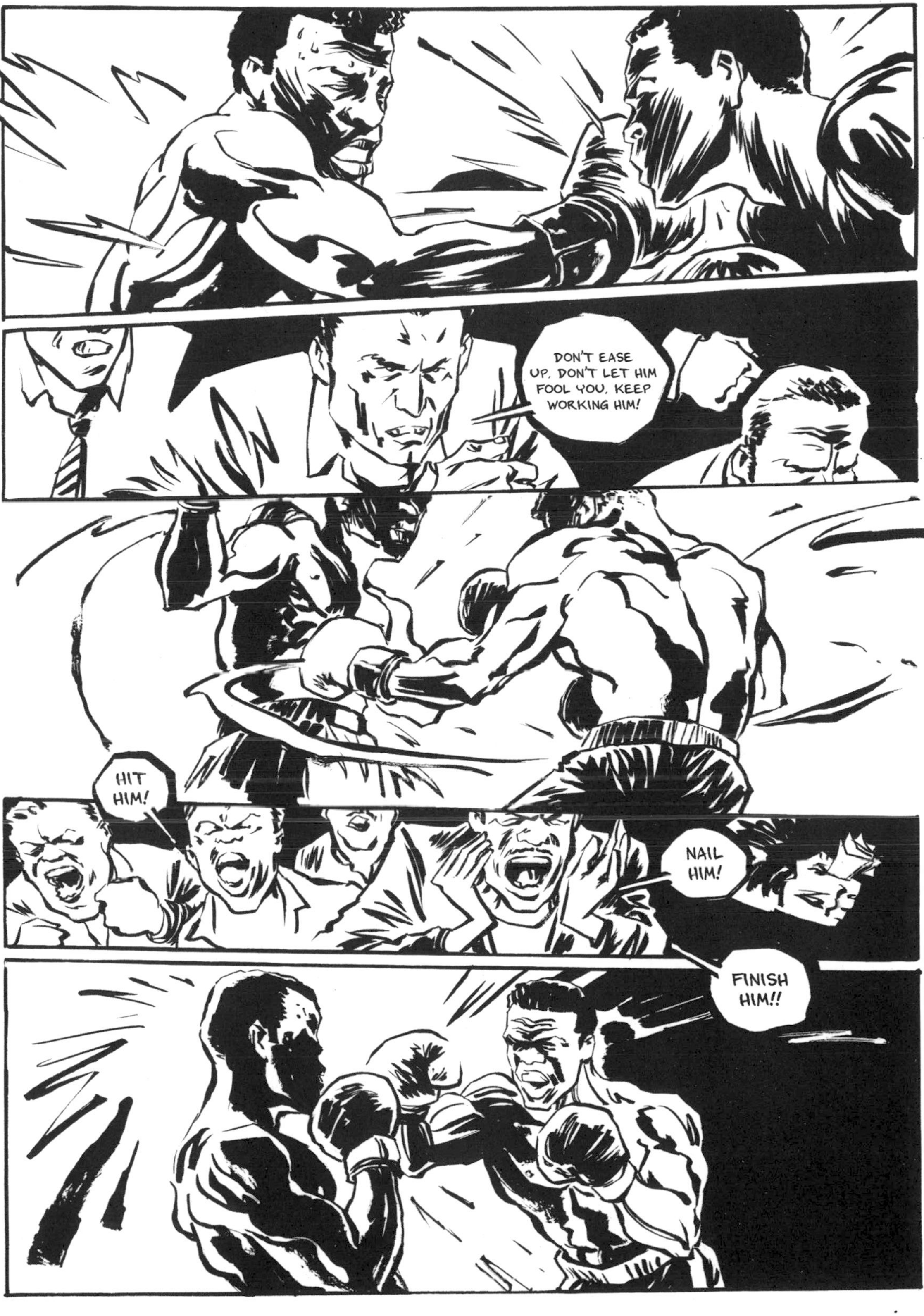
DON'T EASE UP. DON'T LET HIM FOOL YOU. KEEP WORKING HIM!
HIT HIM!
NAIL HIM!
FINISH HIM!!

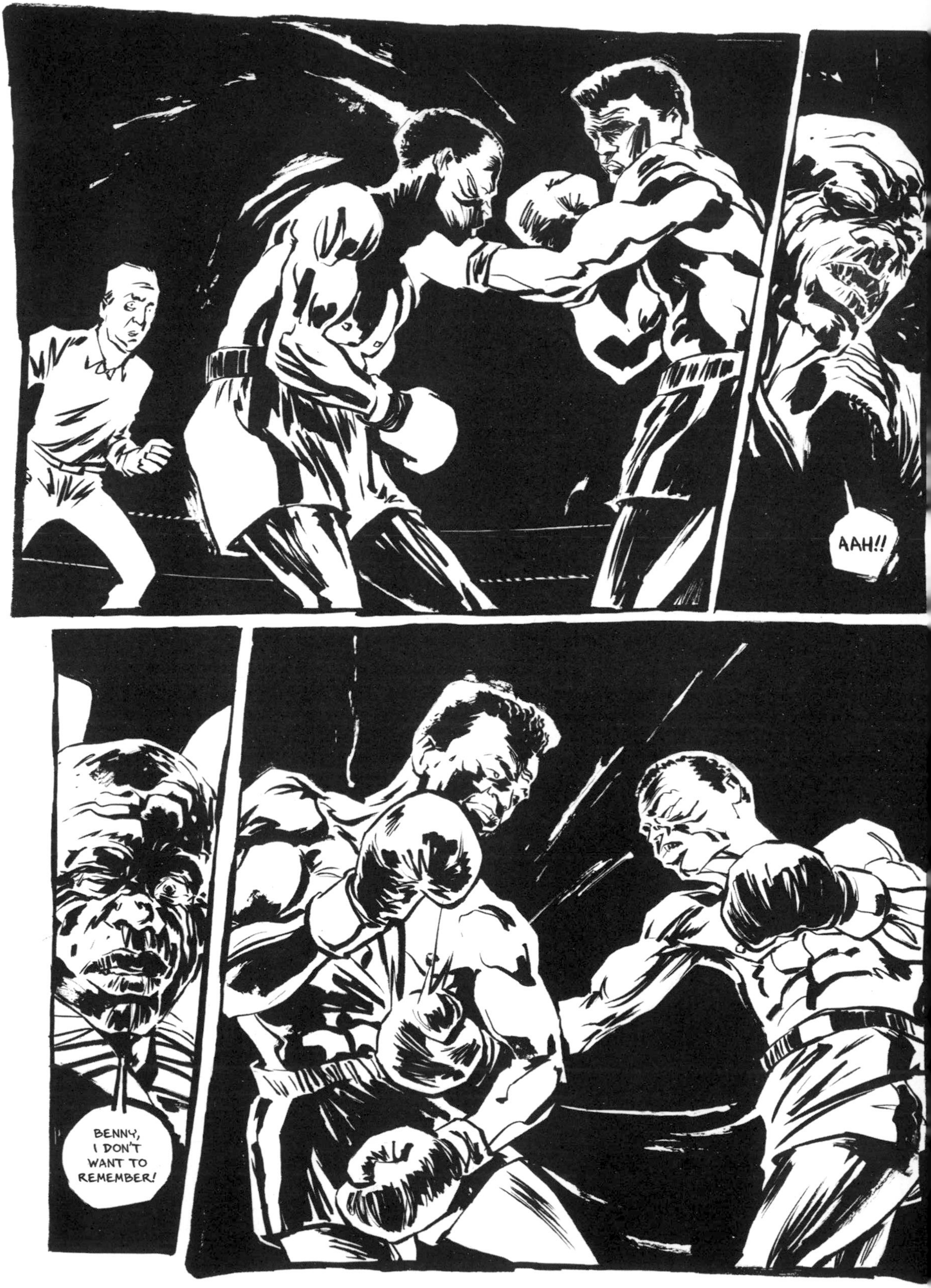
AAH!!
BENNY, I DON'T WANT TO REMEMBER!

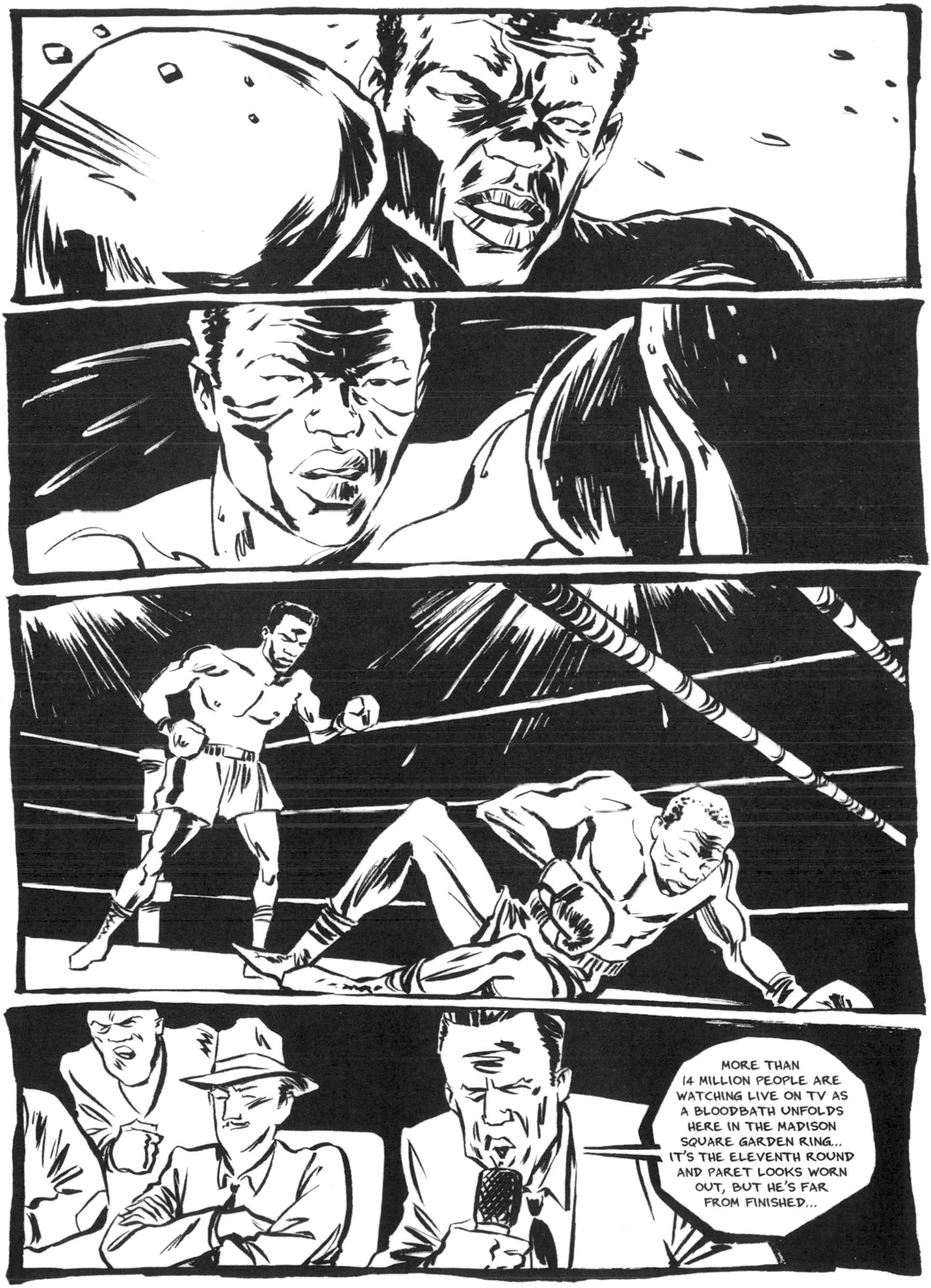
MORE THAN 14 MILLION PEOPLE ARE WATCHING LIVE ON TV AS A BLOODBATH UNFOLDS HERE IN THE MADISON SQUARE GARDEN RING... IT'S THE ELEVENTH ROUND AND PARET LOOKS WORN OUT, BUT HE'S FAR FROM FINISHED...

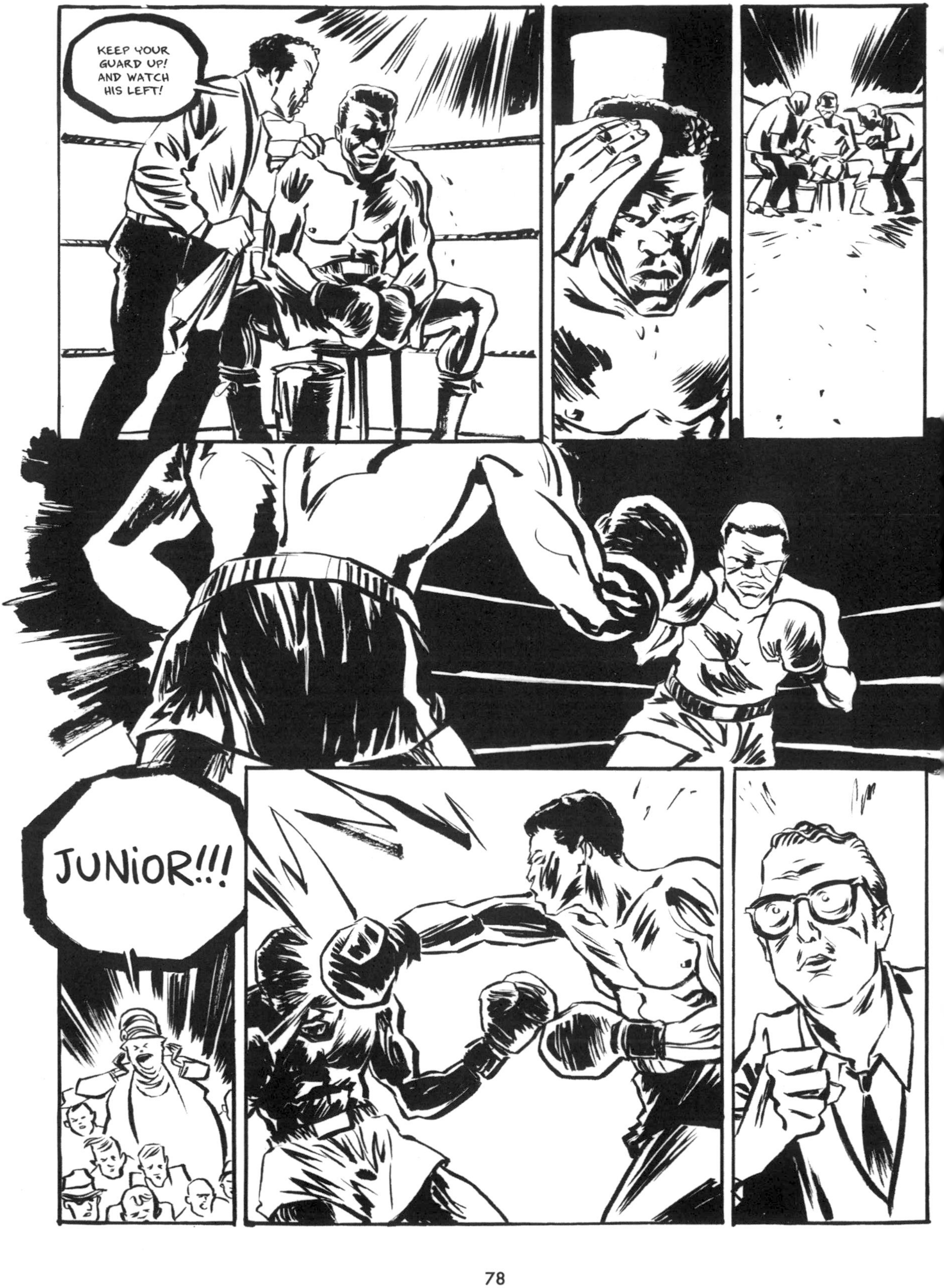
KEEP YOUR GUARD UP! AND WATCH HIS LEFT!
JUNIOR!!!

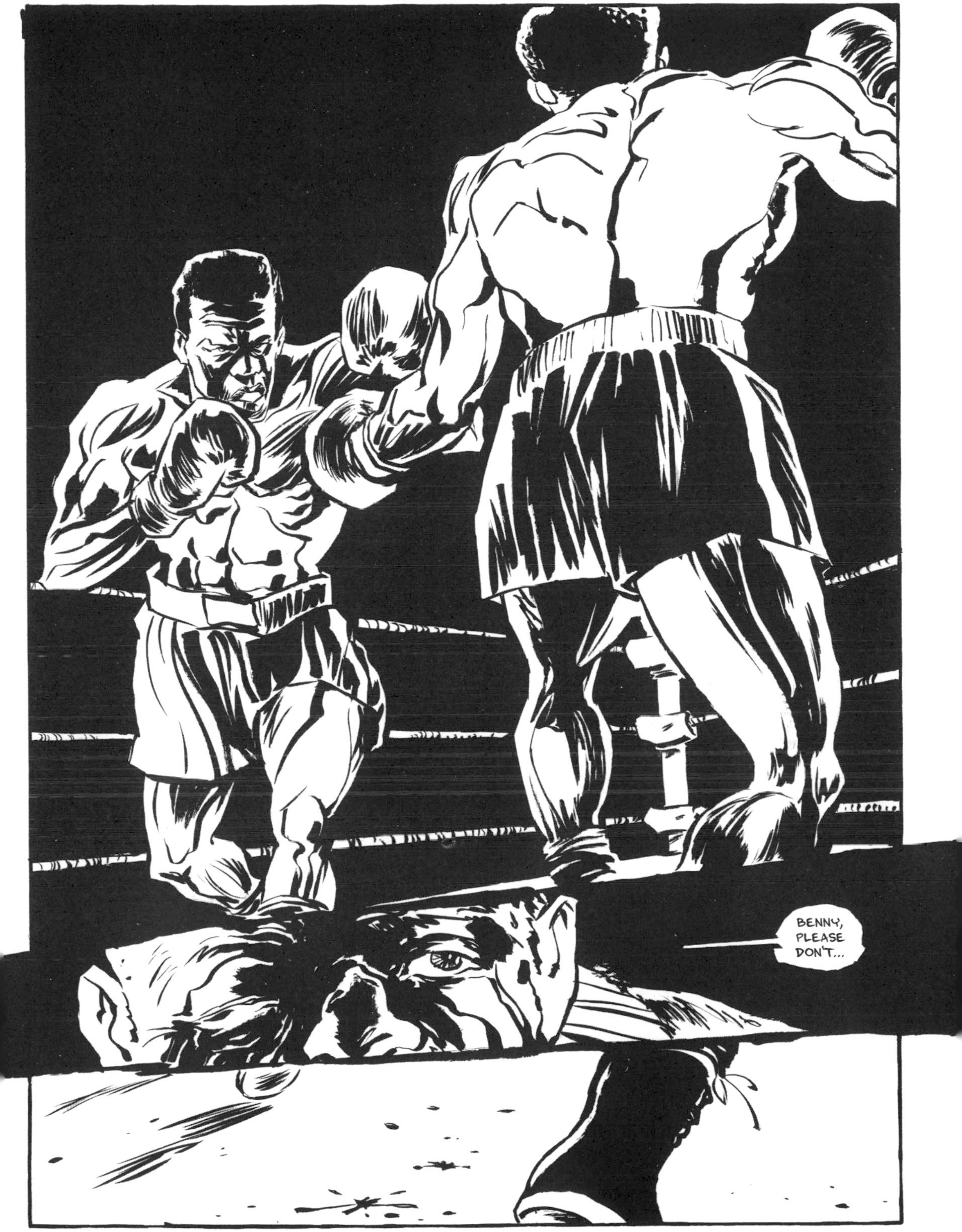
BENNY, PLEASE DON'T...

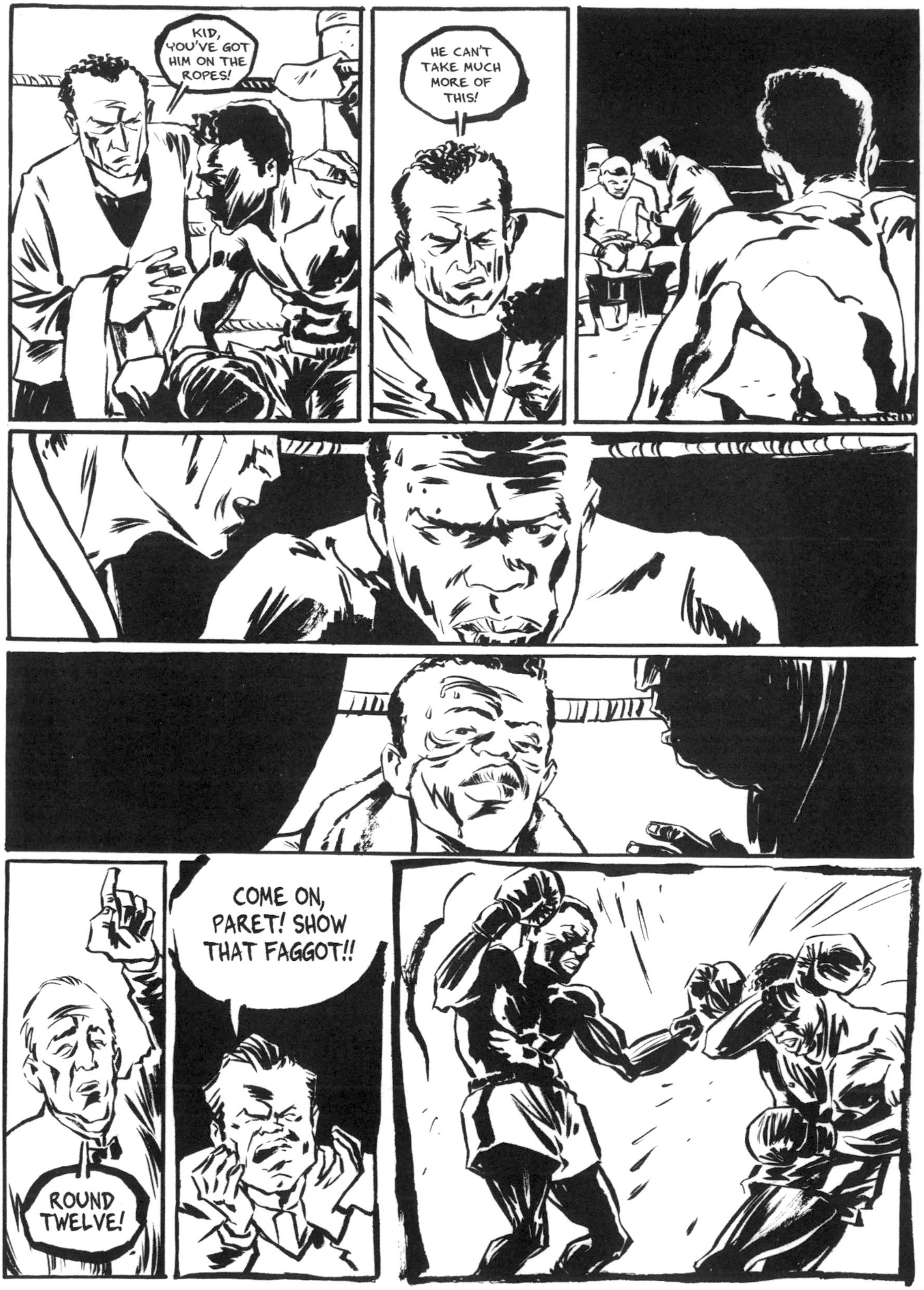
KID, YOU'VE GOT HIM ON THE ROPES!
HE CAN'T TAKE MUCH MORE OF THIS!
ROUND TWELVE!
COME ON, PARET! SHOW THAT FAGGOT!!

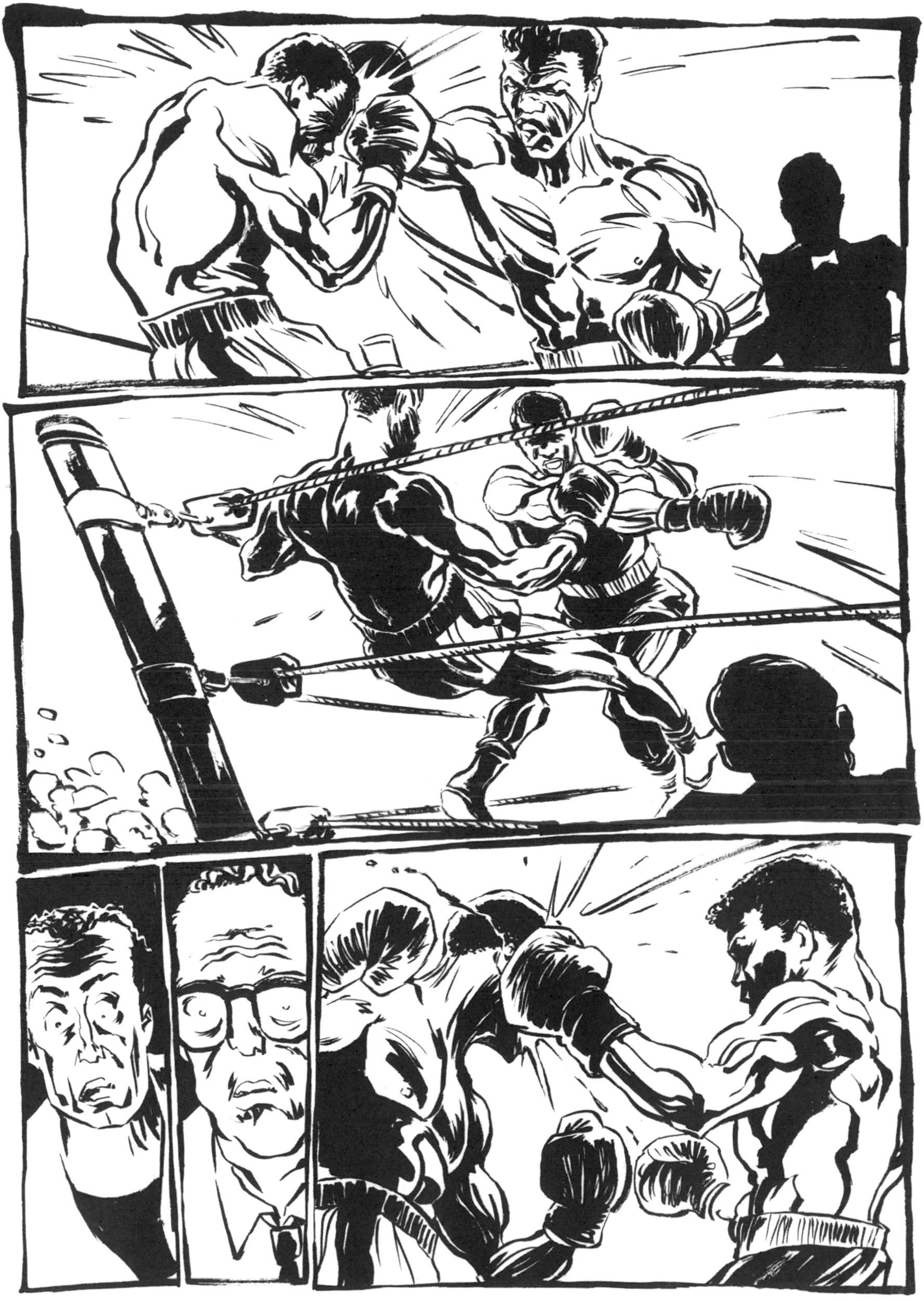

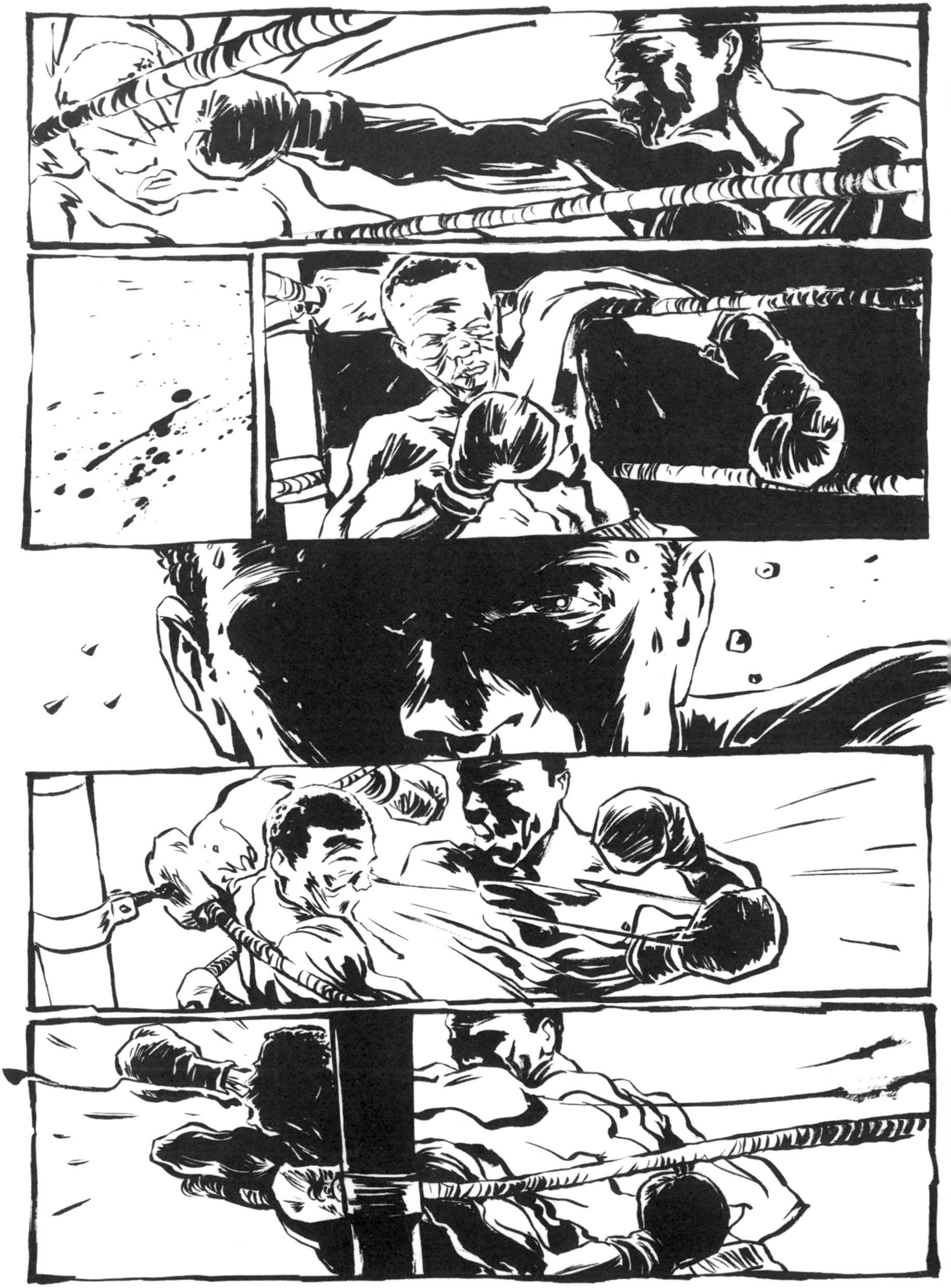

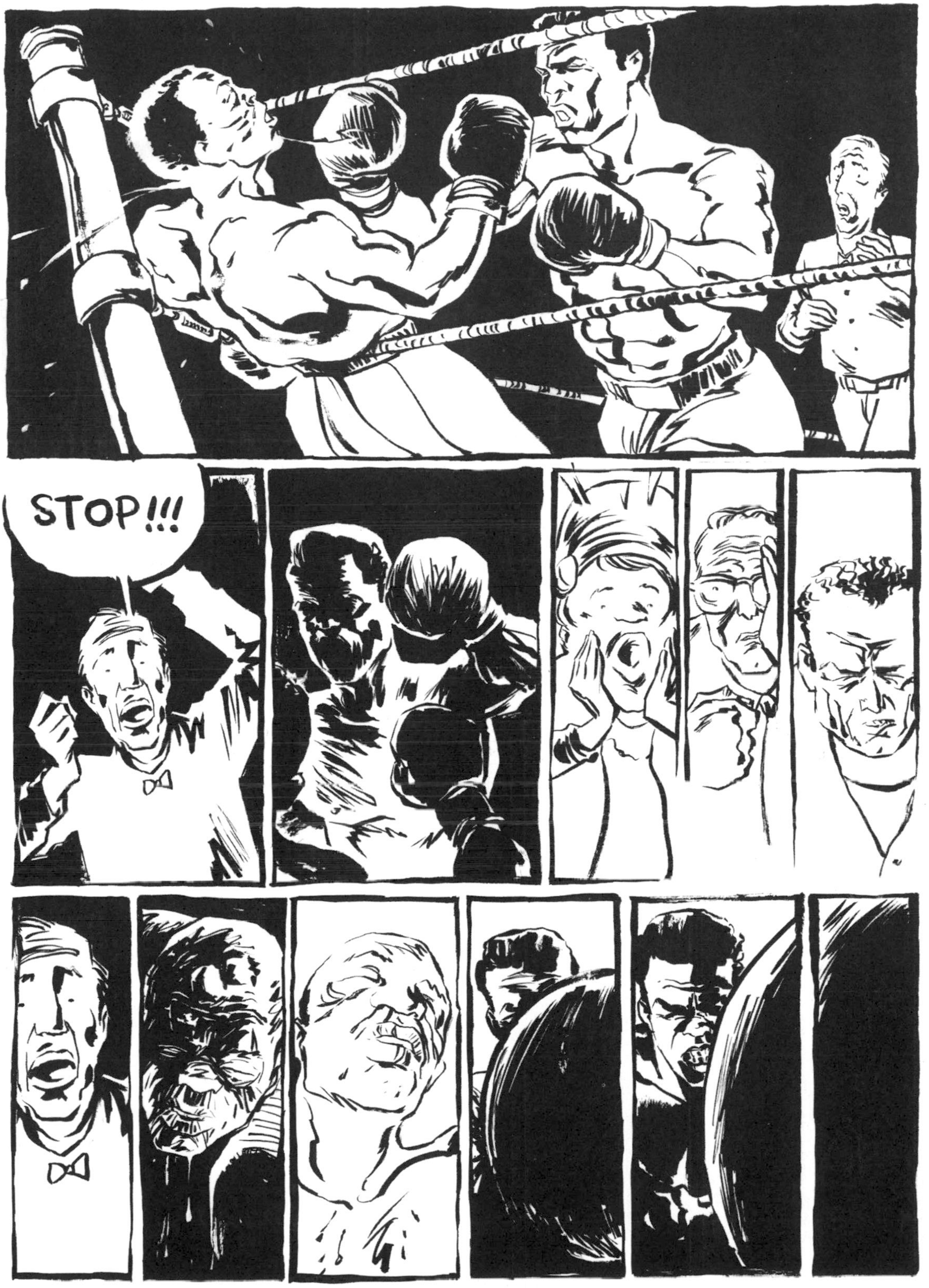
STOP!!!

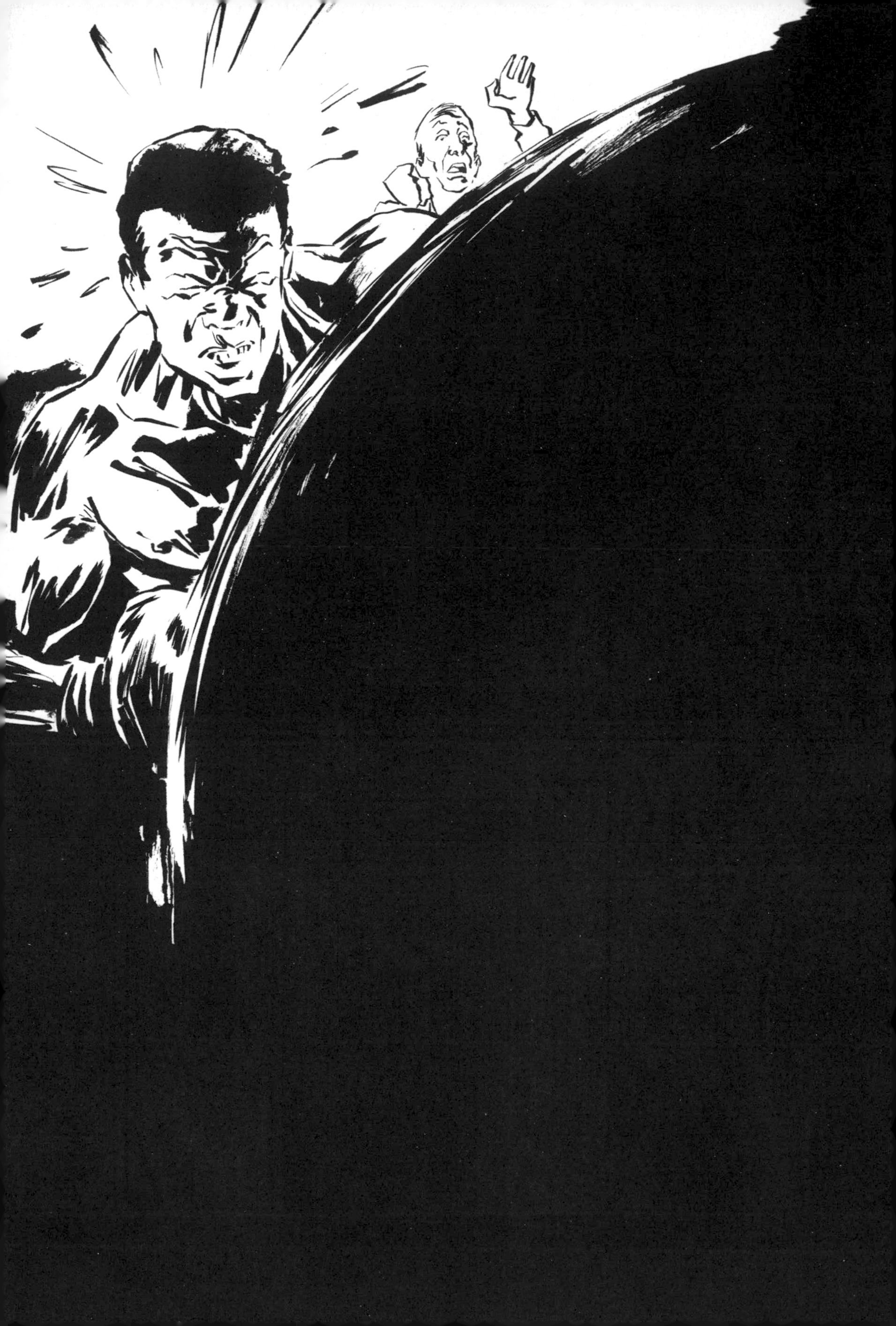

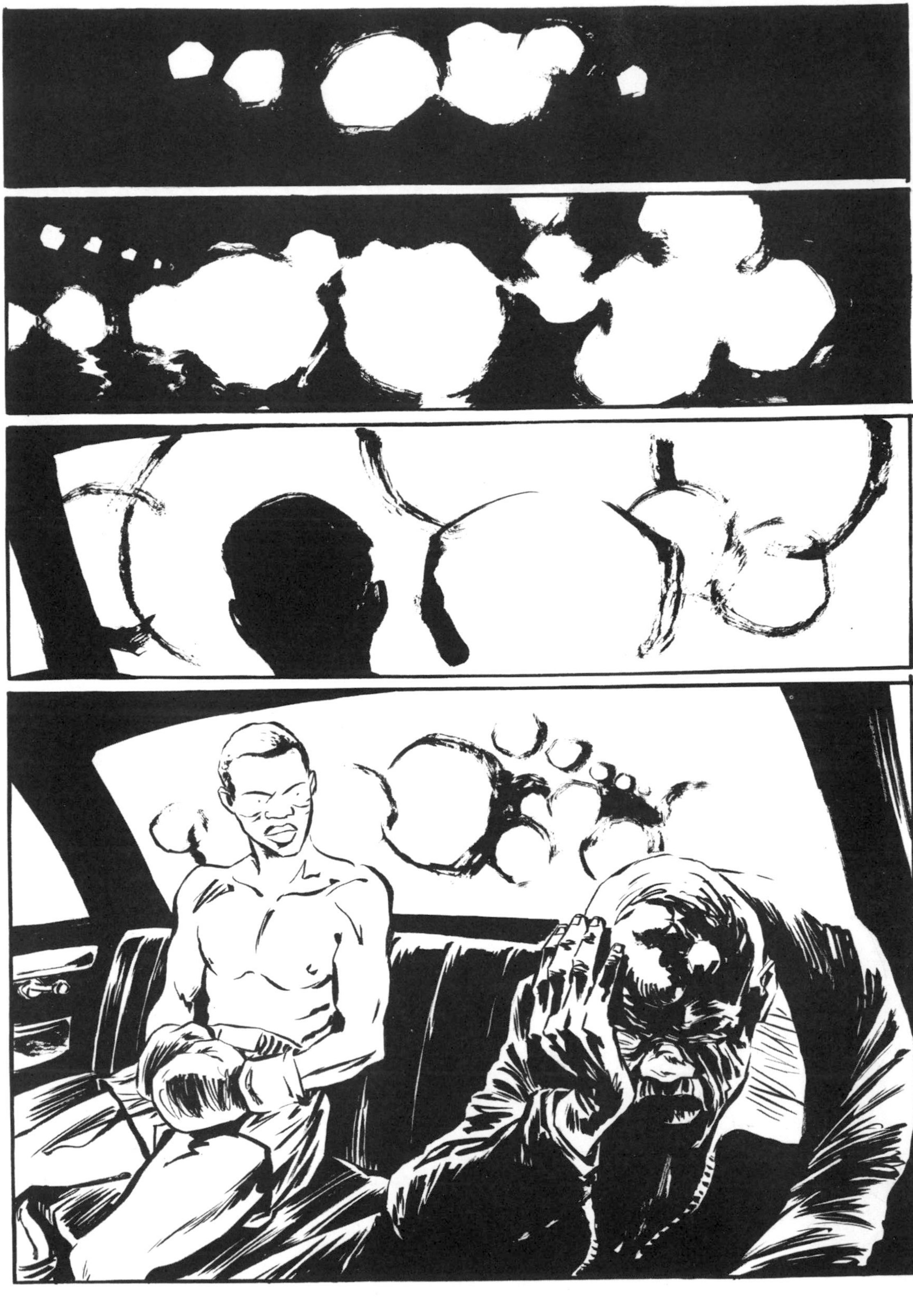

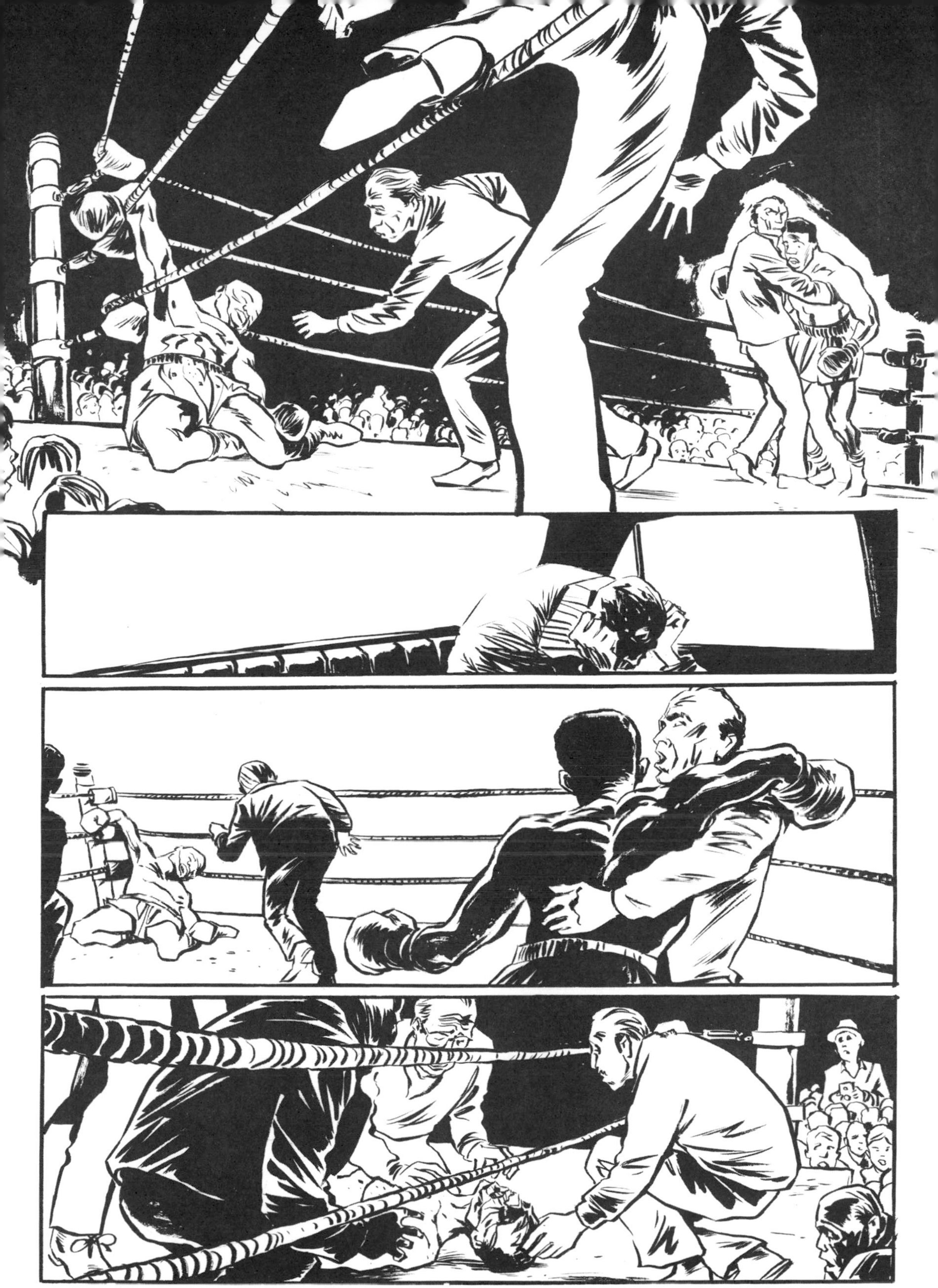

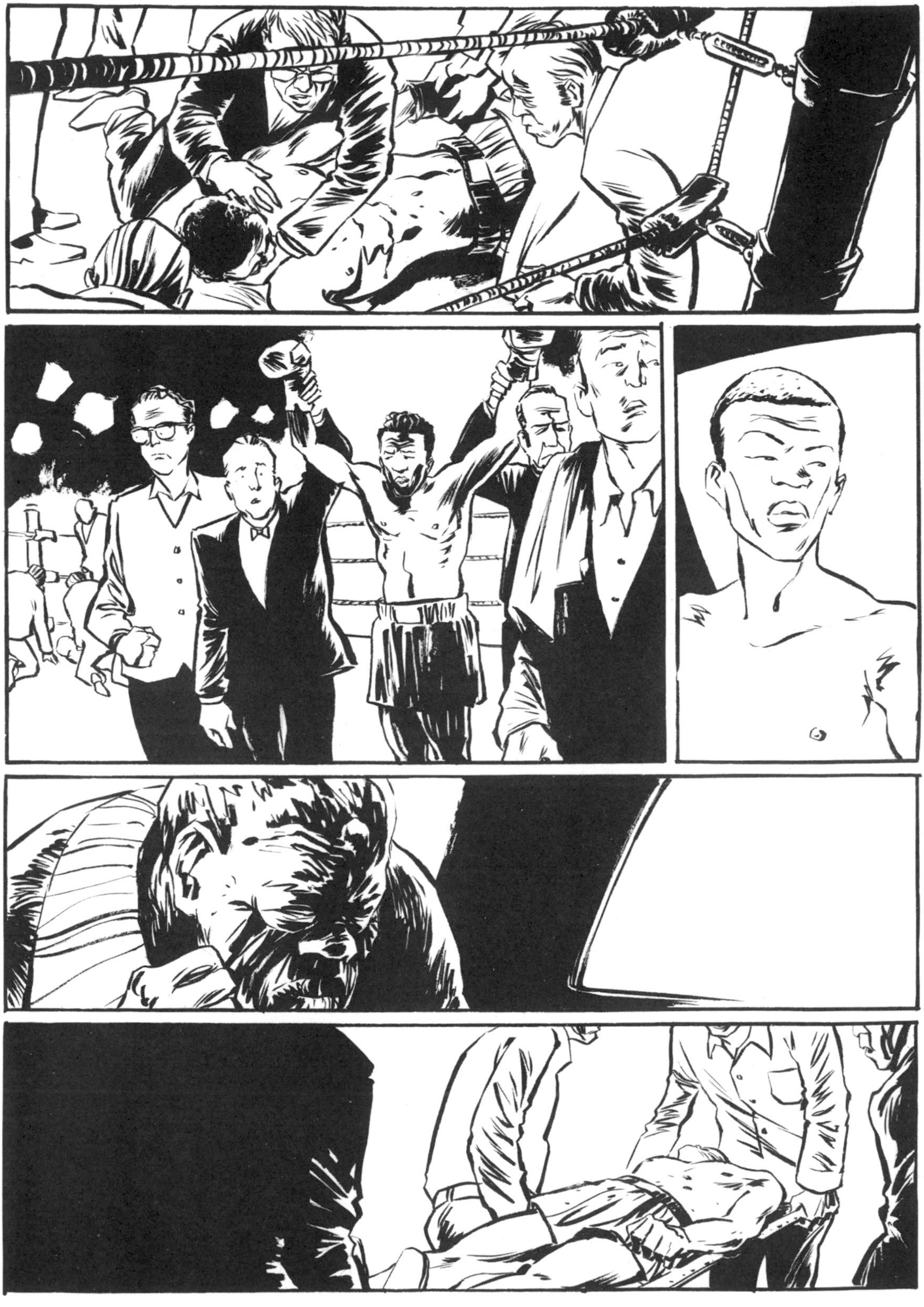

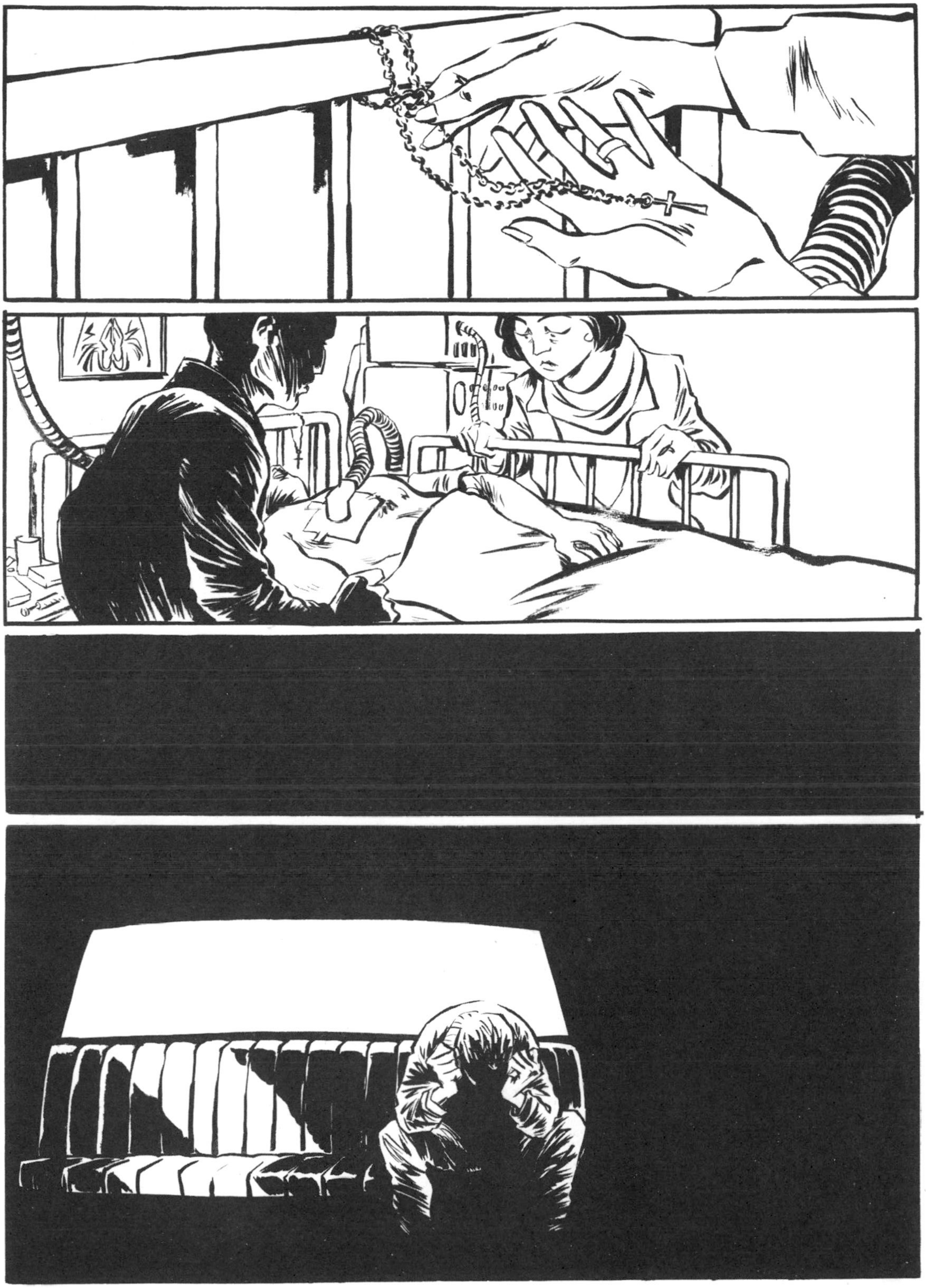

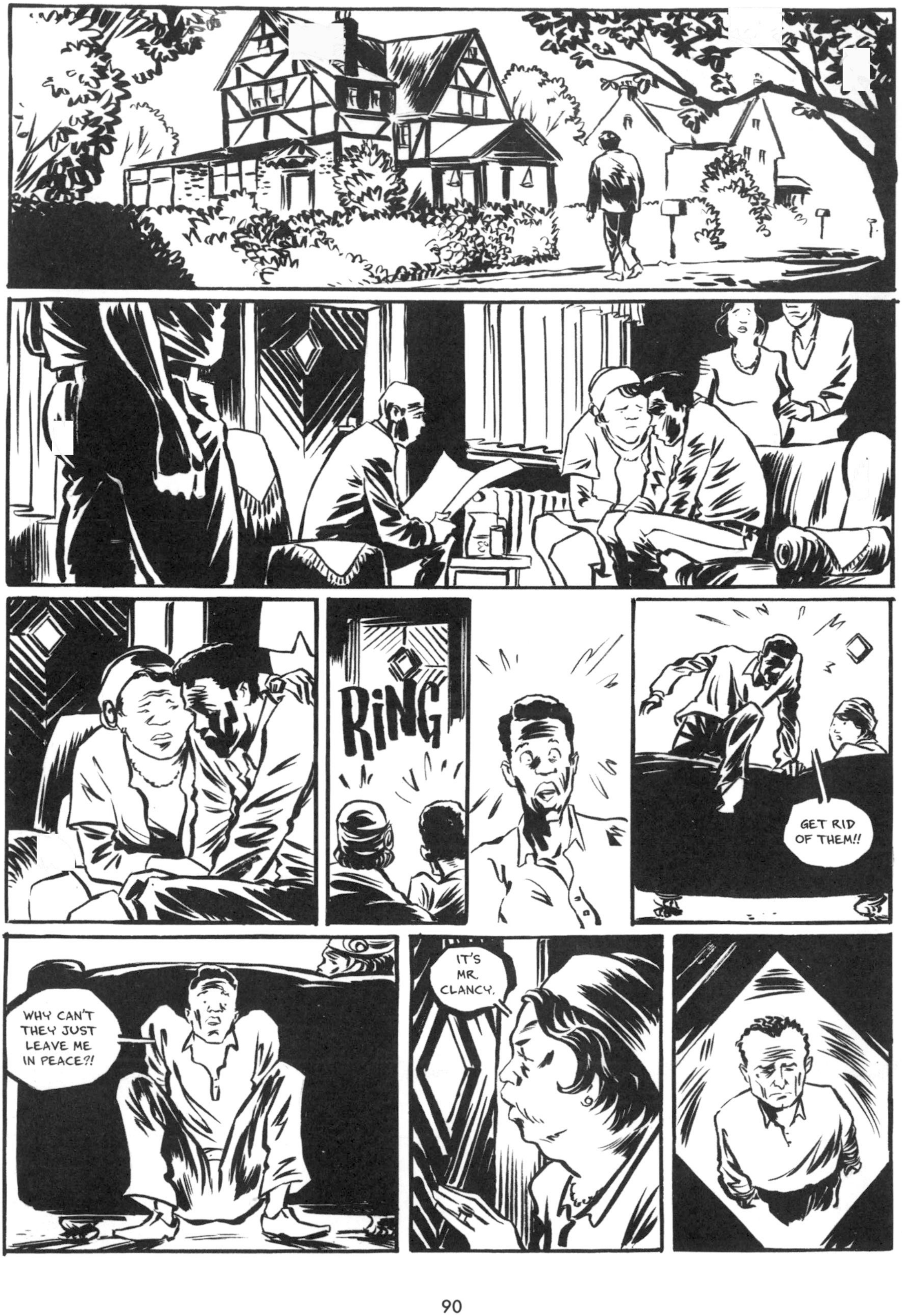
RING
GET RID OF THEM!!
WHY CAN'T THEY JUST LEAVE ME IN PEACE?!
IT'S MR. CLANCY.

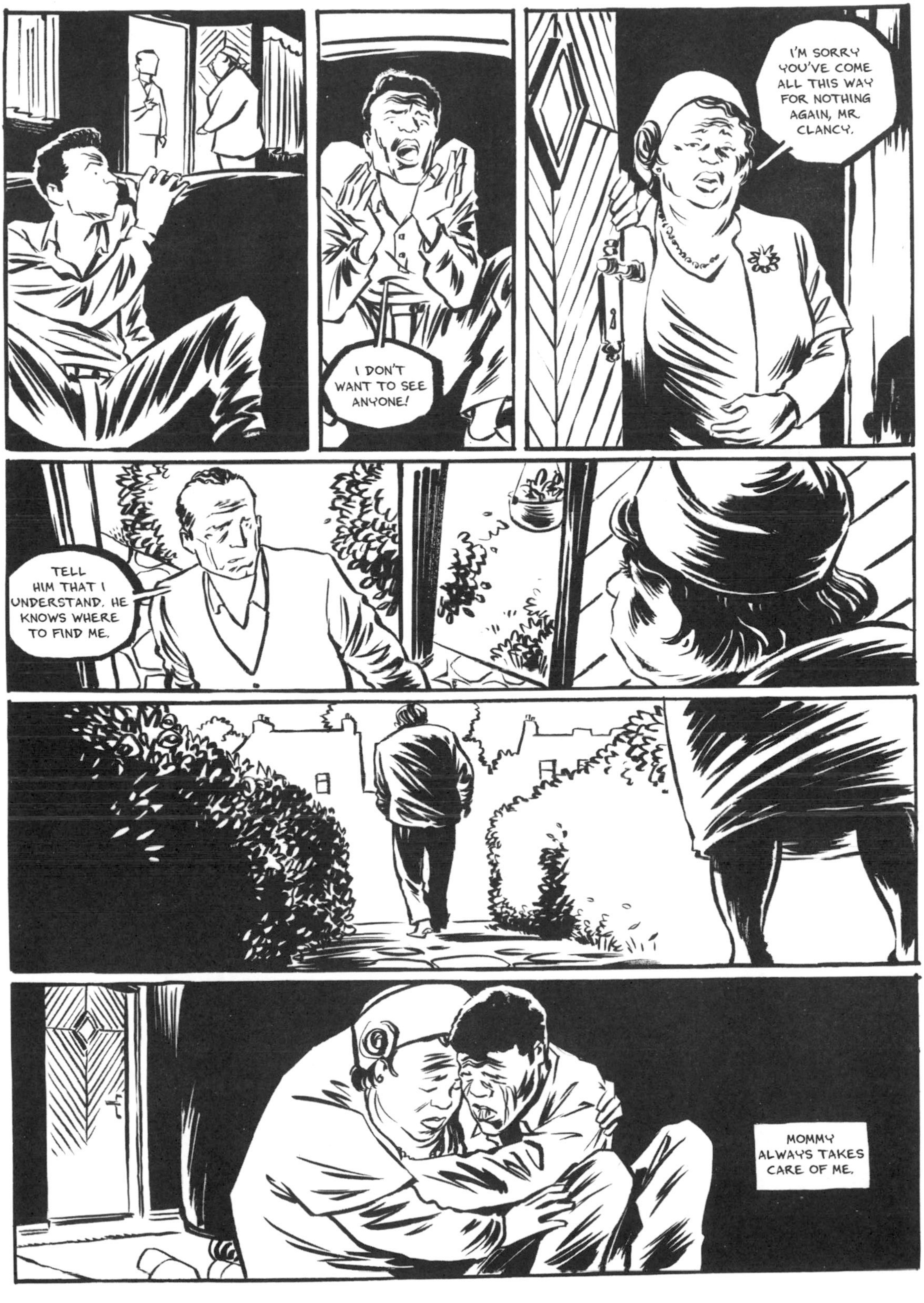
I DON'T WANT TO SEE ANYONE!
I'M SORRY YOU'VE COME ALL THIS WAY FOR NOTHING AGAIN, MR CLANCY.
TELL HIM THAT I UNDERSTAND. HE KNOWS WHERE TO FIND ME.
MOMMY ALWAYS TAKES CARE OF ME.

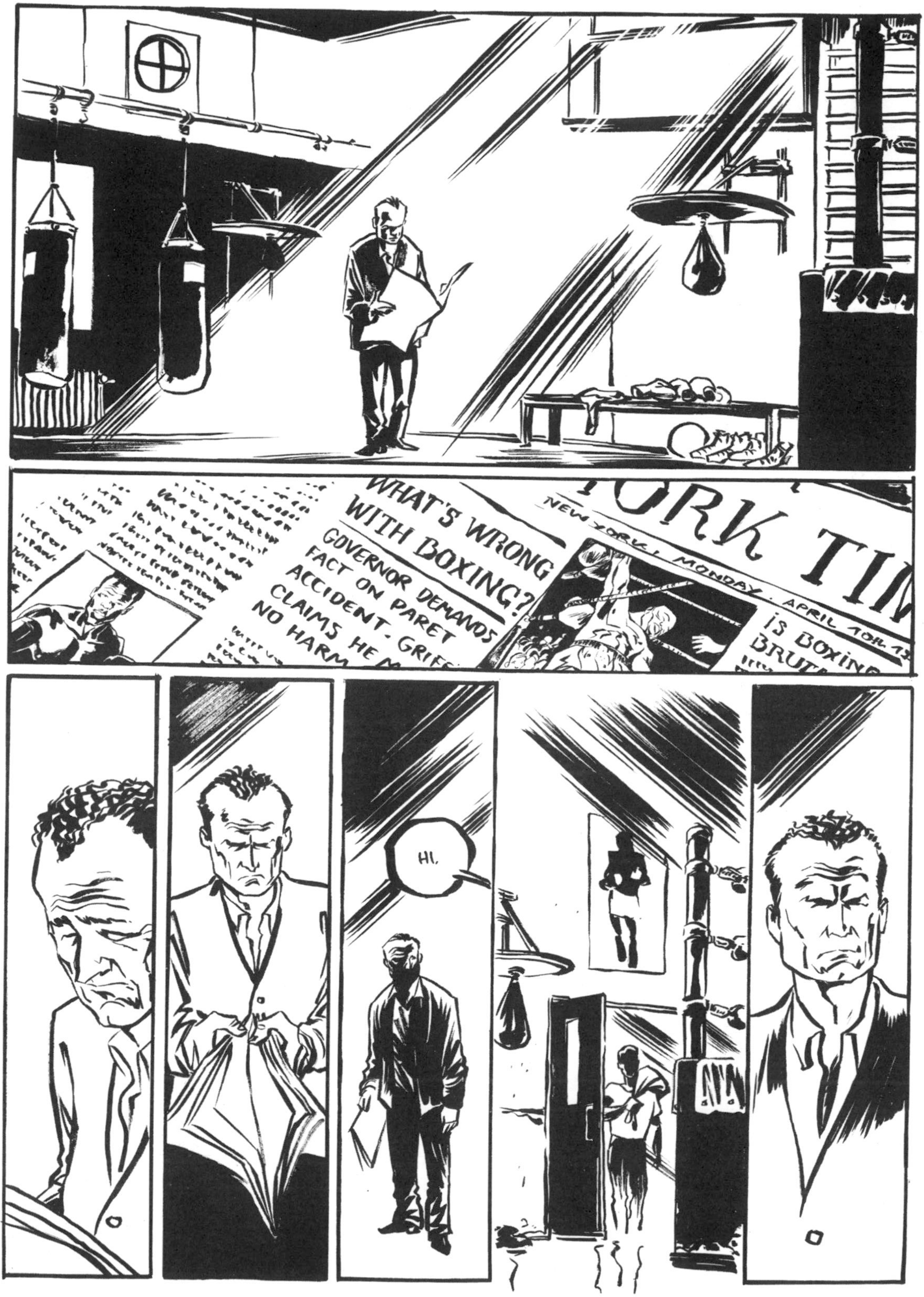
WHAT'S WRONG WITH BOXING?
GOVERNOR DEMANDS FACT ON PARET ACCIDENT -
CLAIMS HE
NO HARM
NEW YORK, MONDAY, APRIL
IS BOXING
HI.

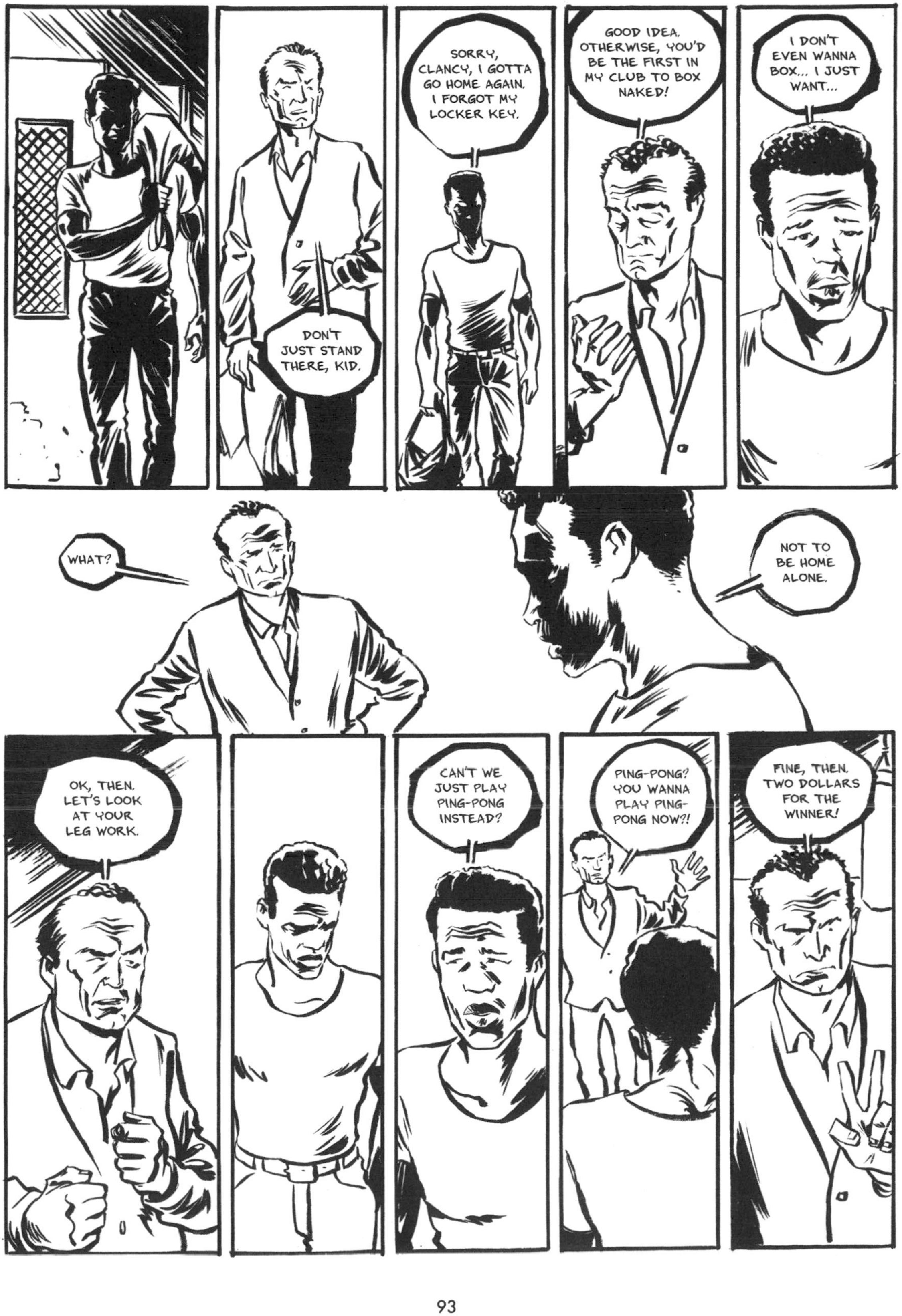
DON'T JUST STAND THERE, KID.
SORRY, CLANCY, I GOTTA GO HOME AGAIN. I FORGOT MY LOCKER KEY.
GOOD IDEA. OTHERWISE, YOU'D BE THE FIRST IN MY CLUB TO BOX NAKED!
I DON'T EVEN WANNA BOX... I JUST WANT...
WHAT?
NOT TO BE HOME ALONE.
OK, THEN. LET'S LOOK AT YOUR LEG WORK.
CAN'T WE JUST PLAY PING-PONG INSTEAD?
PING-PONG? YOU WANNA PLAY PING-PONG NOW?!
FINE, THEN. TWO DOLLARS FOR THE WINNER!

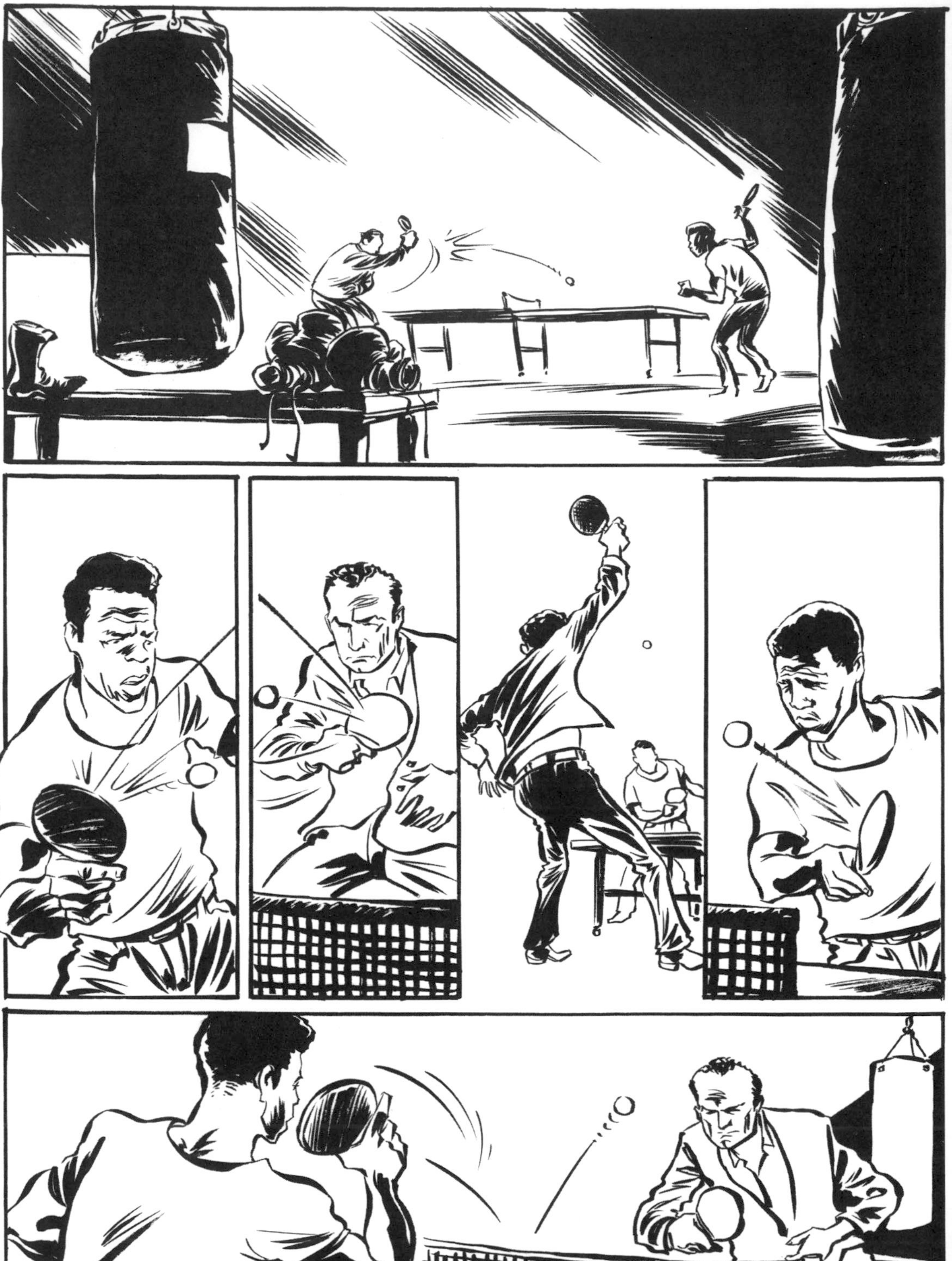

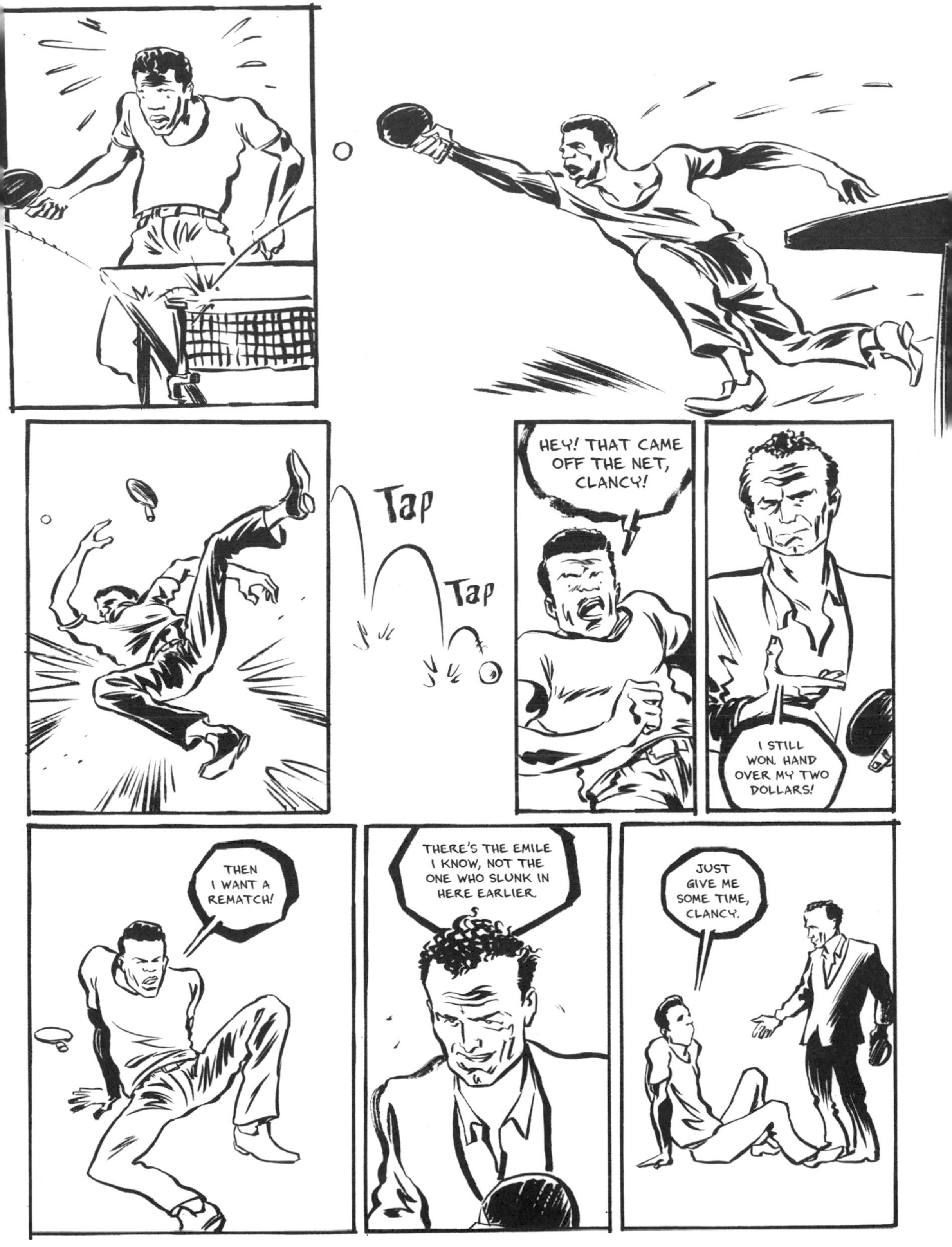
Tap
Tap
HEY! THAT CAME OFF THE NET, CLANCY!
I STILL WON. HAND OVER MY TWO DOLLARS!
THEN I WANT A REMATCH!
THERE'S THE EMILE I KNOW, NOT THE ONE WHO SLUNK IN HERE EARLIER.
JUST GIVE ME SOME TIME, CLANCY.

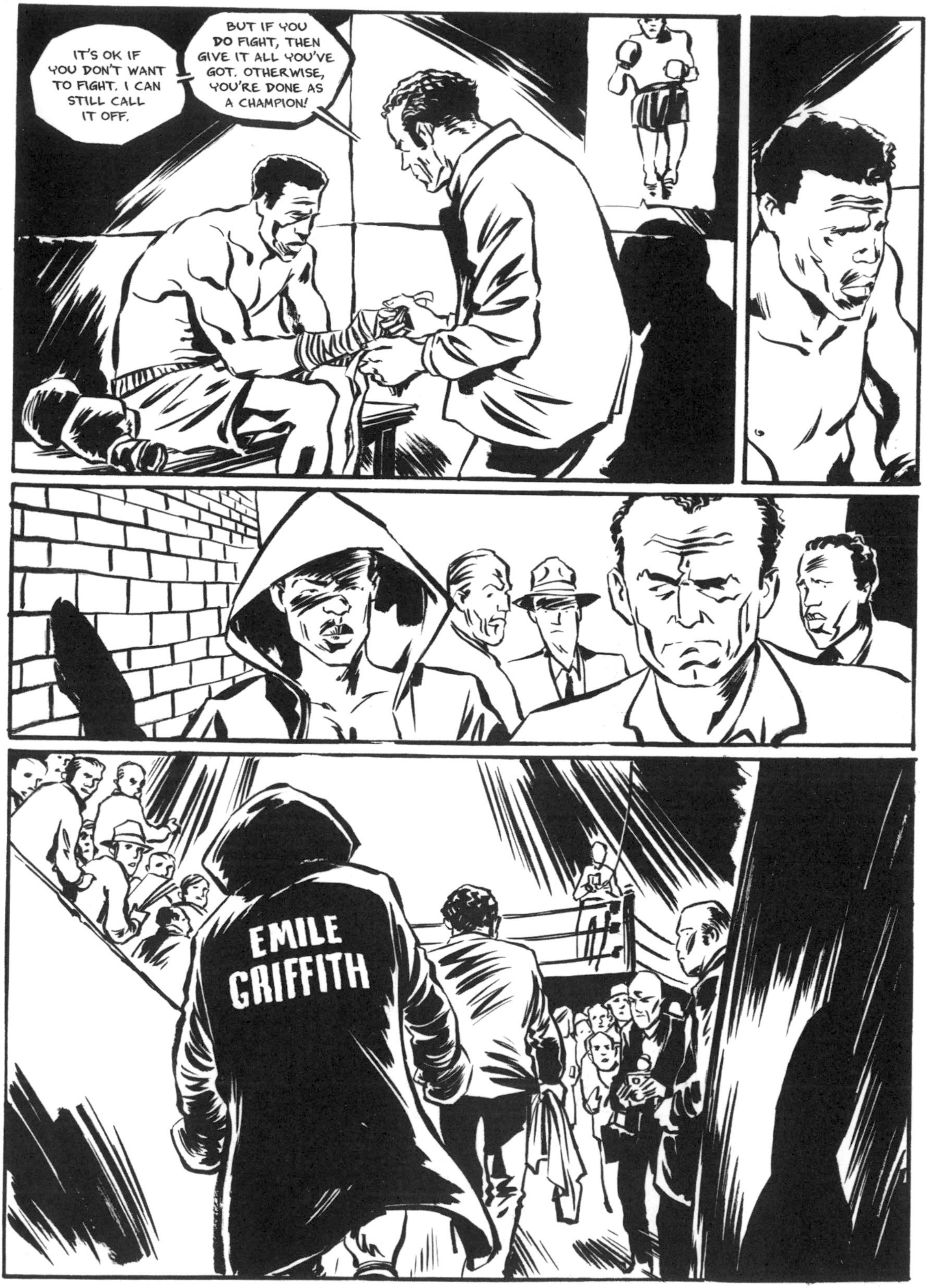
IT'S OK IF YOU DON'T WANT TO FIGHT. I CAN STILL CALL IT OFF.
BUT IF YOU DO FIGHT, THEN GIVE IT ALL YOU'VE GOT. OTHERWISE, YOU'RE DONE AS A CHAMPION!
EMILE GRIFFITH

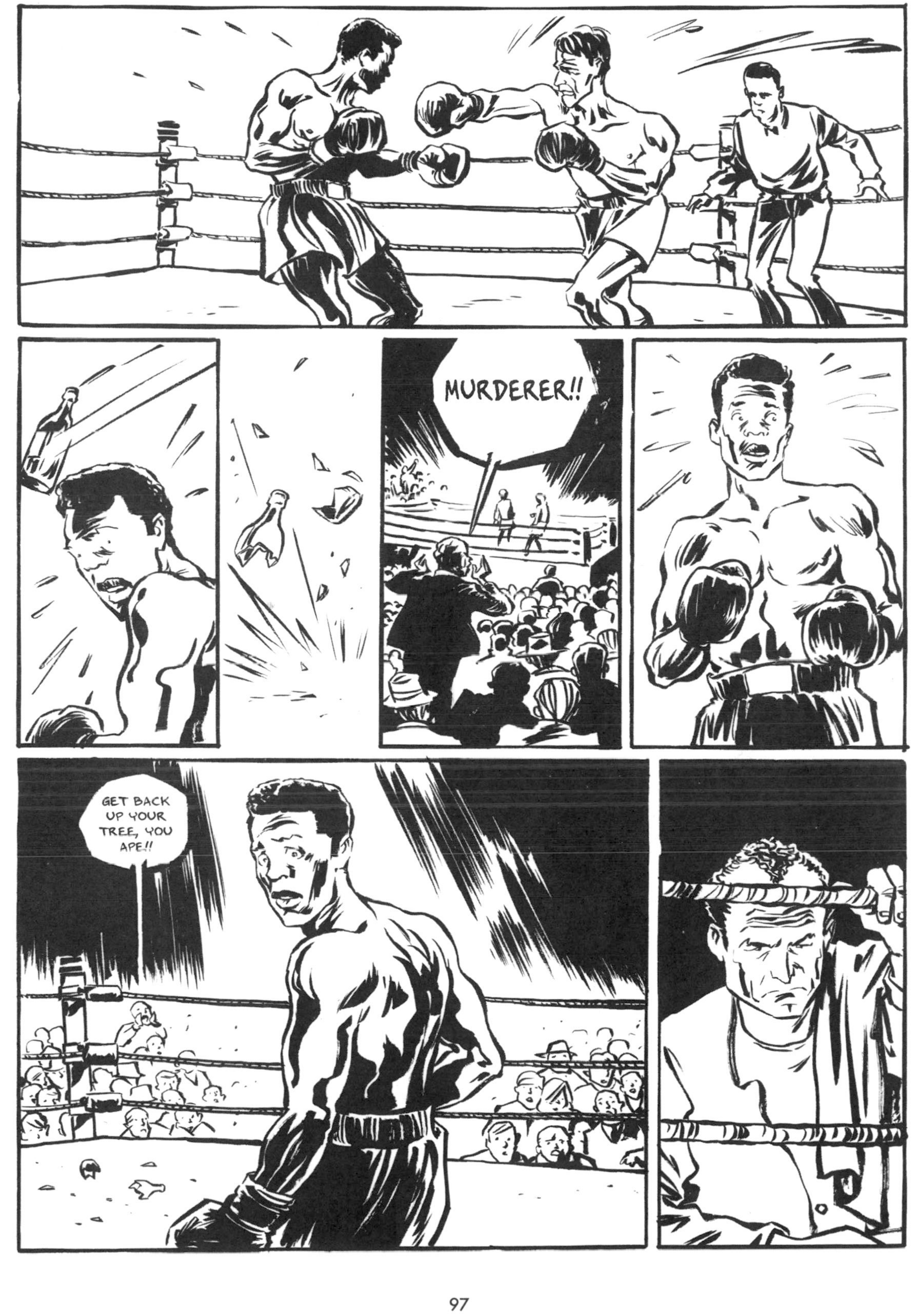
MURDERER!!
GET BACK UP YOUR TREE, YOU APE!!

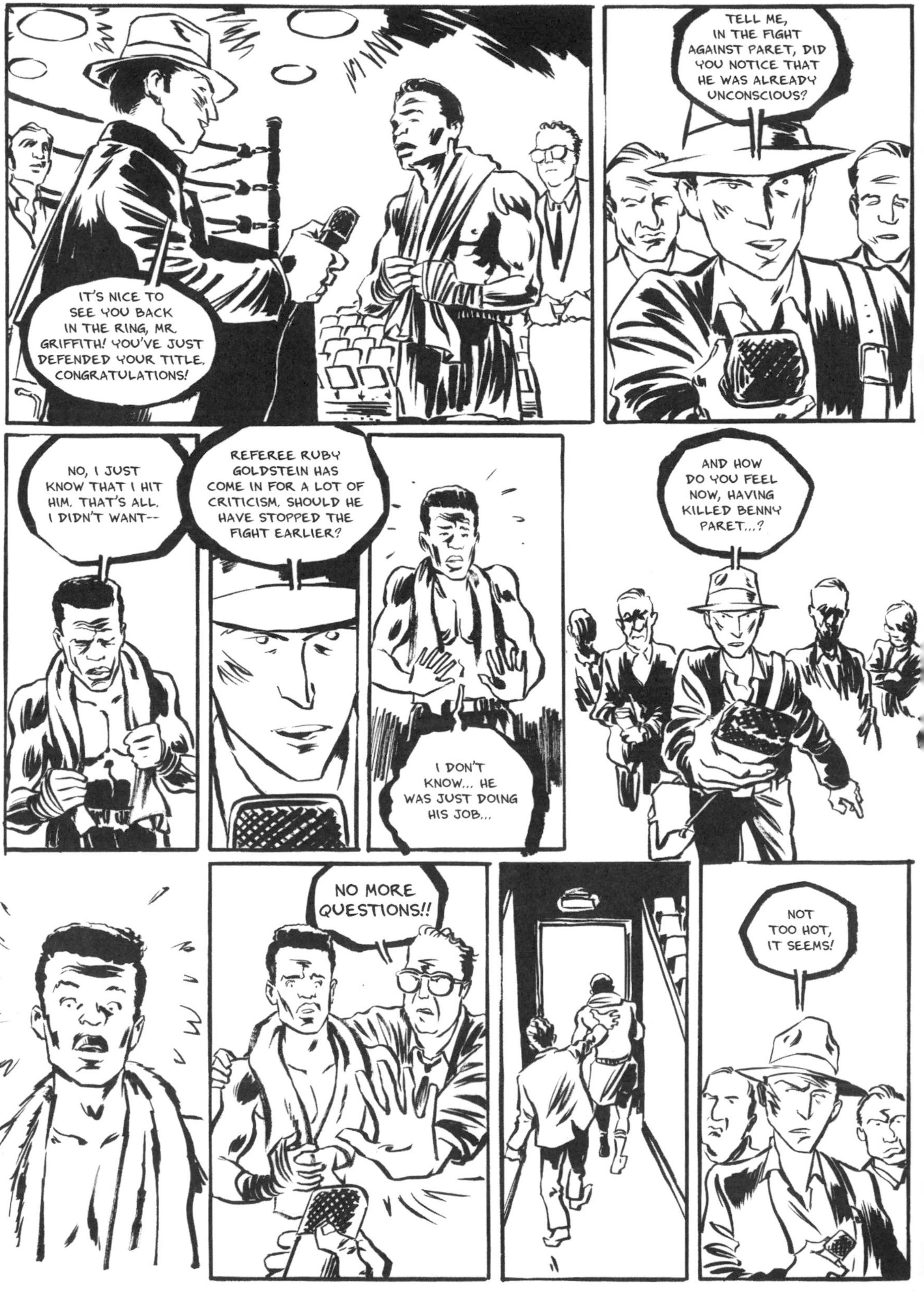
IT'S NICE TO SEE YOU BACK IN THE RING, MR. GRIFFITH! YOU'VE JUST DEFENDED YOUR TITLE. CONGRATULATIONS!
TELL ME, IN THE FIGHT AGAINST PARET, DID YOU NOTICE THAT HE WAS ALREADY UNCONSCIOUS?
NO, I JUST KNOW THAT I HIT HIM. THAT'S ALL. I DIDN'T WANT--
REFEREE RUBY GOLDSTEIN HAS COME IN FOR A LOT OF CRITICISM. SHOULD HE HAVE STOPPED THE FIGHT EARLIER?
I DON'T KNOW... HE WAS JUST DOING HIS JOB...
AND HOW DO YOU FEEL NOW, HAVING KILLED BENNY PARET...?
NO MORE QUESTIONS!!
NOT TOO HOT, IT SEEMS!

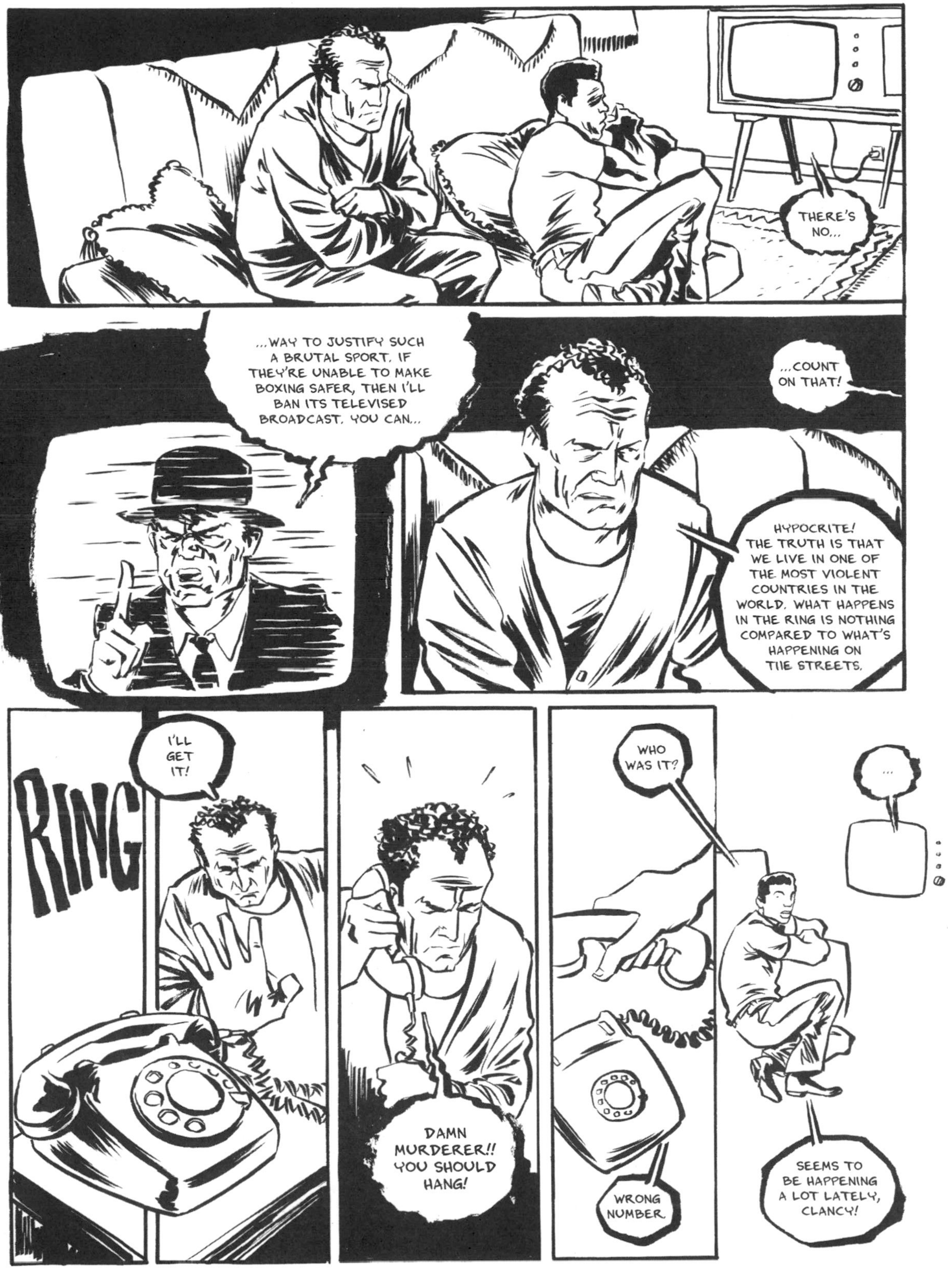
THERE'S NO...
...WAY TO JUSTIFY SUCH A BRUTAL SPORT. IF THEY'RE UNABLE TO MAKE BOXING SAFER, THEN I'LL BAN ITS TELEVISED BROADCAST. YOU CAN...
...COUNT ON THAT!
HYPOCRITE! THE TRUTH IS THAT WE LIVE IN ONE OF THE MOST VIOLENT COUNTRIES IN THE WORLD. WHAT HAPPENS IN THE RING IS NOTHING COMPARED TO WHAT'S HAPPENING ON THE STREETS.
RING
I'LL GET IT!
DAMN MURDERER!! YOU SHOULD HANG!
WHO WAS IT?
...
WRONG NUMBER.
SEEMS TO BE HAPPENING A LOT LATELY, CLANCY!

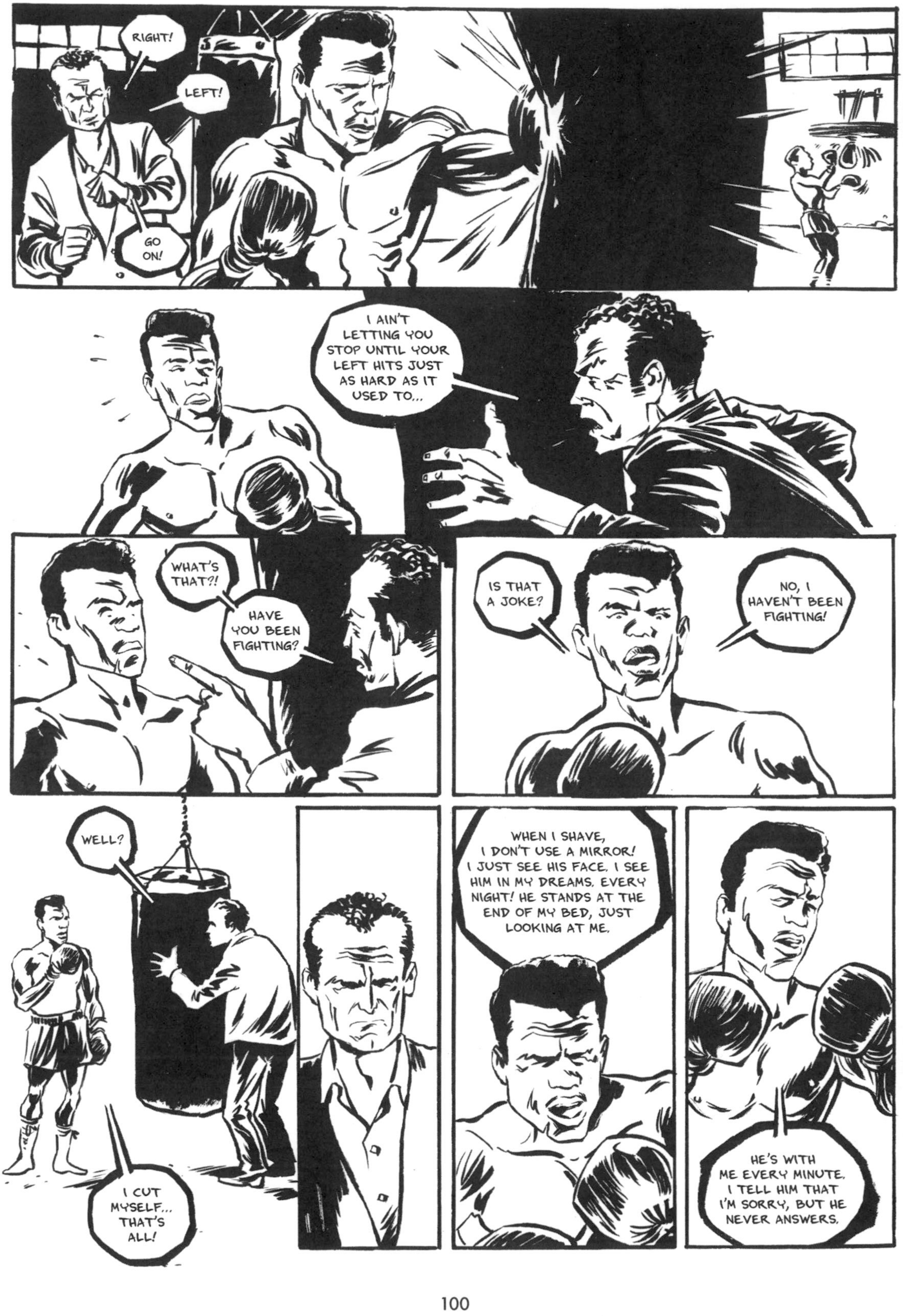
RIGHT!
LEFT!
GO ON!
I AIN'T LETTING YOU STOP UNTIL YOUR LEFT HITS JUST AS HARD AS IT USED TO...
WHAT'S THAT?!
HAVE YOU BEEN FIGHTING?
IS THAT A JOKE?
NO, I HAVEN'T BEEN FIGHTING!
WELL?
I CUT MYSELF... THAT'S ALL!
WHEN I SHAVE, I DON'T USE A MIRROR! I JUST SEE HIS FACE. I SEE HIM IN MY DREAMS. EVERY NIGHT! HE STANDS AT THE END OF MY BED, JUST LOOKING AT ME.
HE'S WITH ME EVERY MINUTE. I TELL HIM THAT I'M SORRY, BUT HE NEVER ANSWERS.

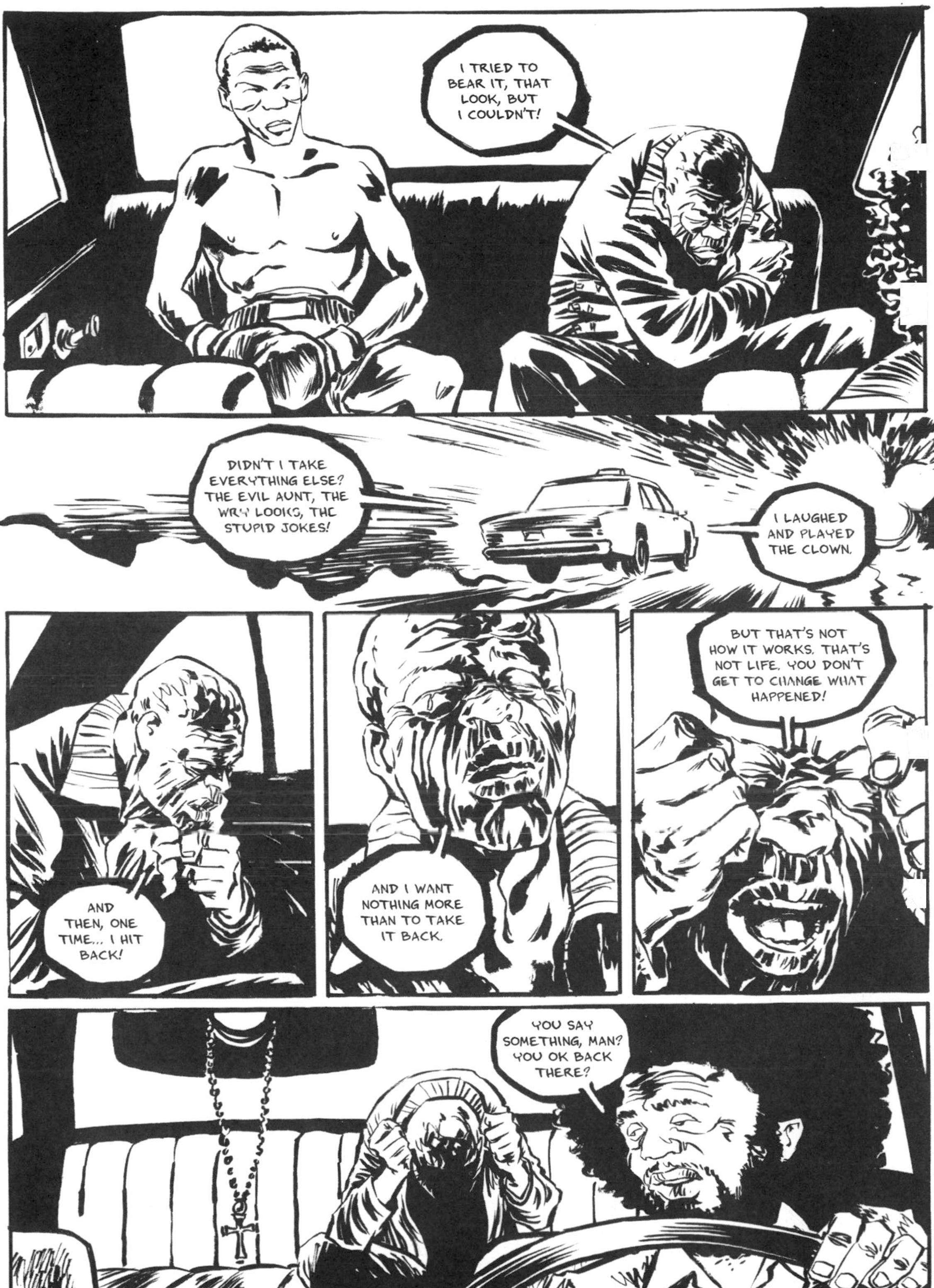
I TRIED TO BEAR IT, THAT LOOK, BUT I COULDN'T!
DIDN'T I TAKE EVERYTHING ELSE? THE EVIL AUNT, THE WRY LOOKS, THE STUPID JOKES!
I LAUGHED AND PLAYED THE CLOWN.
AND THEN, ONE TIME... I HIT BACK!
AND I WANT NOTHING MORE THAN TO TAKE IT BACK.
BUT THAT'S NOT HOW IT WORKS. THAT'S NOT LIFE. YOU DON'T GET TO CHANGE WHAT HAPPENED!
YOU SAY SOMETHING, MAN? YOU OK BACK THERE?

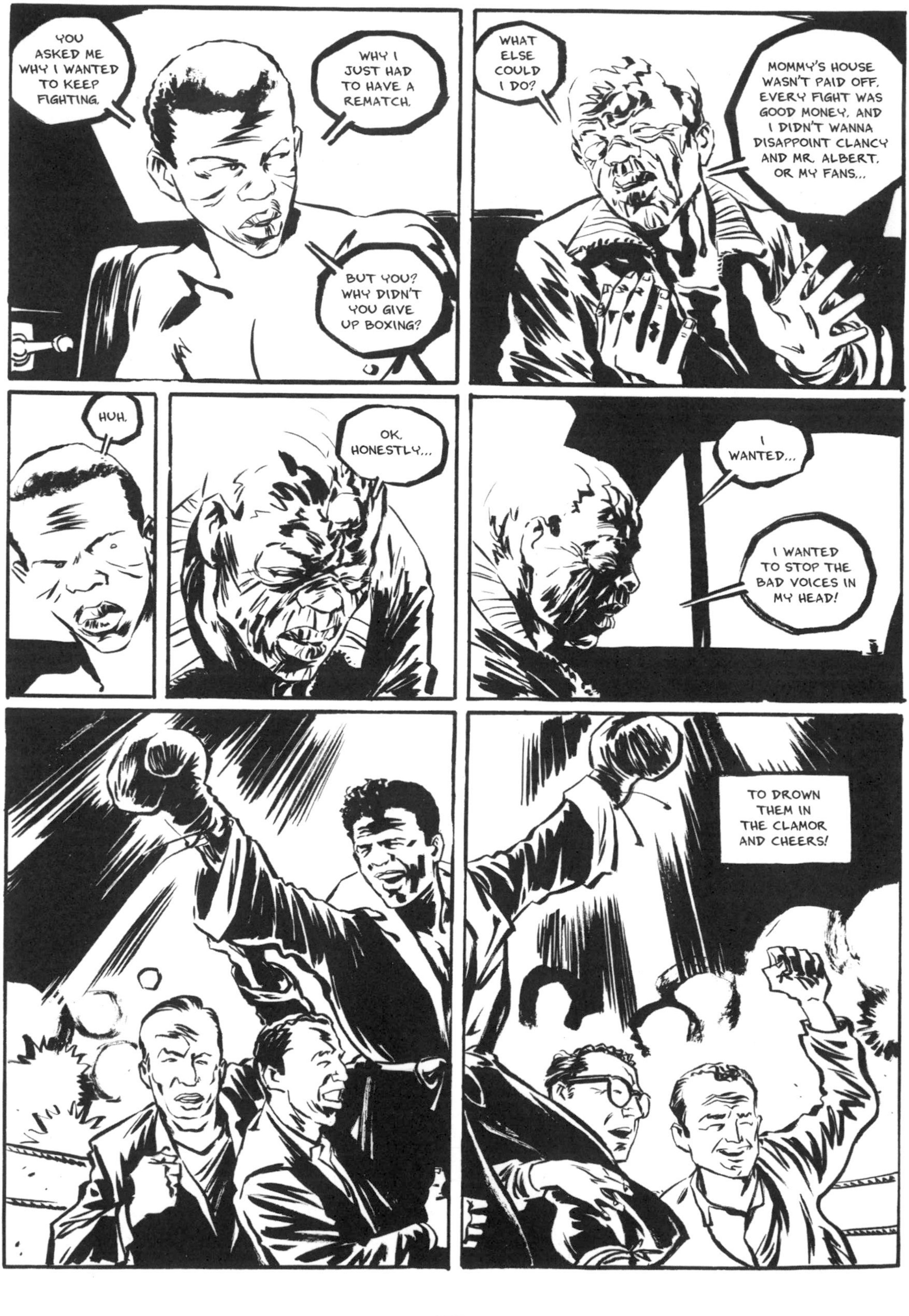
YOU ASKED ME WHY I WANTED TO KEEP FIGHTING.
WHY I JUST HAD TO HAVE A REMATCH.
BUT YOU? WHY DIDN'T YOU GIVE UP BOXING?
WHAT ELSE COULD I DO?
MOMMY'S HOUSE WASN'T PAID OFF. EVERY FIGHT WAS GOOD MONEY, AND I DIDN'T WANNA DISAPPOINT CLANCY AND MR. ALBERT. OR MY FANS...
HUH.
OK. HONESTLY...
I WANTED...
I WANTED TO STOP THE BAD VOICES IN MY HEAD!
TO DROWN THEM IN THE CLAMOR AND CHEERS!

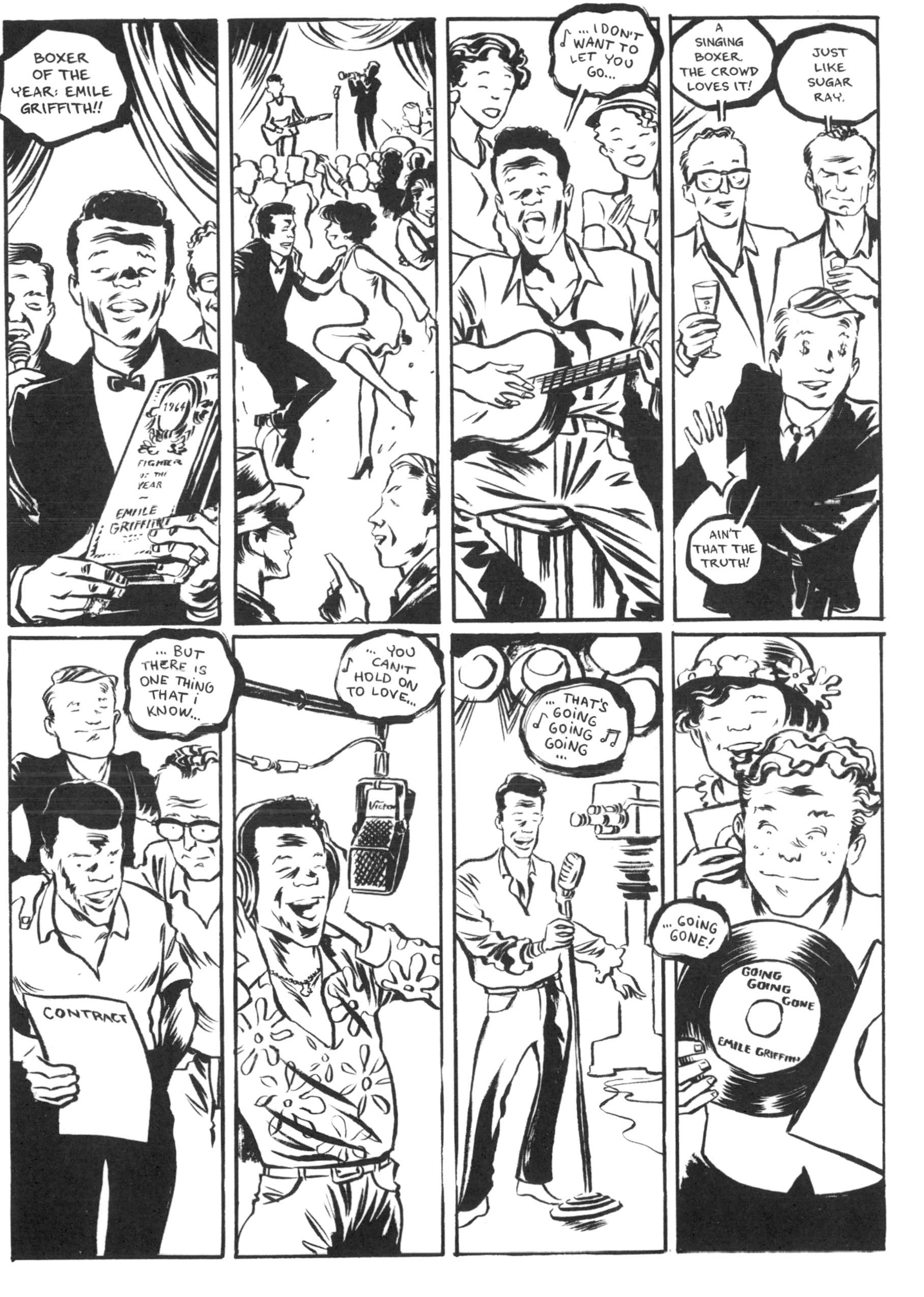
BOXER OF THE YEAR: EMILE GRIFFITH!!
1964
FIGHTER OF THE YEAR
EMILE
... I DON'T WANT TO LET YOU GO...
A SINGING BOXER. THE CROWD LOVES IT!
JUST LIKE SUGAR RAY.
AIN'T THAT THE TRUTH!
... BUT THERE IS ONE THING THAT I KNOW...
CONTRACT
... YOU CAN'T HOLD ON TO LOVE...
Victor
... THAT'S GOING GOING GOING ...
... GOING GONE!
GOING GOING GONE
EMILE GRIFFITH

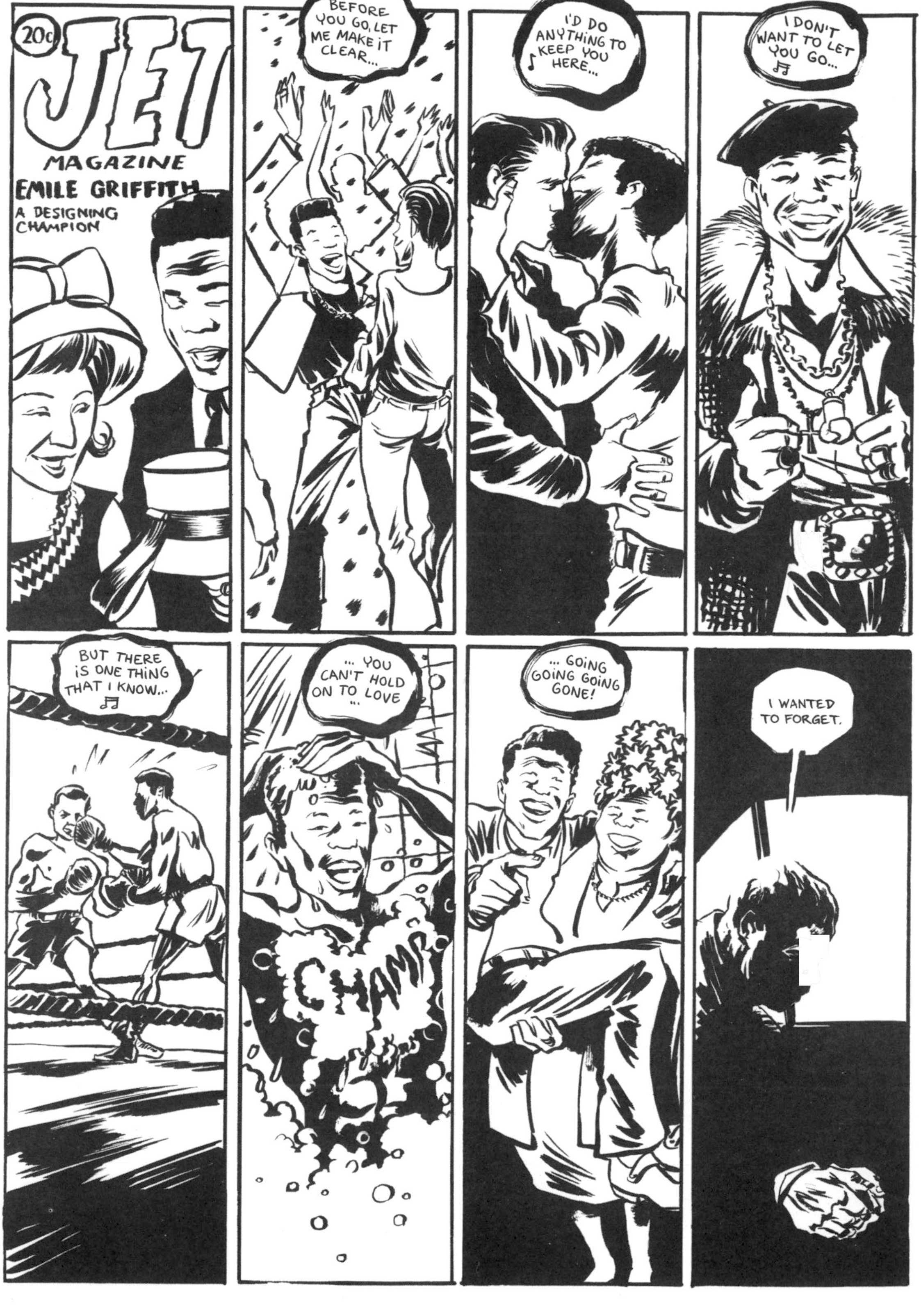
20¢
JET
MAGAZINE
EMILE GRIFFITH
A DESIGNING CHAMPION
BEFORE YOU GO, LET ME MAKE IT CLEAR...
I'D DO ANYTHING TO KEEP YOU HERE...
I DON'T WANT TO LET YOU GO...
BUT THERE IS ONE THING THAT I KNOW...
... YOU CAN'T HOLD ON TO LOVE ...
CHAMP
... GOING GOING GOING GONE!
I WANTED TO FORGET.

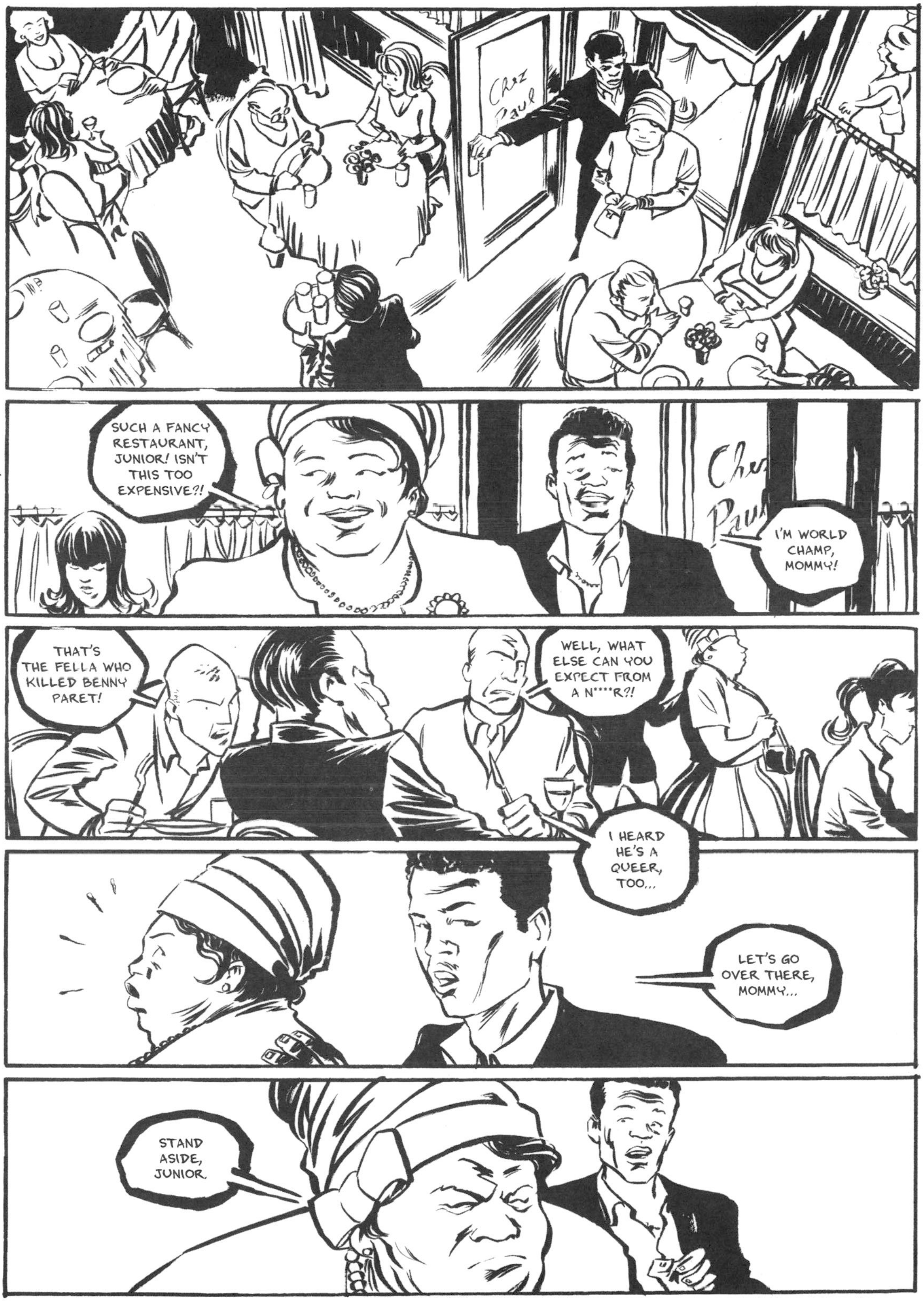
SUCH A FANCY RESTAURANT, JUNIOR! ISN'T THIS TOO EXPENSIVE?!
I'M WORLD CHAMP, MOMMY!
THAT'S THE FELLA WHO KILLED BENNY PARET!
WELL, WHAT ELSE CAN YOU EXPECT FROM A N****R?!
I HEARD HE'S A QUEER, TOO...
LET'S GO OVER THERE, MOMMY...
STAND ASIDE, JUNIOR.

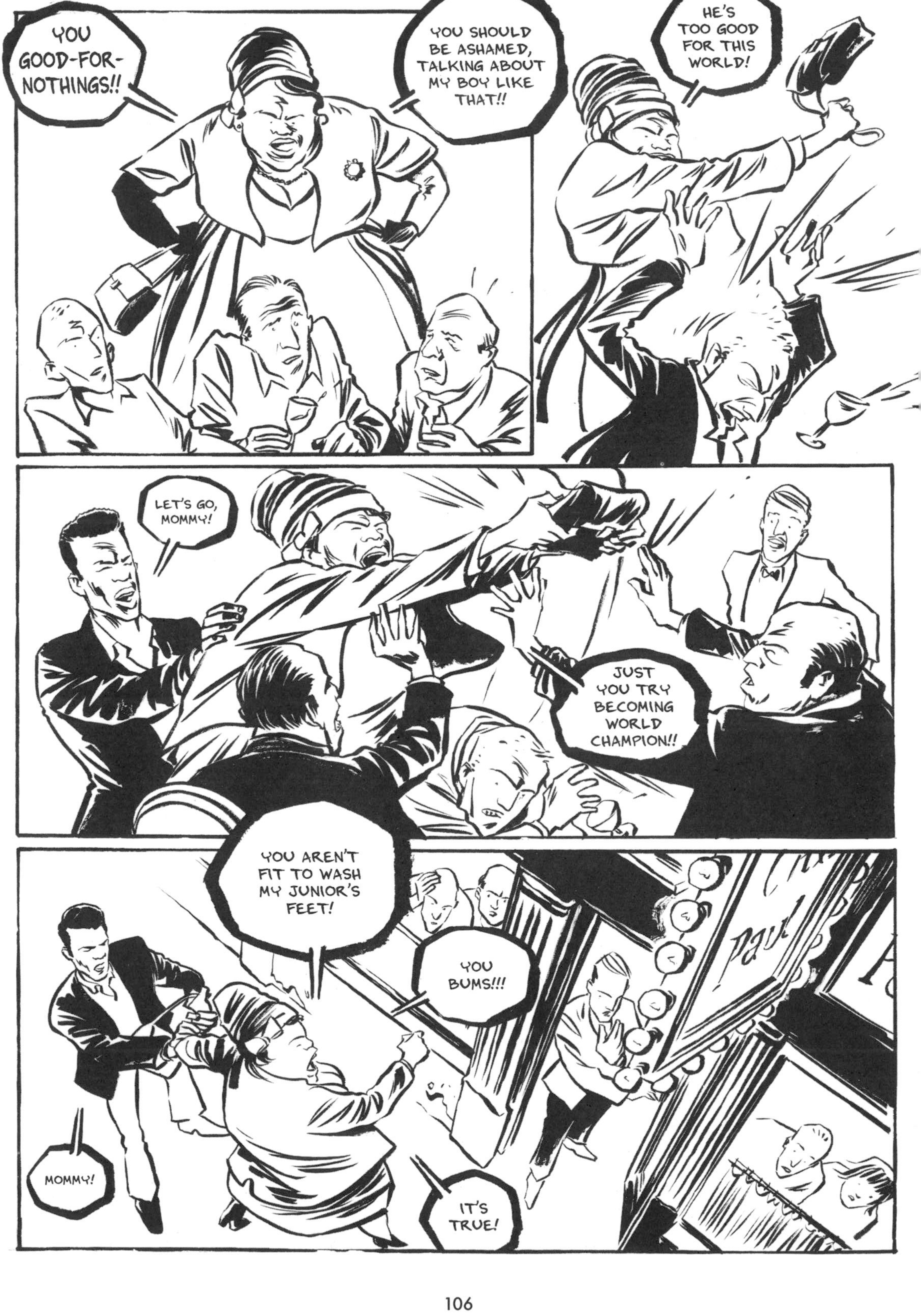
YOU GOOD-FOR-NOTHINGS!!
YOU SHOULD BE ASHAMED, TALKING ABOUT MY BOY LIKE THAT!!
HE'S TOO GOOD FOR THIS WORLD!
LET'S GO, MOMMY!
JUST YOU TRY BECOMING WORLD CHAMPION!!
YOU AREN'T FIT TO WASH MY JUNIOR'S FEET!
YOU BUMS!!!
MOMMY!
IT'S TRUE!

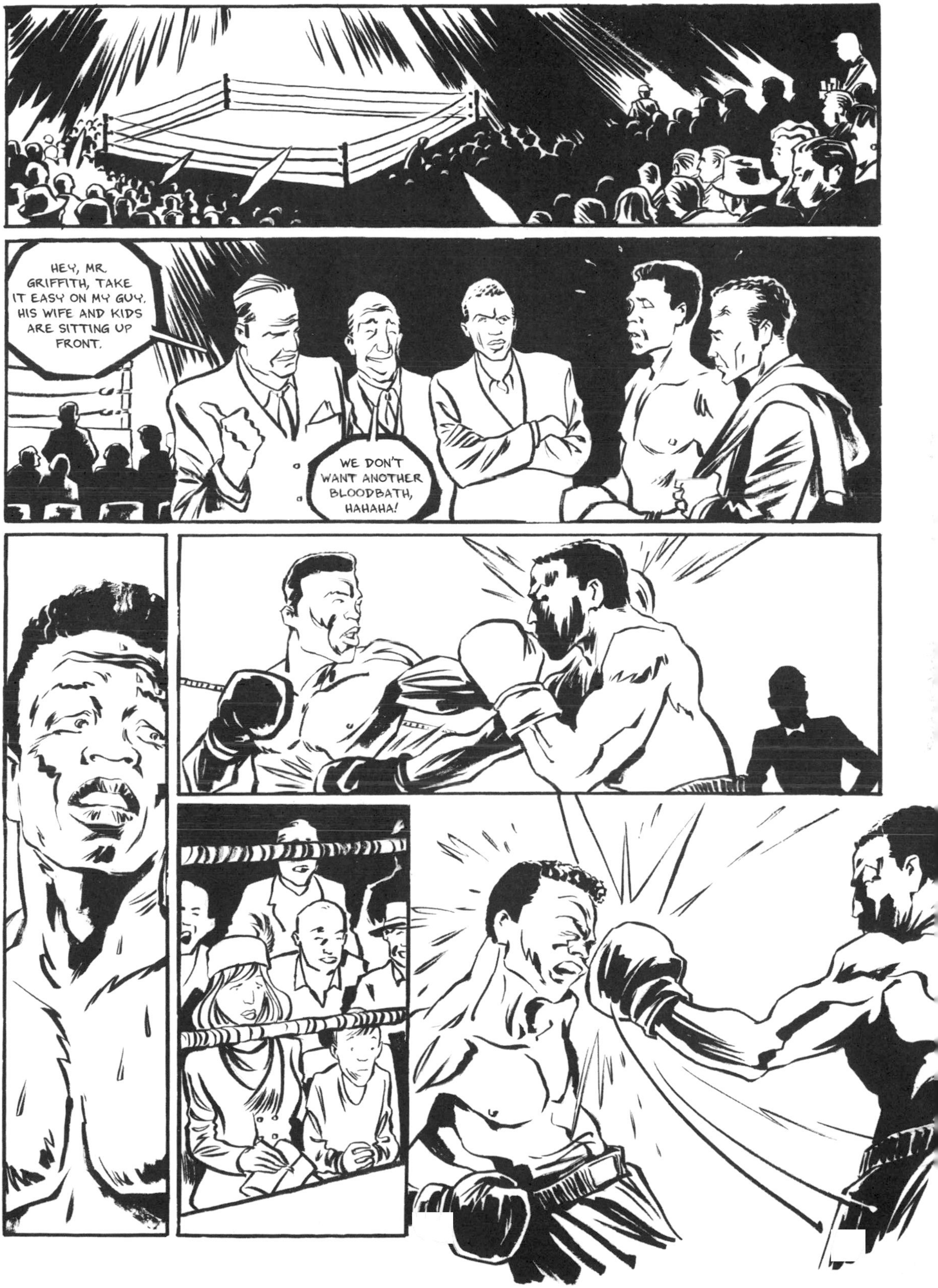
HEY, MR. GRIFFITH, TAKE IT EASY ON MY GUY. HIS WIFE AND KIDS ARE SITTING UP FRONT.
WE DON'T WANT ANOTHER BLOODBATH, HAHAHA!

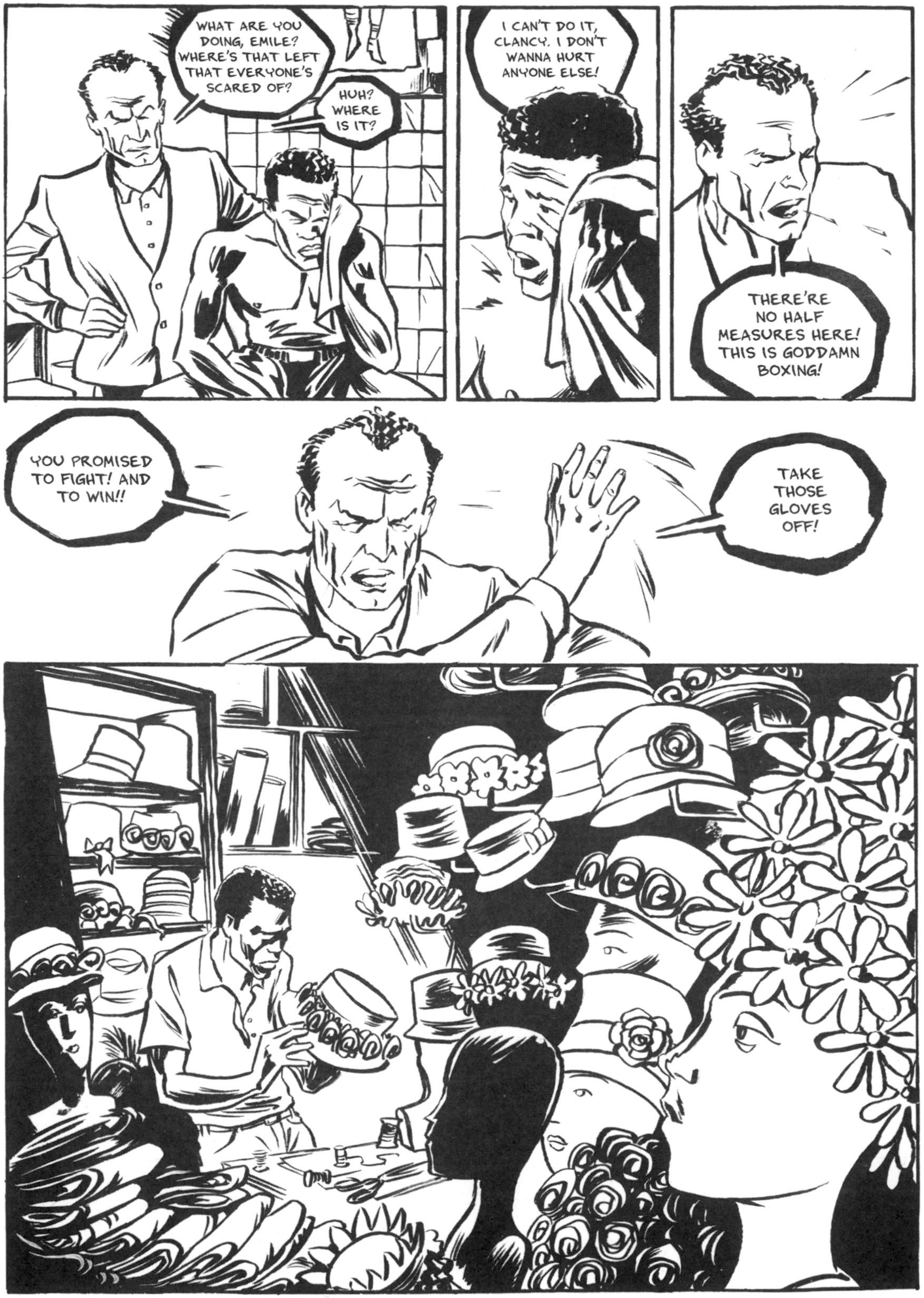
WHAT ARE YOU DOING, EMILE? WHERE'S THAT LEFT THAT EVERYONE'S SCARED OF?
HUH? WHERE IS IT?
I CAN'T DO IT, CLANCY. I DON'T WANNA HURT ANYONE ELSE!
THERE'RE NO HALF MEASURES HERE! THIS IS GODDAMN BOXING!
YOU PROMISED TO FIGHT! AND TO WIN!!
TAKE THOSE GLOVES OFF!

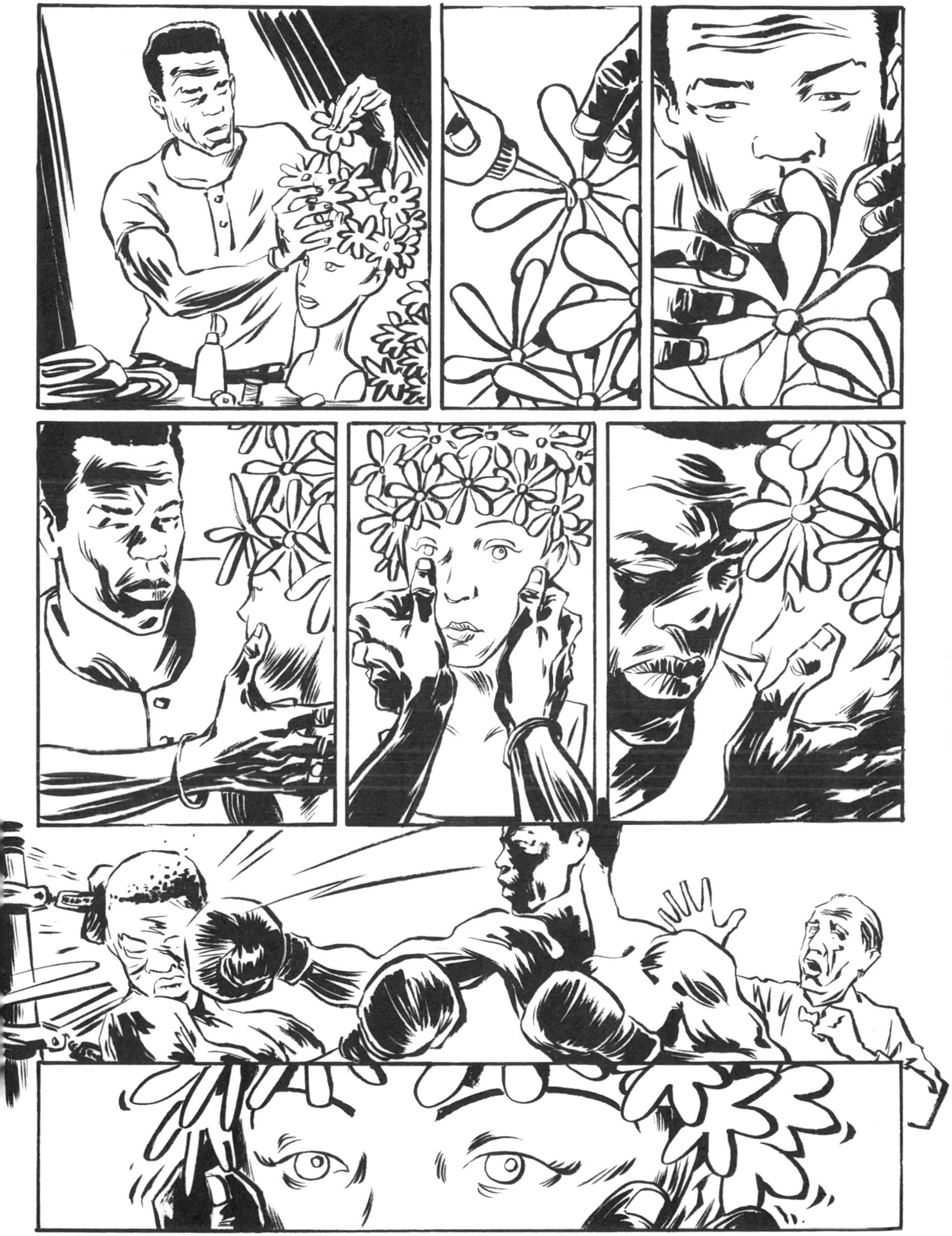

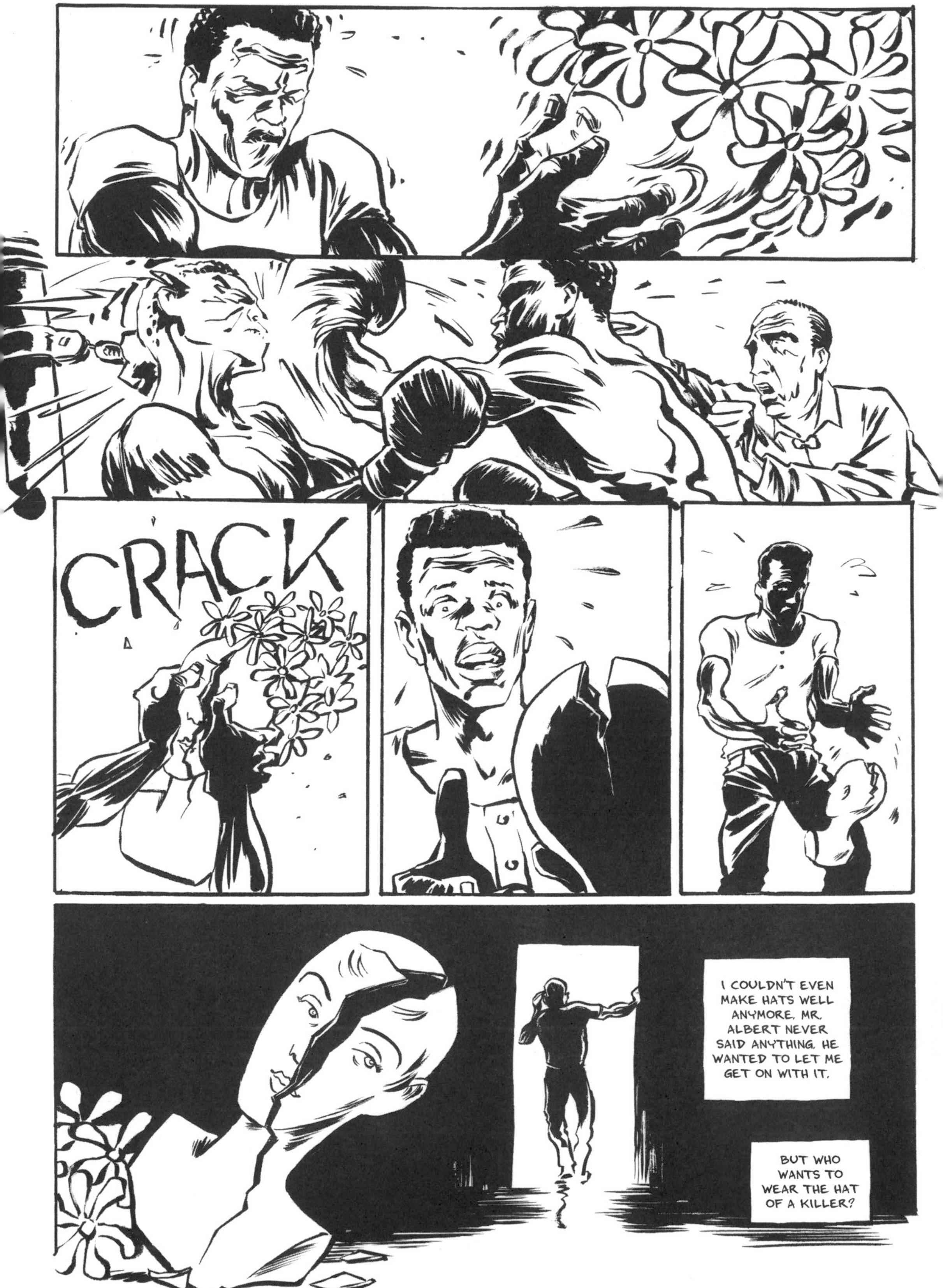
CRACK
I COULDN'T EVEN MAKE HATS WELL ANYMORE. MR. ALBERT NEVER SAID ANYTHING. HE WANTED TO LET ME GET ON WITH IT.
BUT WHO WANTS TO WEAR THE HAT OF A KILLER?

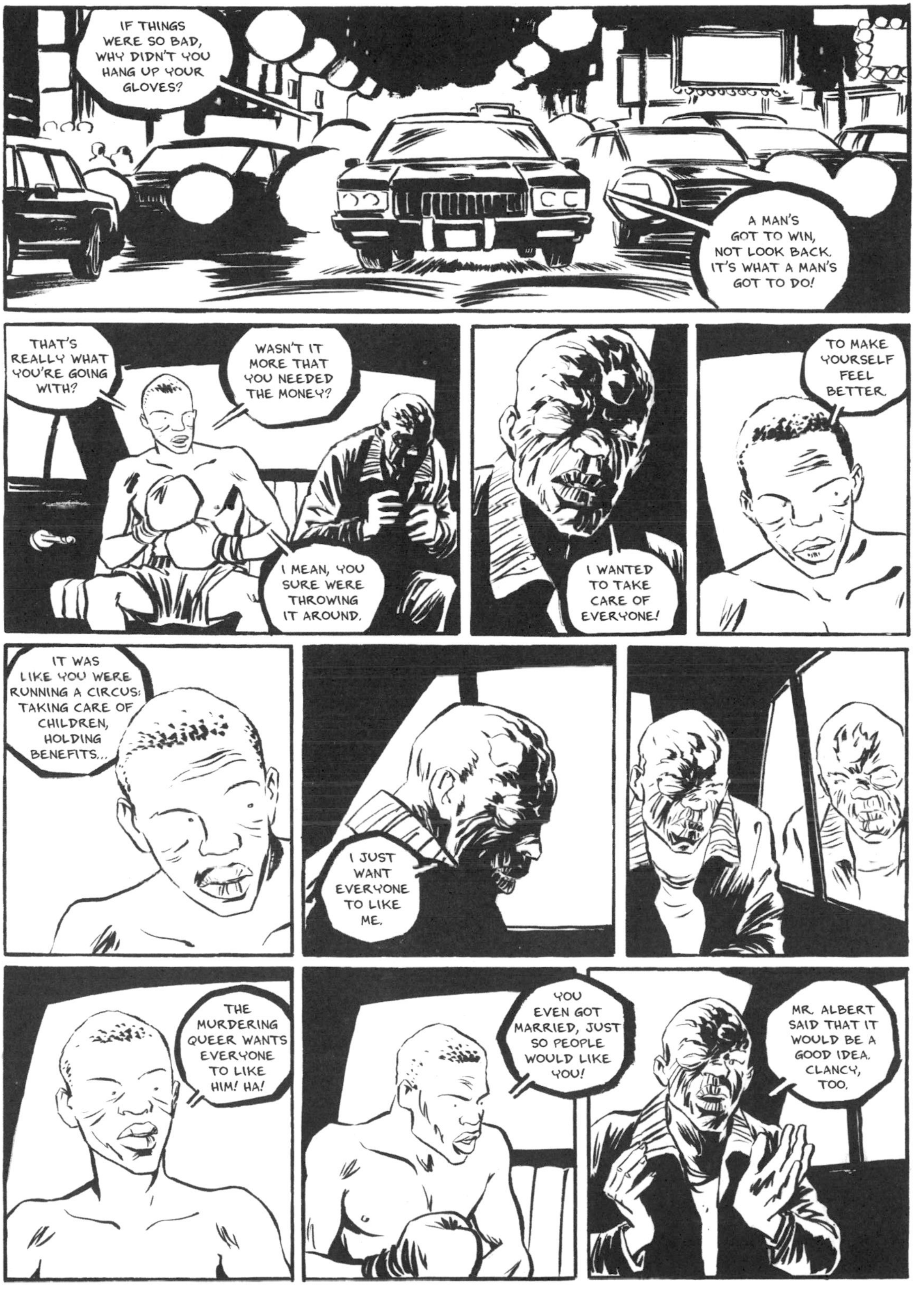
IF THINGS WERE SO BAD, WHY DIDN'T YOU HANG UP YOUR GLOVES?
A MAN'S GOT TO WIN, NOT LOOK BACK. IT'S WHAT A MAN'S GOT TO DO!
THAT'S REALLY WHAT YOU'RE GOING WITH?
WASN'T IT MORE THAT YOU NEEDED THE MONEY?
I MEAN, YOU SURE WERE THROWING IT AROUND.
I WANTED TO TAKE CARE OF EVERYONE!
TO MAKE YOURSELF FEEL BETTER.
IT WAS LIKE YOU WERE RUNNING A CIRCUS: TAKING CARE OF CHILDREN, HOLDING BENEFITS...
I JUST WANT EVERYONE TO LIKE ME.
THE MURDERING QUEER WANTS EVERYONE TO LIKE HIM! HA!
YOU EVEN GOT MARRIED, JUST SO PEOPLE WOULD LIKE YOU!
MR. ALBERT SAID THAT IT WOULD BE A GOOD IDEA. CLANCY, TOO.

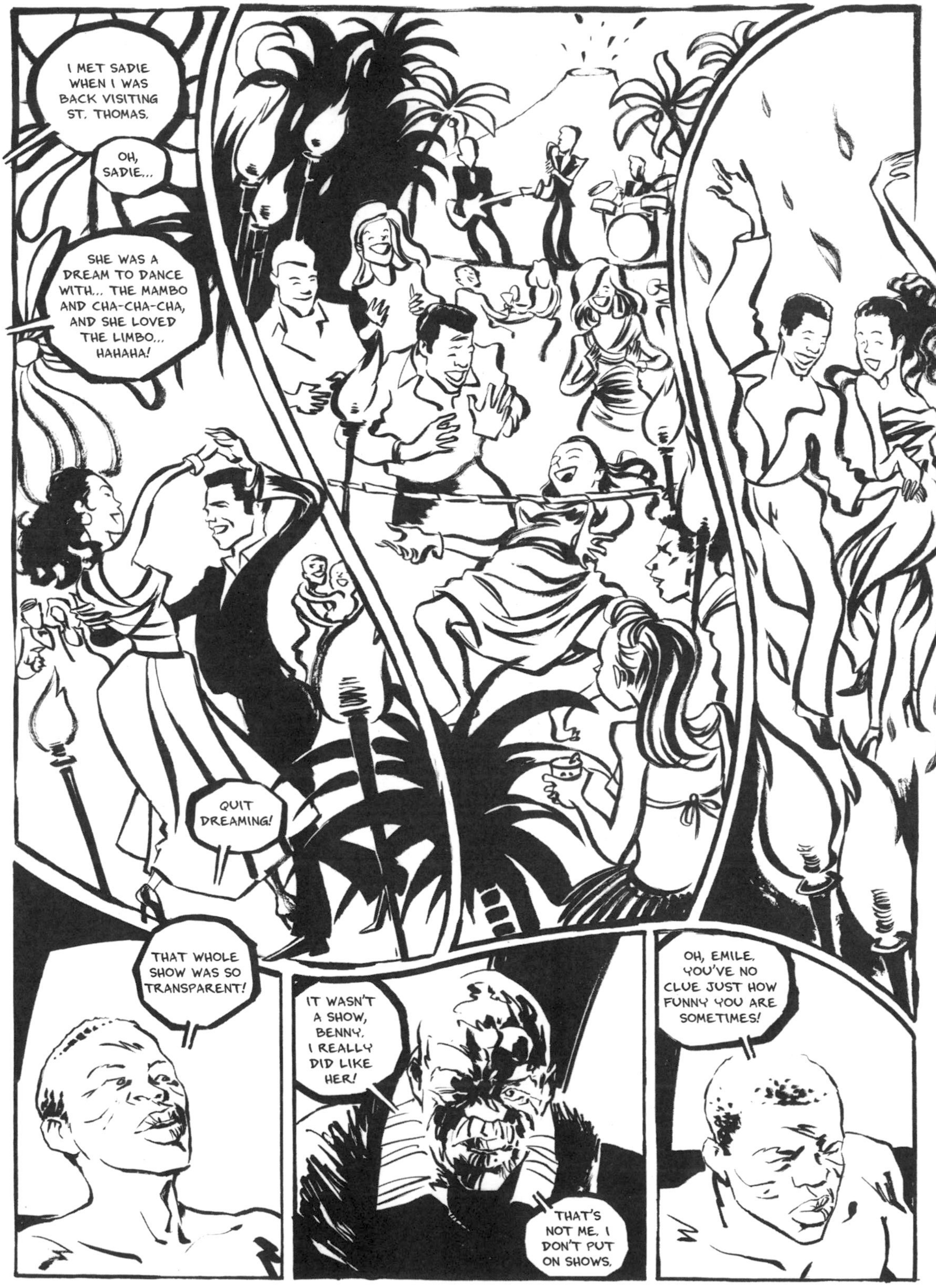
I MET SADIE WHEN I WAS BACK VISITING ST. THOMAS.
OH, SADIE...
SHE WAS A DREAM TO DANCE WITH... THE MAMBO AND CHA-CHA-CHA, AND SHE LOVED THE LIMBO... HAHAHA!
QUIT DREAMING!
THAT WHOLE SHOW WAS SO TRANSPARENT!
IT WASN'T A SHOW, BENNY. I REALLY DID LIKE HER!
THAT'S NOT ME. I DON'T PUT ON SHOWS.
OH, EMILE. YOU'VE NO CLUE JUST HOW FUNNY YOU ARE SOMETIMES!

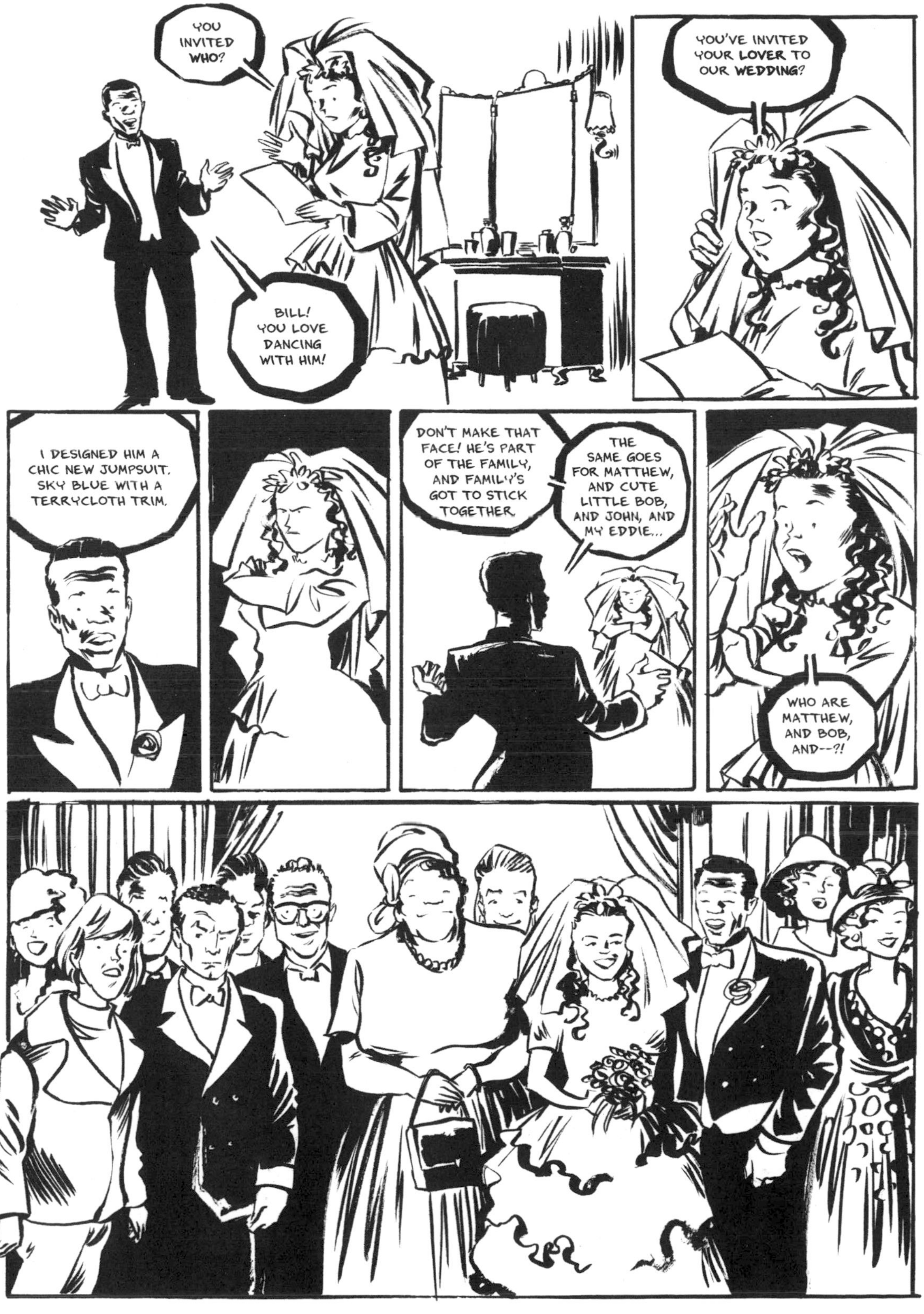
YOU INVITED WHO?
BILL! YOU LOVE DANCING WITH HIM!
YOU'VE INVITED YOUR LOVER TO OUR WEDDING?
I DESIGNED HIM A CHIC NEW JUMPSUIT. SKY BLUE WITH A TERRYCLOTH TRIM.
DON'T MAKE THAT FACE! HE'S PART OF THE FAMILY, AND FAMILY'S GOT TO STICK TOGETHER.
THE SAME GOES FOR MATTHEW, AND CUTE LITTLE BOB, AND JOHN, AND MY EDDIE...
WHO ARE MATTHEW, AND BOB, AND--?!

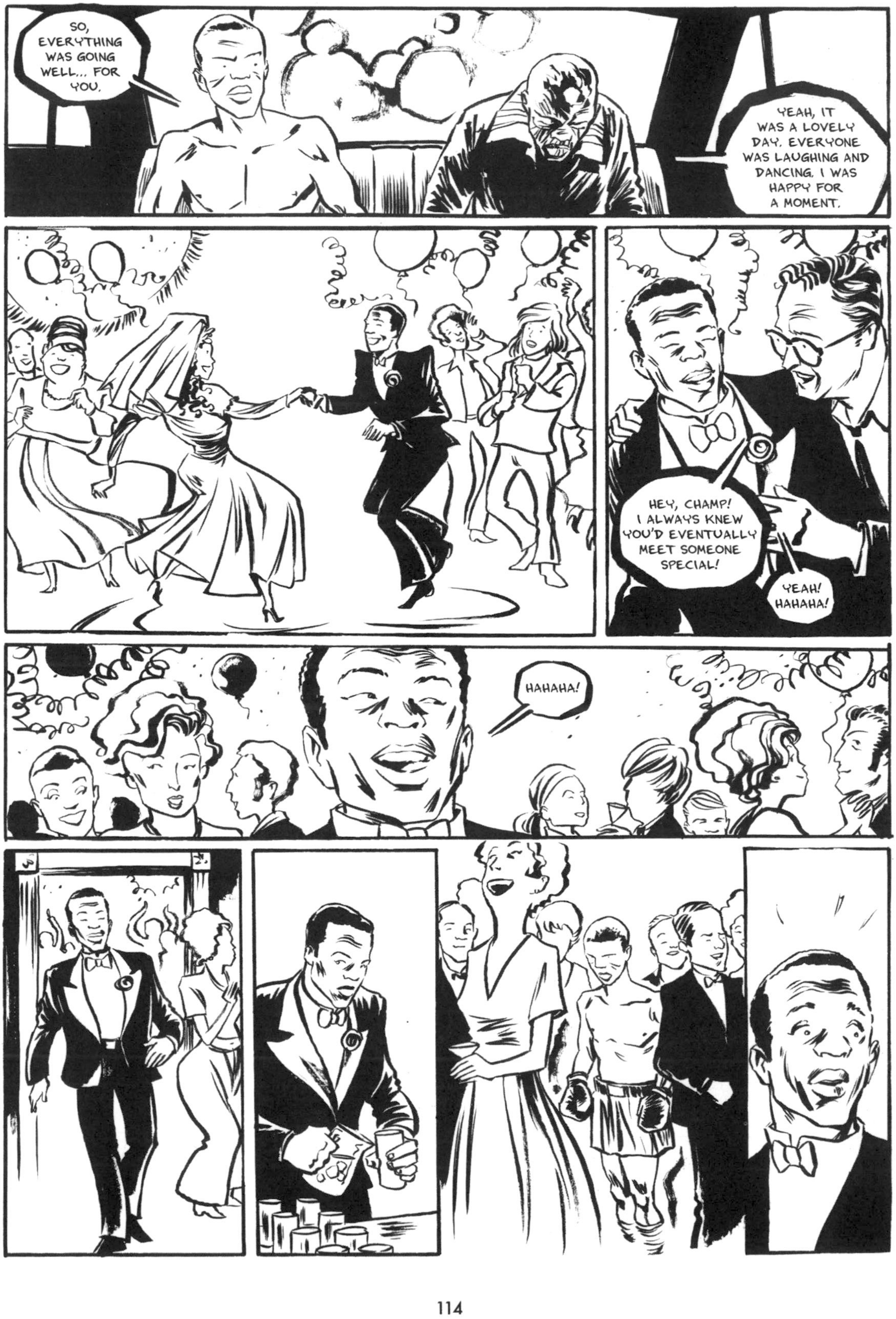
SO, EVERYTHING WAS GOING WELL... FOR YOU.
YEAH, IT WAS A LOVELY DAY. EVERYONE WAS LAUGHING AND DANCING. I WAS HAPPY FOR A MOMENT.
HEY, CHAMP! I ALWAYS KNEW YOU'D EVENTUALLY MEET SOMEONE SPECIAL!
YEAH! HAHAHA!
HAHAHA!

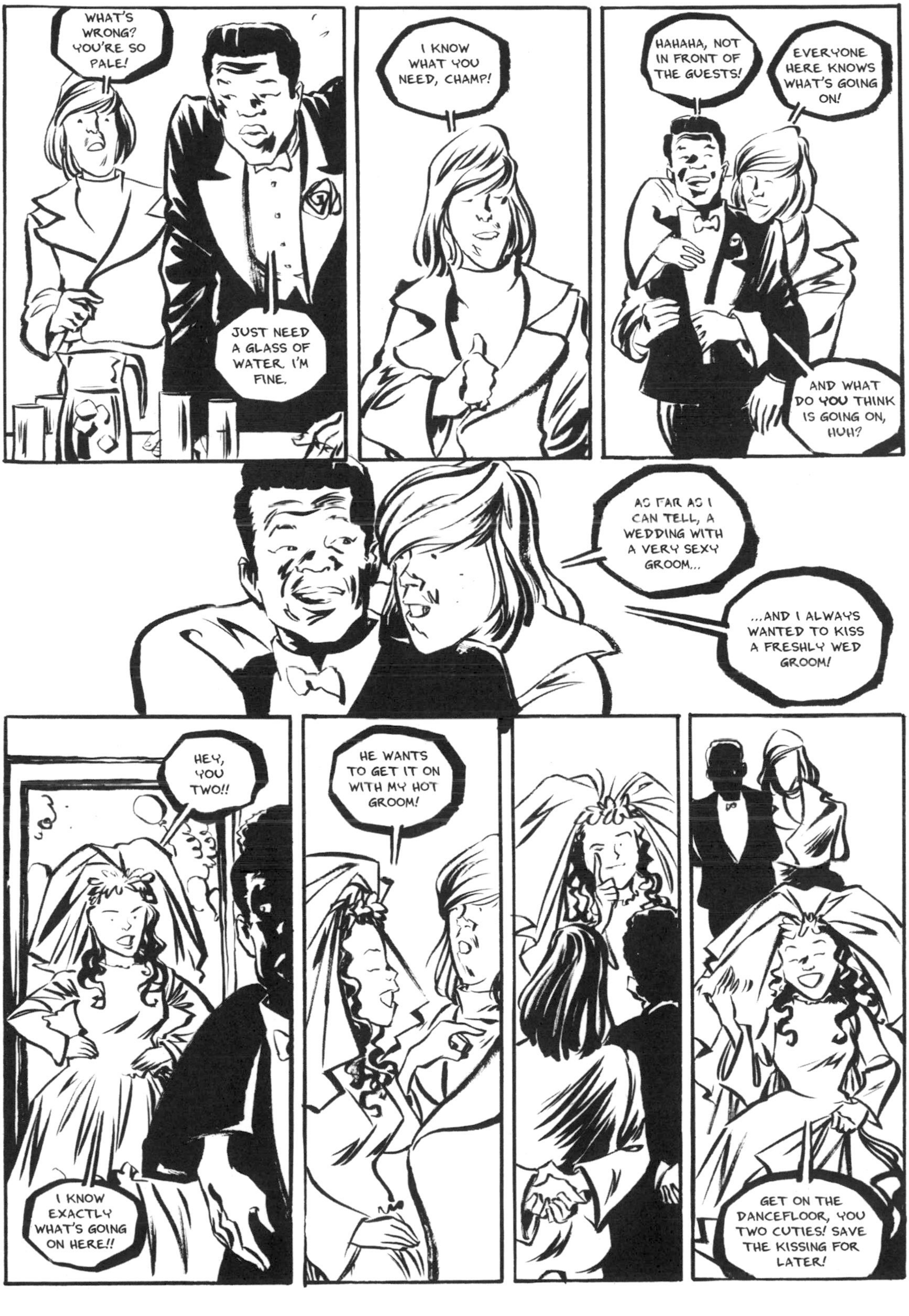
WHAT'S WRONG? YOU'RE SO PALE!
JUST NEED A GLASS OF WATER. I'M FINE.
I KNOW WHAT YOU NEED, CHAMP!
HAHAHA, NOT IN FRONT OF THE GUESTS!
EVERYONE HERE KNOWS WHAT'S GOING ON!
AND WHAT DO YOU THINK IS GOING ON, HUH?
AS FAR AS I CAN TELL, A WEDDING WITH A VERY SEXY GROOM...
...AND I ALWAYS WANTED TO KISS A FRESHLY WED GROOM!
HEY, YOU TWO!!
I KNOW EXACTLY WHAT'S GOING ON HERE!!
HE WANTS TO GET IT ON WITH MY HOT GROOM!
GET ON THE DANCEFLOOR, YOU TWO CUTIES! SAVE THE KISSING FOR LATER!

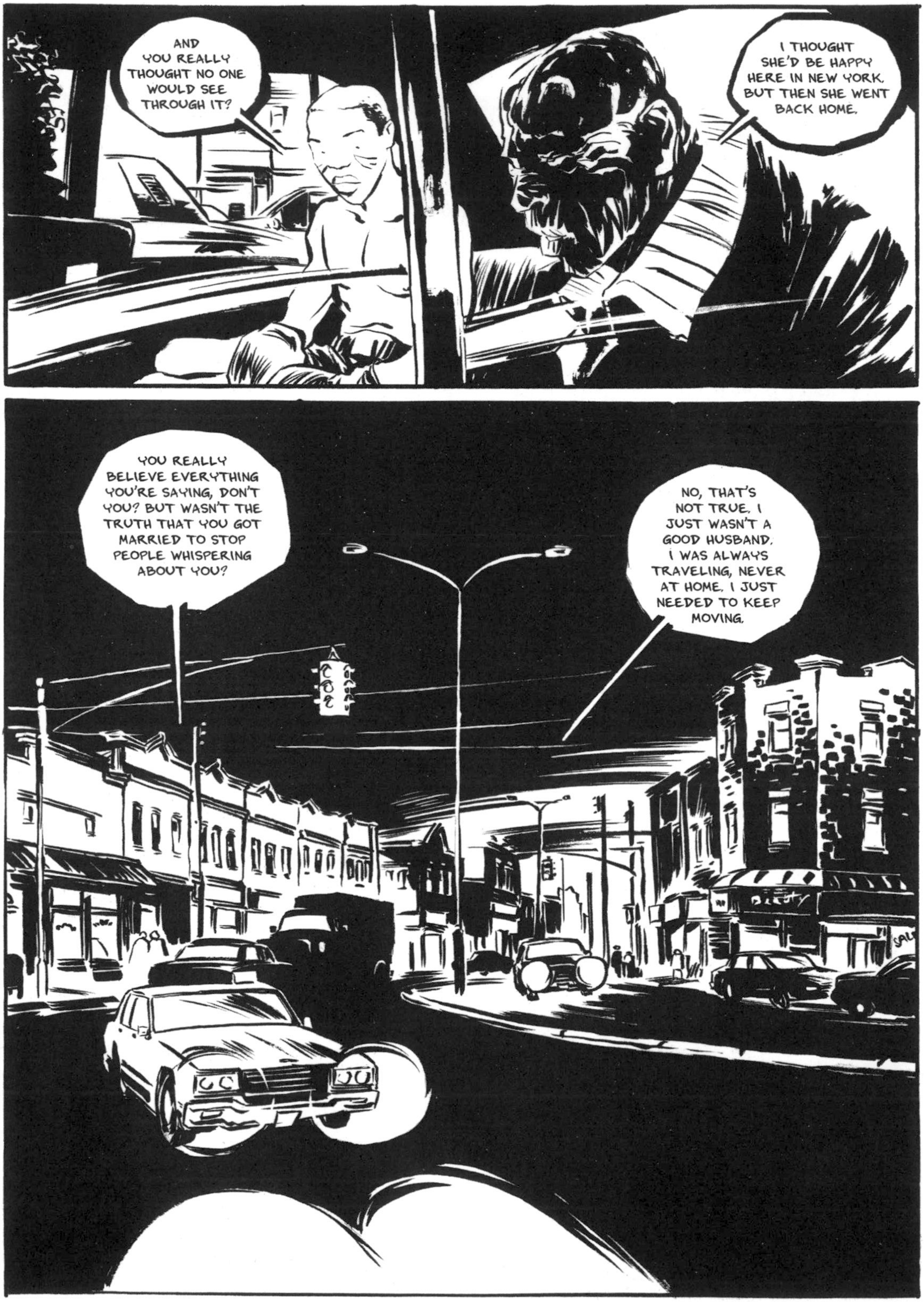
AND YOU REALLY THOUGHT NO ONE WOULD SEE THROUGH IT?
I THOUGHT SHE'D BE HAPPY HERE IN NEW YORK. BUT THEN SHE WENT BACK HOME.
YOU REALLY BELIEVE EVERYTHING YOU'RE SAYING, DON'T YOU? BUT WASN'T THE TRUTH THAT YOU GOT MARRIED TO STOP PEOPLE WHISPERING ABOUT YOU?
NO, THAT'S NOT TRUE. I JUST WASN'T A GOOD HUSBAND. I WAS ALWAYS TRAVELING, NEVER AT HOME. I JUST NEEDED TO KEEP MOVING.

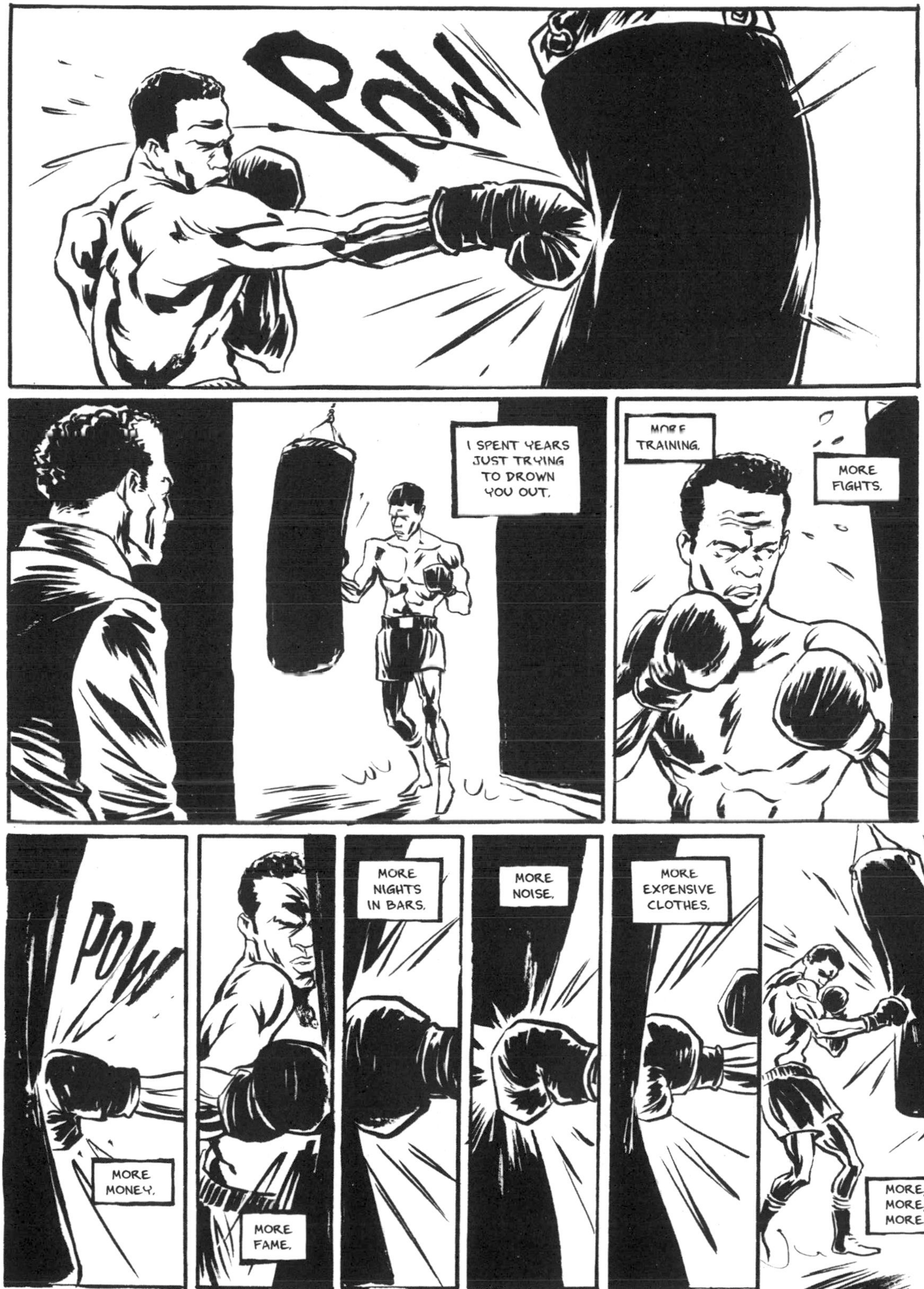
POW
I SPENT YEARS JUST TRYING TO DROWN YOU OUT.
MORE TRAINING.
MORE FIGHTS.
POW
MORE MONEY.
MORE FAME.
MORE NIGHTS IN BARS.
MORE NOISE.
MORE EXPENSIVE CLOTHES.
MORE, MORE, MORE.

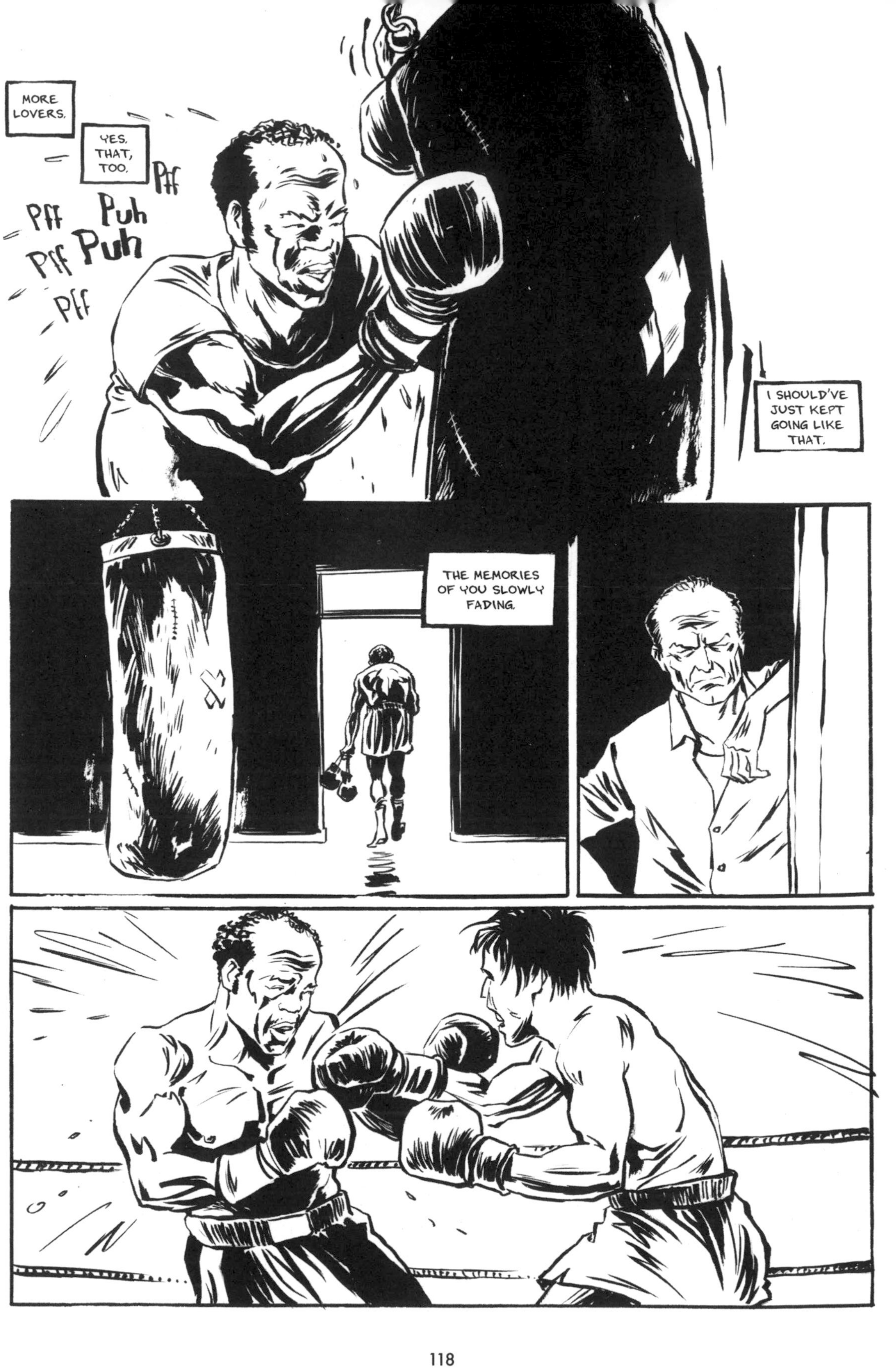
MORE LOVERS.
YES, THAT, TOO.
Pff
Pff
Puh
Pff Puh
Pff
I SHOULD'VE JUST KEPT GOING LIKE THAT.
THE MEMORIES OF YOU SLOWLY FADING.

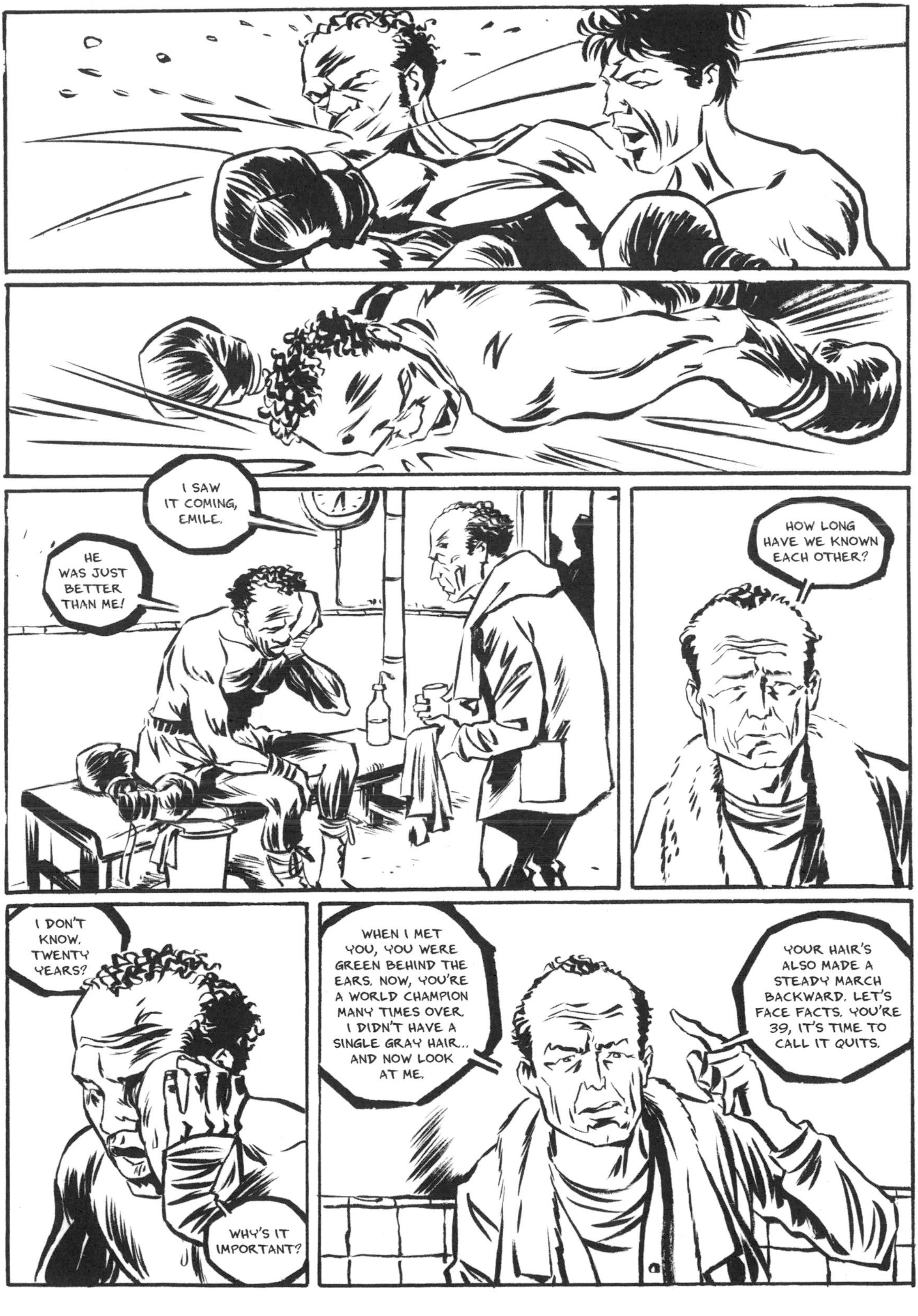

I SAW IT COMING, EMILE.
HE WAS JUST BETTER THAN ME!
HOW LONG HAVE WE KNOWN EACH OTHER?
I DON'T KNOW. TWENTY YEARS?
WHY'S IT IMPORTANT?
WHEN I MET YOU, YOU WERE GREEN BEHIND THE EARS. NOW, YOU'RE A WORLD CHAMPION MANY TIMES OVER. I DIDN'T HAVE A SINGLE GRAY HAIR... AND NOW LOOK AT ME.
YOUR HAIR'S ALSO MADE A STEADY MARCH BACKWARD. LET'S FACE FACTS. YOU'RE 39, IT'S TIME TO CALL IT QUITS.

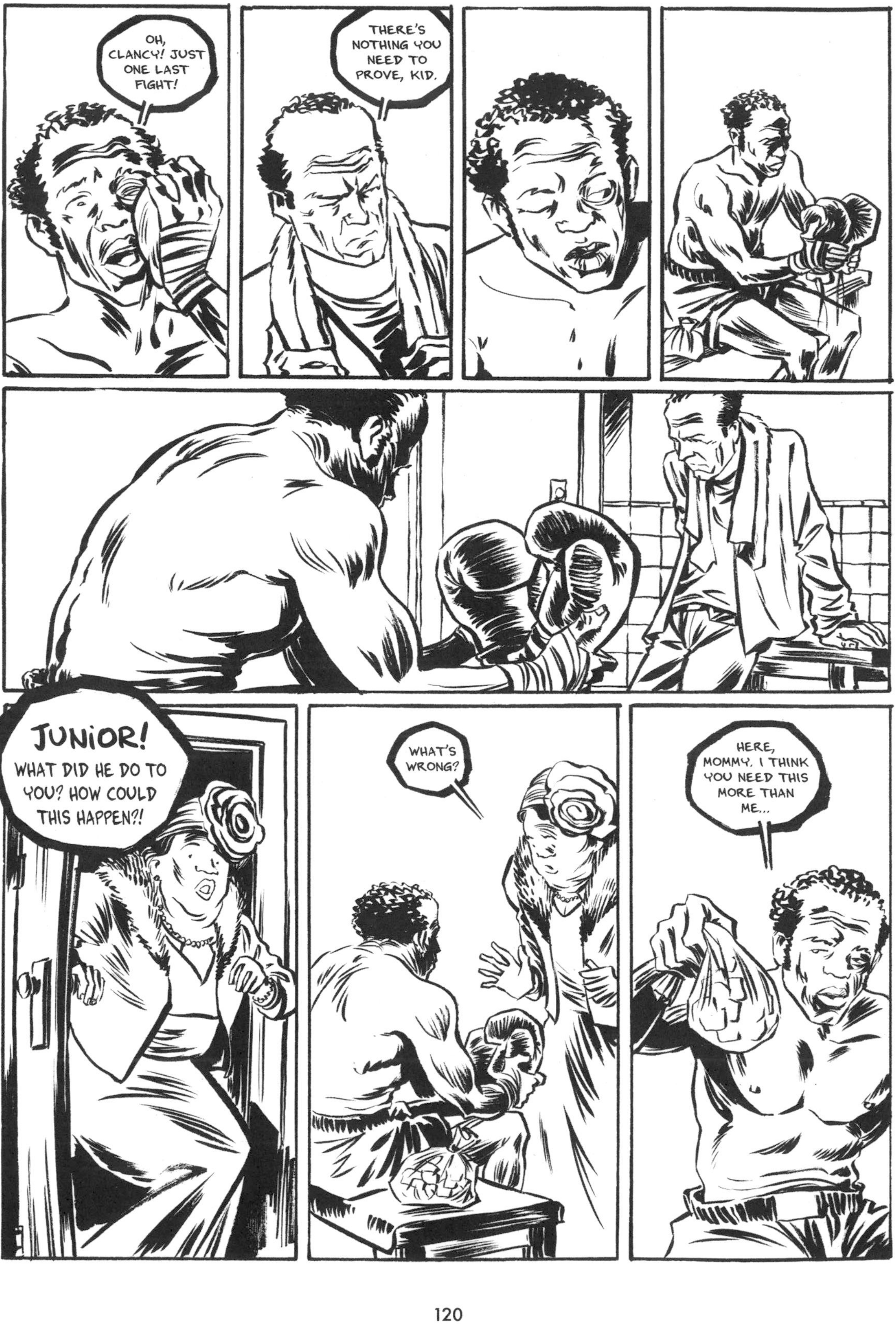
OH, CLANCY! JUST ONE LAST FIGHT!
THERE'S NOTHING YOU NEED TO PROVE, KID.
JUNIOR! WHAT DID HE DO TO YOU? HOW COULD THIS HAPPEN?!
WHAT'S WRONG?
HERE, MOMMY. I THINK YOU NEED THIS MORE THAN ME...

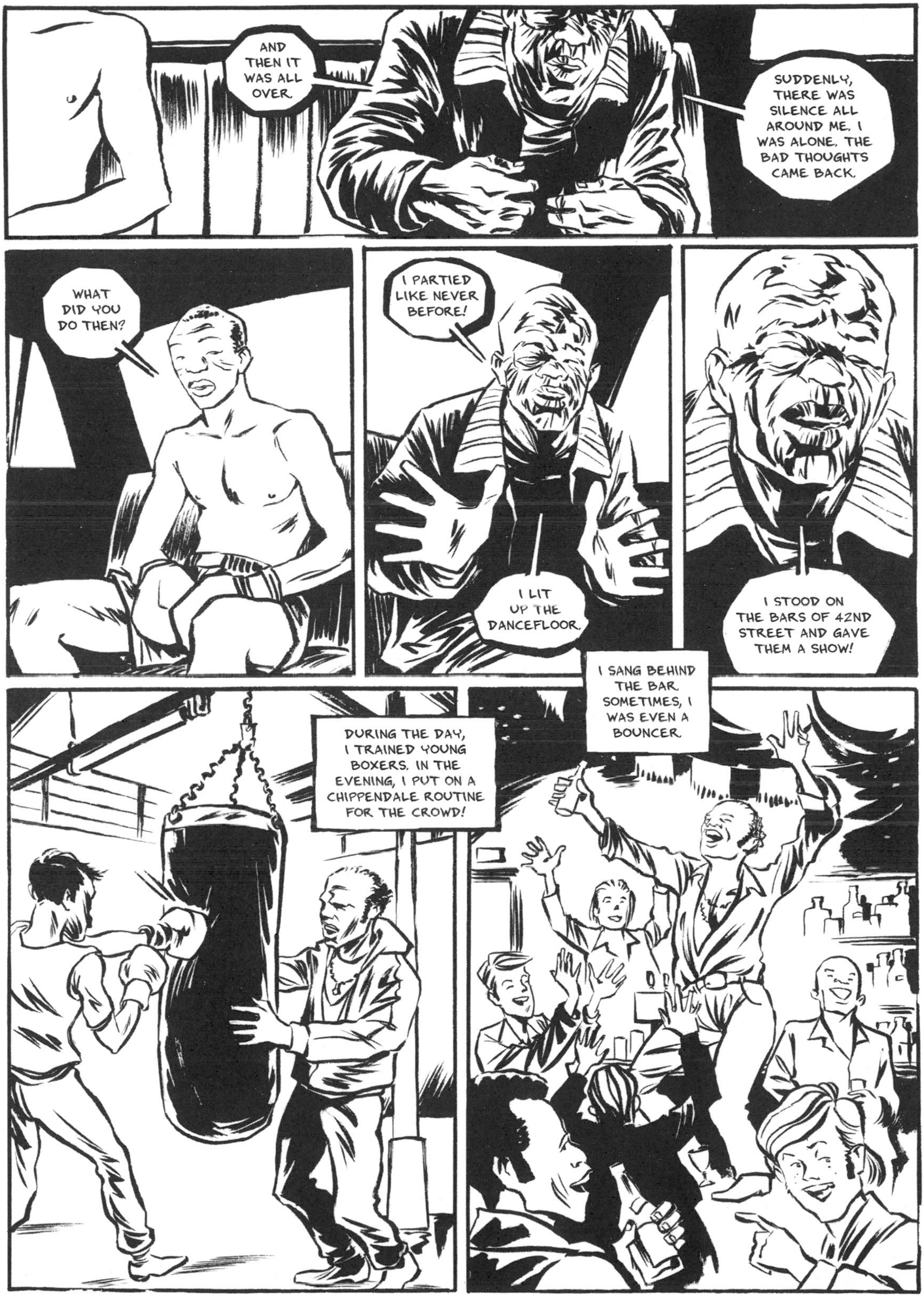
AND THEN IT WAS ALL OVER.
SUDDENLY, THERE WAS SILENCE ALL AROUND ME. I WAS ALONE. THE BAD THOUGHTS CAME BACK.
WHAT DID YOU DO THEN?
I PARTIED LIKE NEVER BEFORE!
I LIT UP THE DANCEFLOOR.
I STOOD ON THE BARS OF 42ND STREET AND GAVE THEM A SHOW!
DURING THE DAY, I TRAINED YOUNG BOXERS. IN THE EVENING, I PUT ON A CHIPPENDALE ROUTINE FOR THE CROWD!
I SANG BEHIND THE BAR. SOMETIMES, I WAS EVEN A BOUNCER.

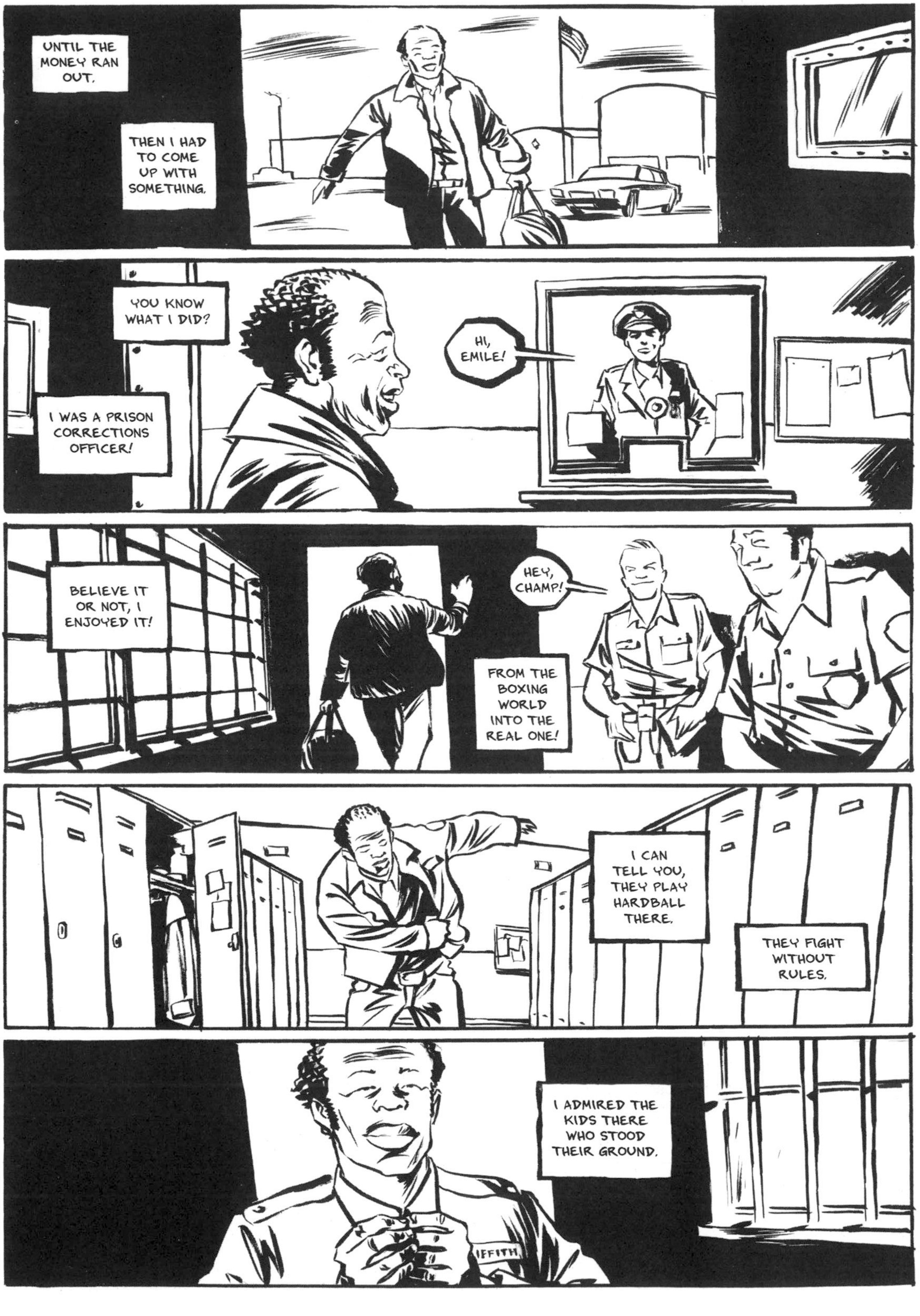
UNTIL THE MONEY RAN OUT.
THEN I HAD TO COME UP WITH SOMETHING.
YOU KNOW WHAT I DID?
HI, EMILE!
I WAS A PRISON CORRECTIONS OFFICER!
BELIEVE IT OR NOT, I ENJOYED IT!
HEY, CHAMP!
FROM THE BOXING WORLD INTO THE REAL ONE!
I CAN TELL YOU, THEY PLAY HARDBALL THERE.
THEY FIGHT WITHOUT RULES.
I ADMIRED THE KIDS THERE WHO STOOD THEIR GROUND.

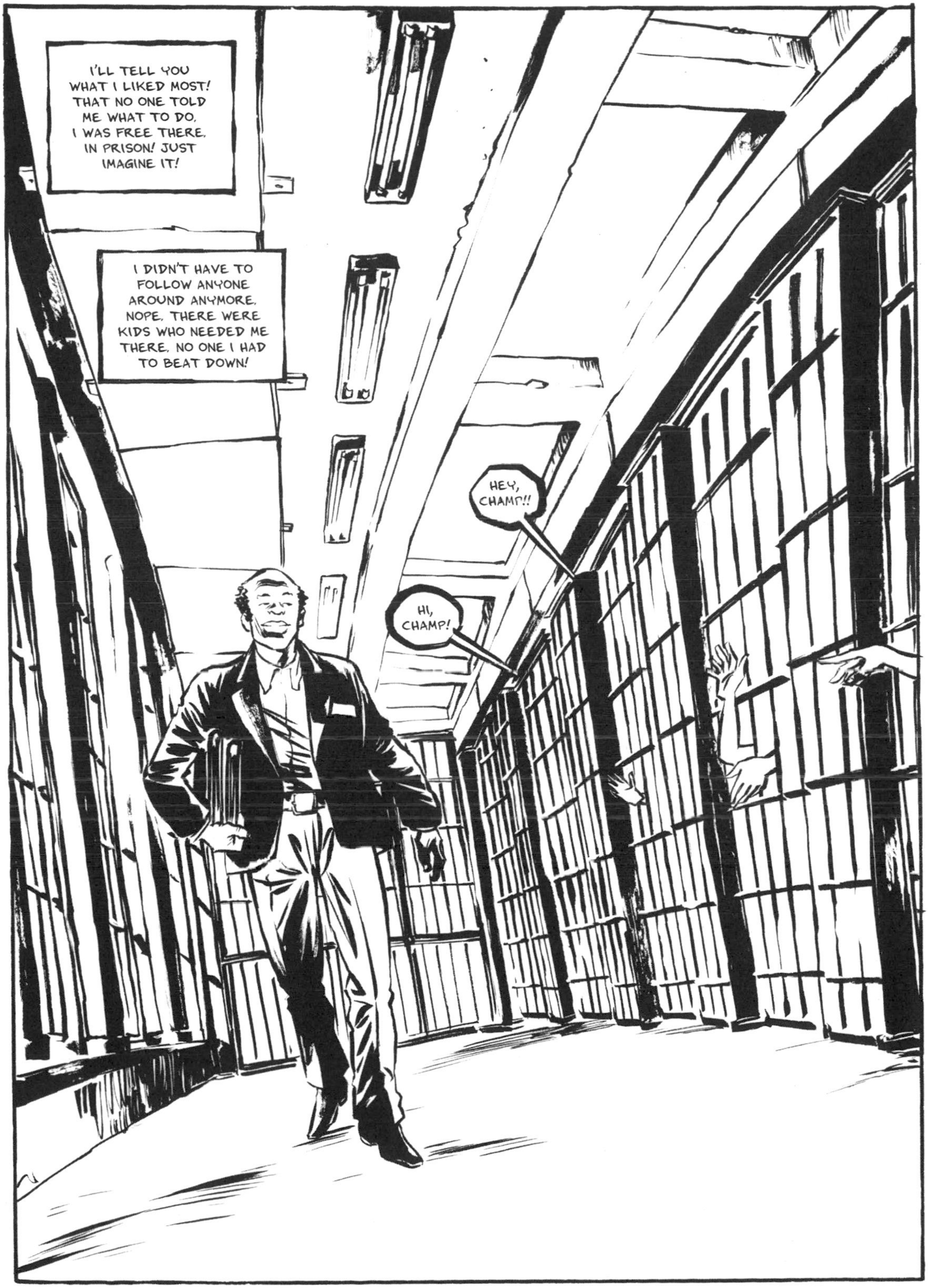
I'LL TELL YOU WHAT I LIKED MOST! THAT NO ONE TOLD ME WHAT TO DO. I WAS FREE THERE. IN PRISON! JUST IMAGINE IT!
I DIDN'T HAVE TO FOLLOW ANYONE AROUND ANYMORE. NOPE. THERE WERE KIDS WHO NEEDED ME THERE. NO ONE I HAD TO BEAT DOWN!
HEY, CHAMP!!
HI, CHAMP!

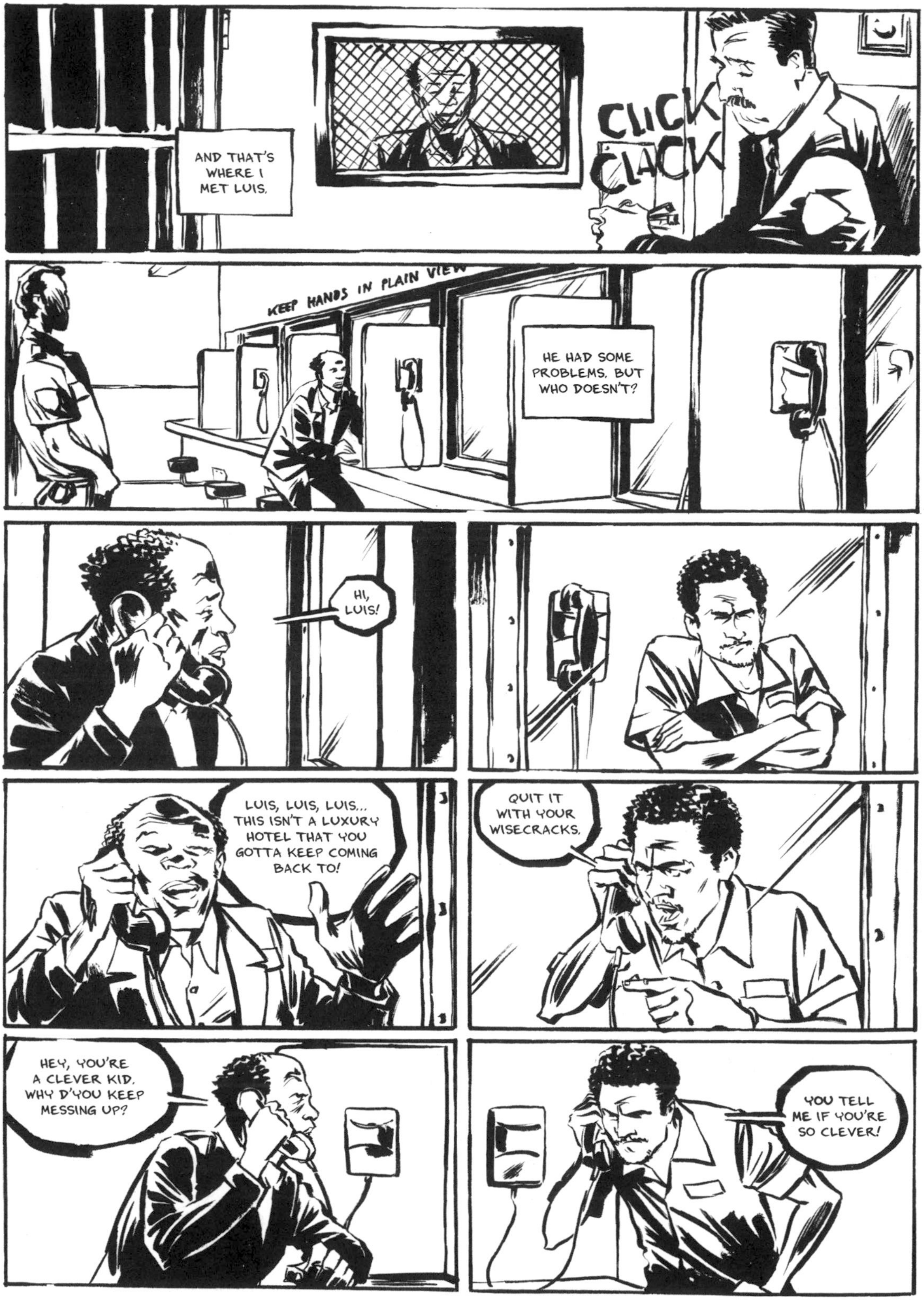
AND THAT'S WHERE I MET LUIS.
CLICK CLACK
KEEP HANDS IN PLAIN VIEW
HE HAD SOME PROBLEMS. BUT WHO DOESN'T?
HI, LUIS!
LUIS, LUIS, LUIS... THIS ISN'T A LUXURY HOTEL THAT YOU GOTTA KEEP COMING BACK TO!
QUIT IT WITH YOUR WISECRACKS.
HEY, YOU'RE A CLEVER KID. WHY D'YOU KEEP MESSING UP?
YOU TELL ME IF YOU'RE SO CLEVER!

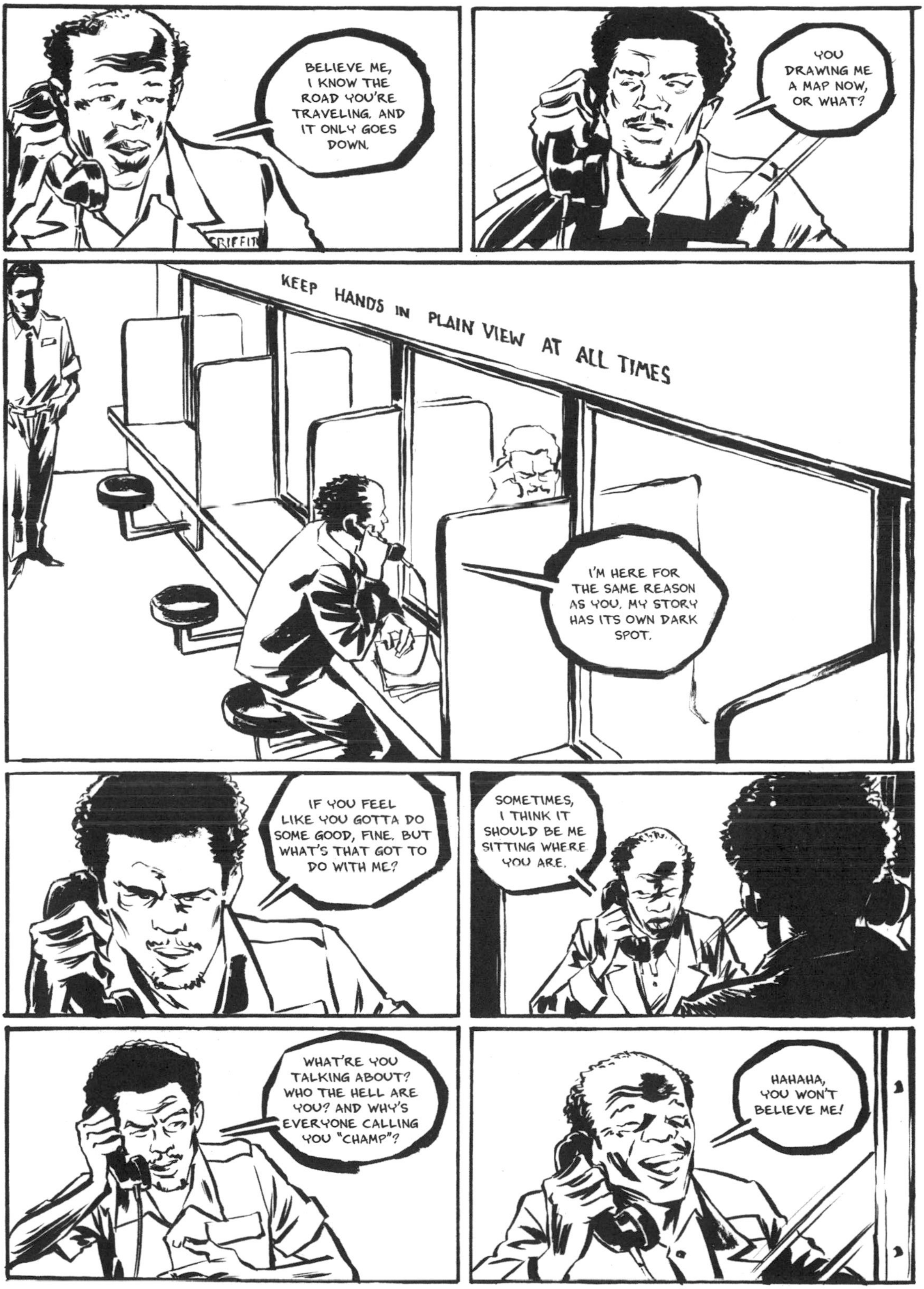
BELIEVE ME, I KNOW THE ROAD YOU'RE TRAVELING, AND IT ONLY GOES DOWN.
YOU DRAWING ME A MAP NOW, OR WHAT?
KEEP HANDS IN PLAIN VIEW AT ALL TIMES
I'M HERE FOR THE SAME REASON AS YOU. MY STORY HAS ITS OWN DARK SPOT.
IF YOU FEEL LIKE YOU GOTTA DO SOME GOOD, FINE. BUT WHAT'S THAT GOT TO DO WITH ME?
SOMETIMES, I THINK IT SHOULD BE ME SITTING WHERE YOU ARE.
WHAT'RE YOU TALKING ABOUT? WHO THE HELL ARE YOU? AND WHY'S EVERYONE CALLING YOU "CHAMP"?
HAHAHA, YOU WON'T BELIEVE ME!

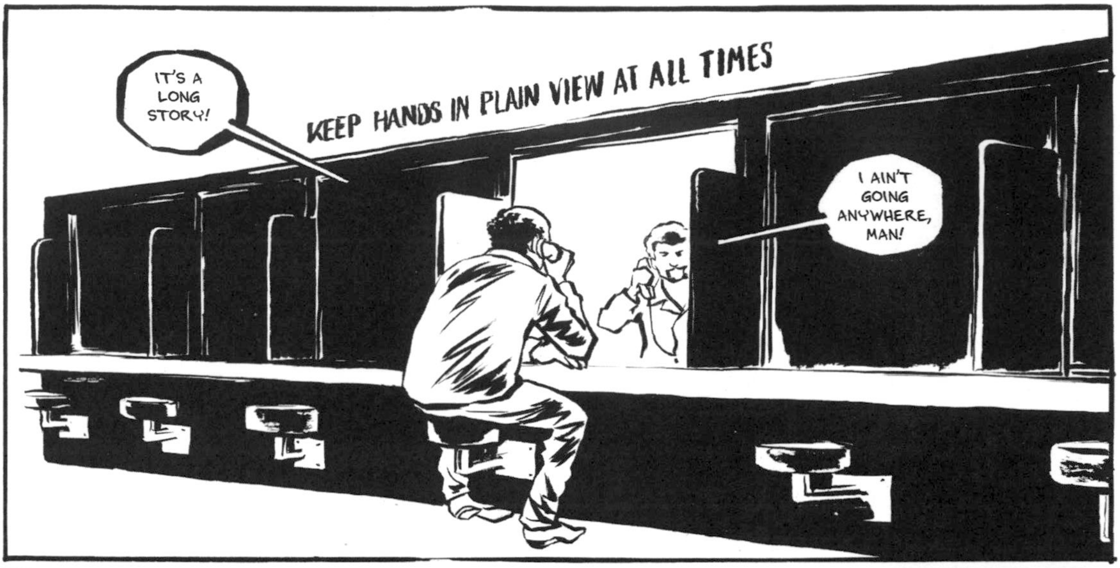
IT'S A LONG STORY!
KEEP HANDS IN PLAIN VIEW AT ALL TIMES
I AIN'T GOING ANYWHERE, MAN!

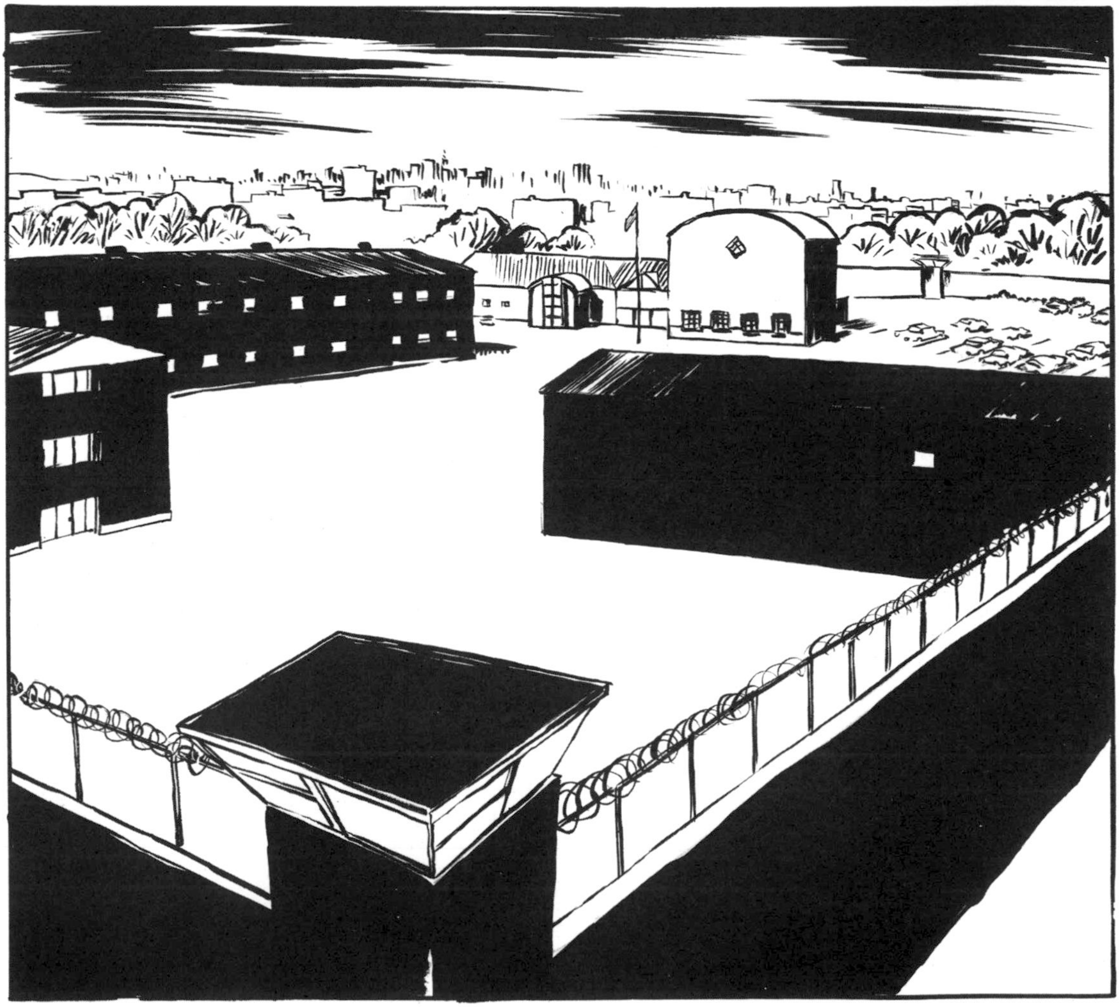

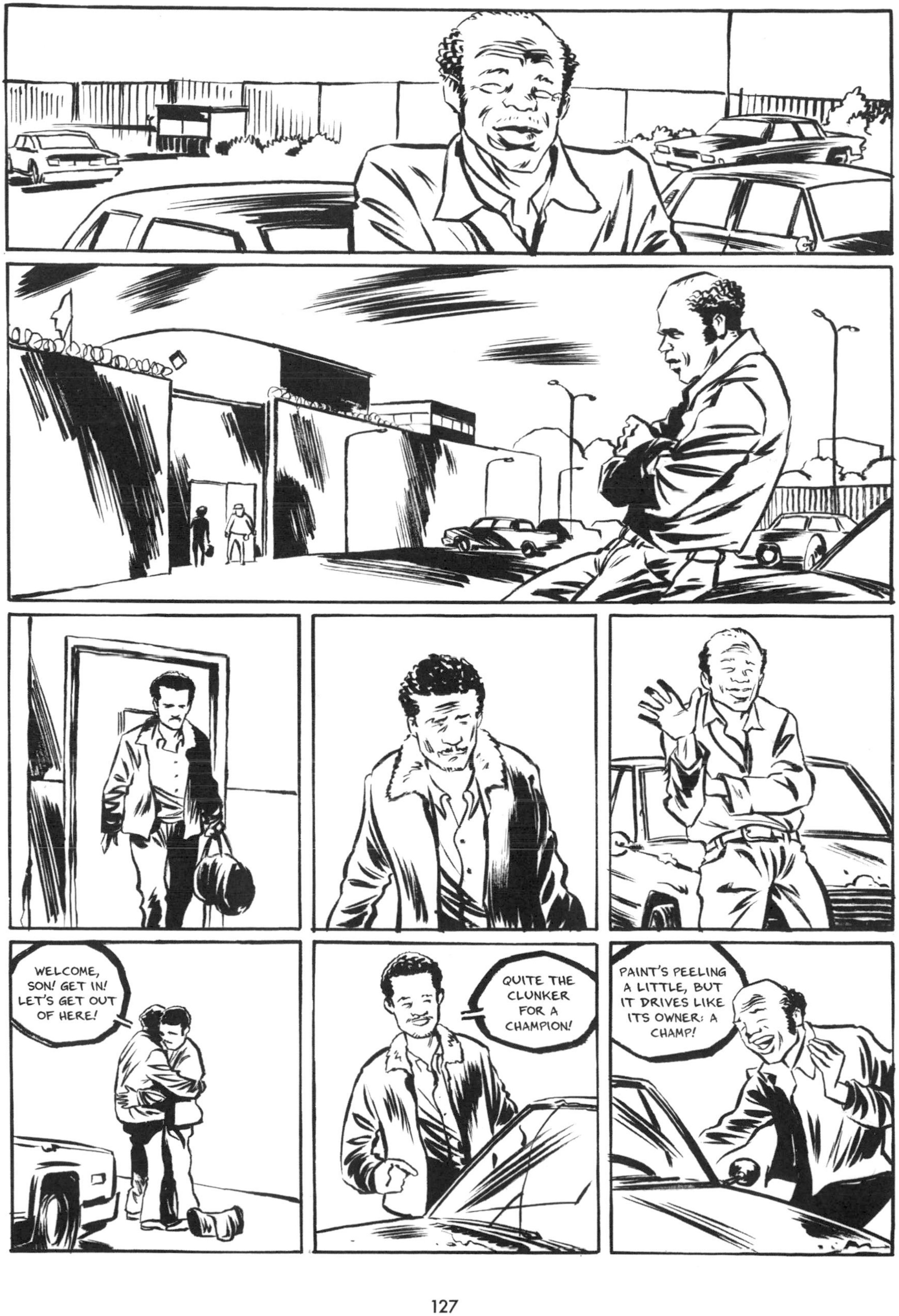
WELCOME, SON! GET IN! LET'S GET OUT OF HERE!
QUITE THE CLUNKER FOR A CHAMPION!
PAINT'S PEELING A LITTLE, BUT IT DRIVES LIKE ITS OWNER: A CHAMP!

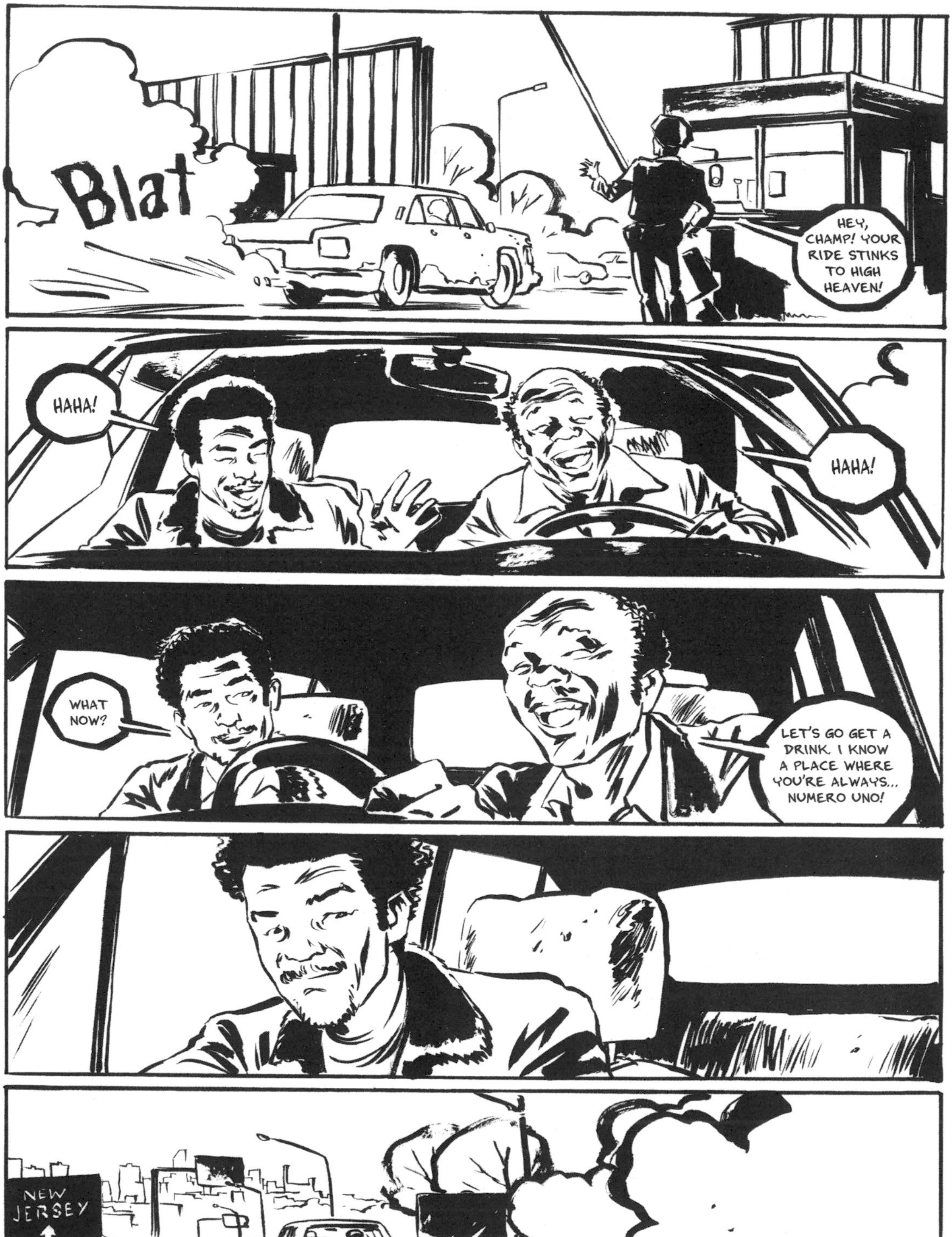
Blat
HEY, CHAMP! YOUR RIDE STINKS TO HIGH HEAVEN!
HAHA!
HAHA!
WHAT NOW?
LET'S GO GET A DRINK. I KNOW A PLACE WHERE YOU'RE ALWAYS... NUMERO UNO!
NEW JERSEY

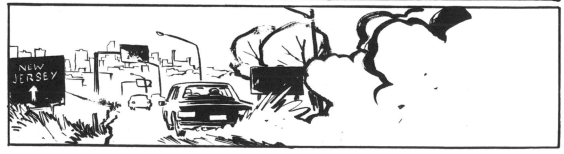

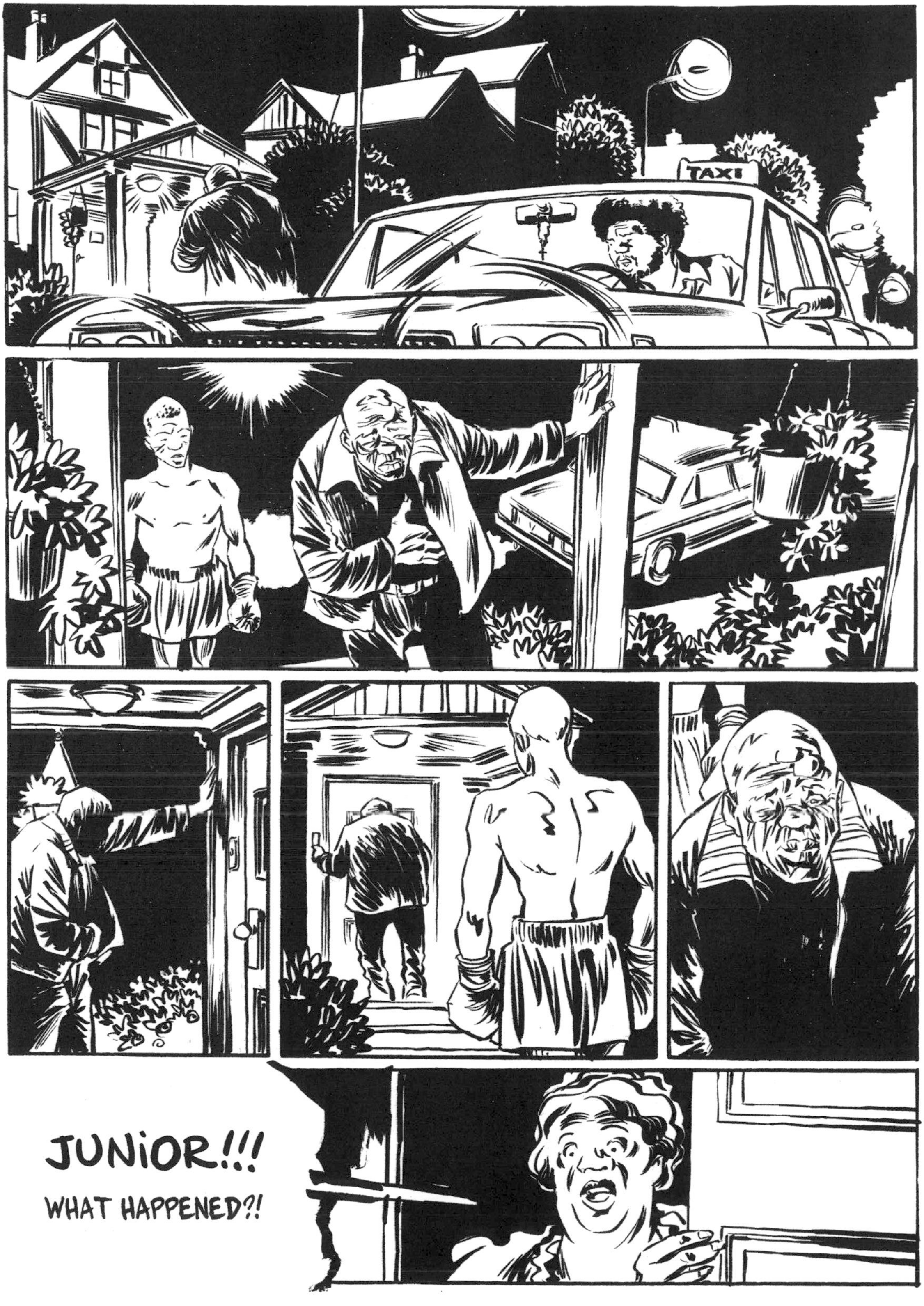
TAXI
JUNIOR!!!
WHAT HAPPENED?!

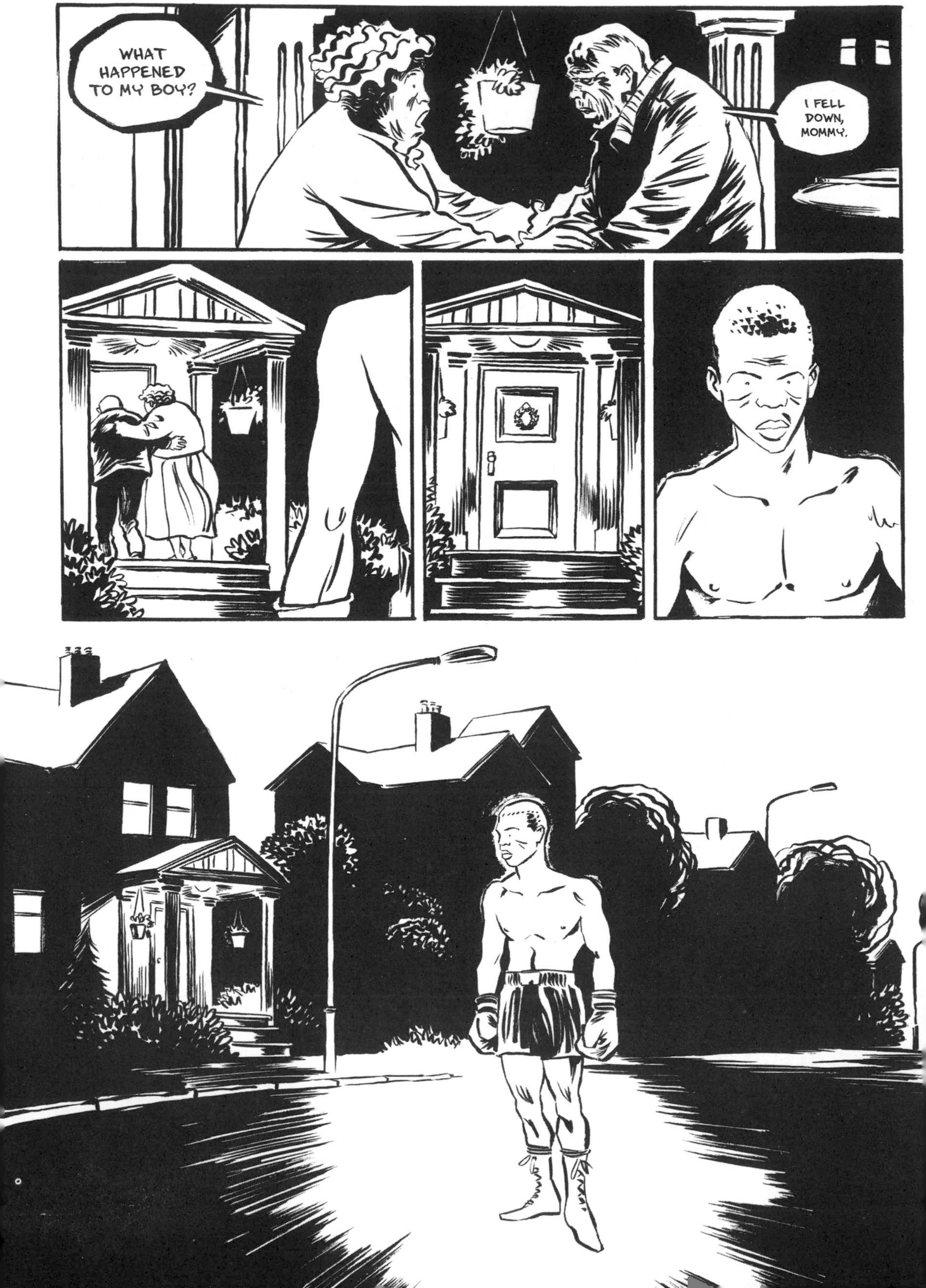
WHAT HAPPENED TO MY BOY?
I FELL DOWN, MOMMY.

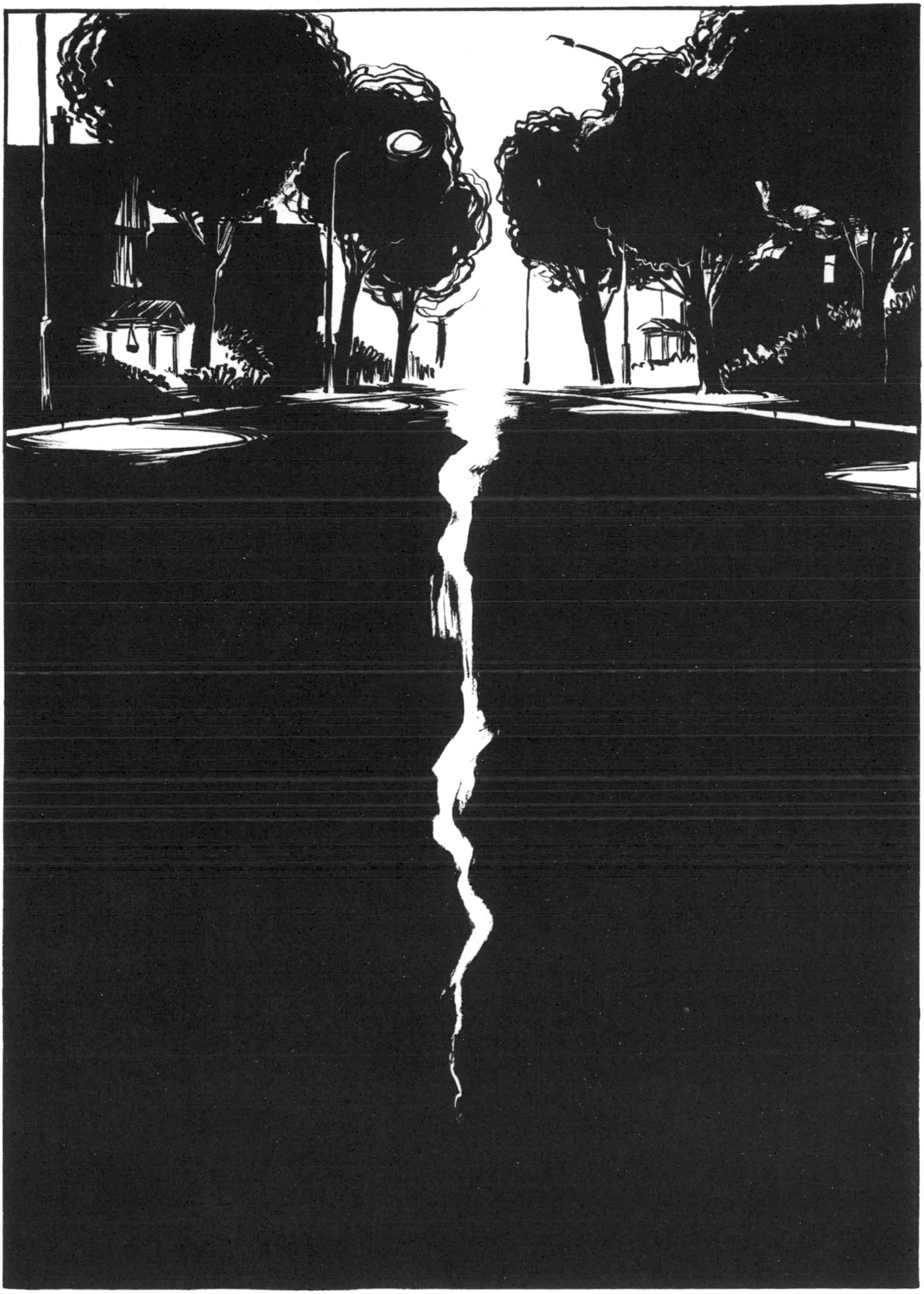

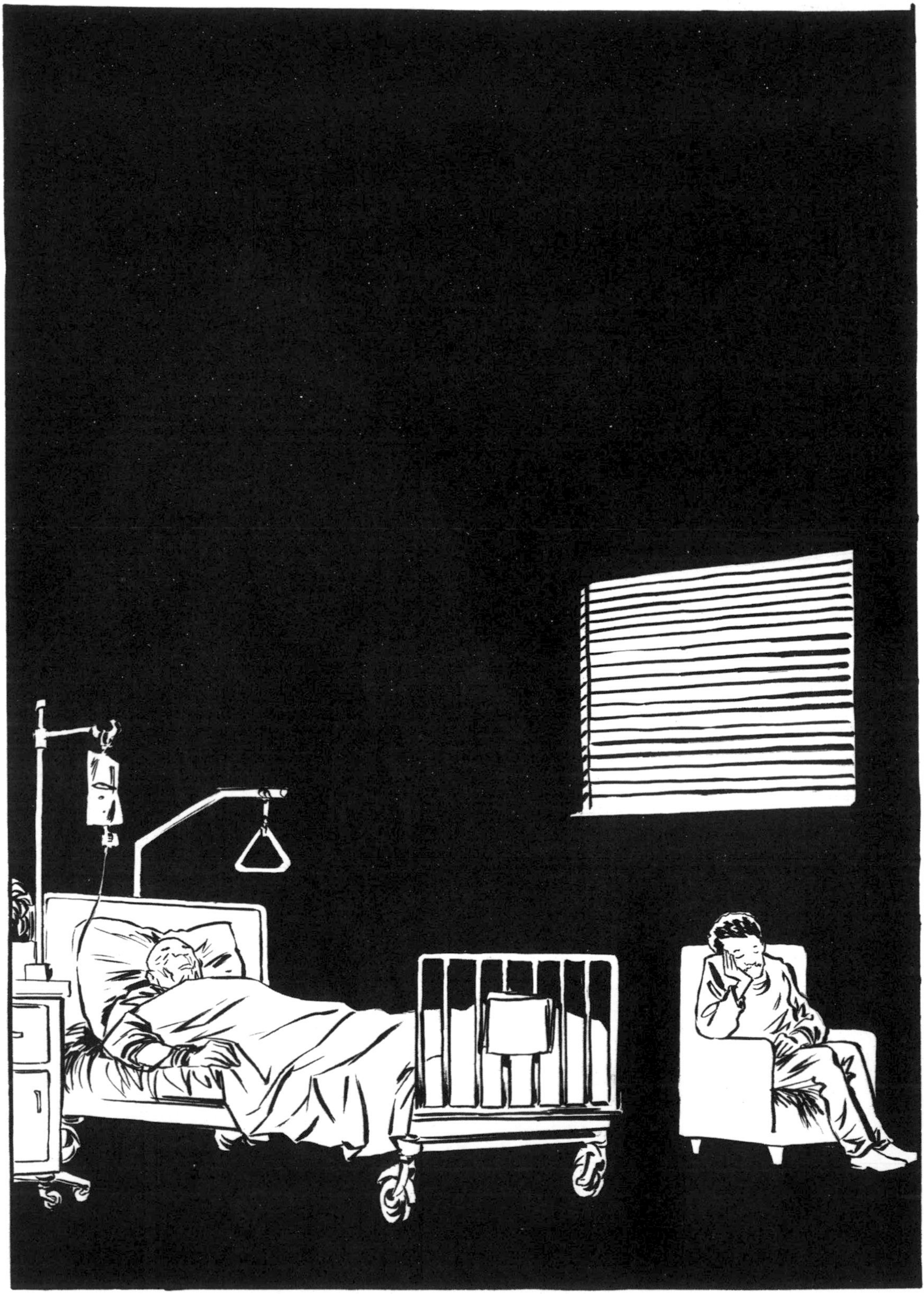

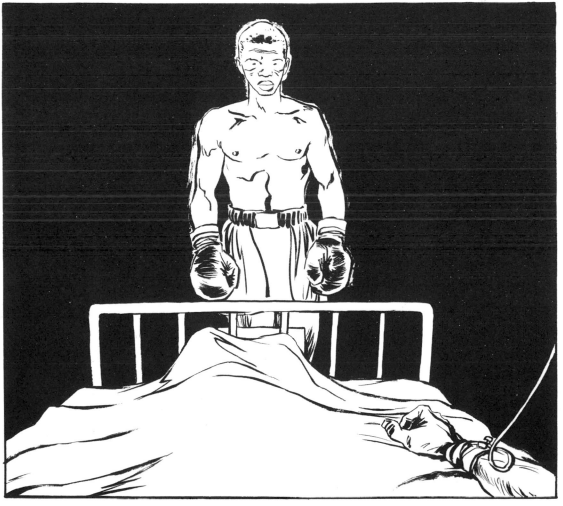

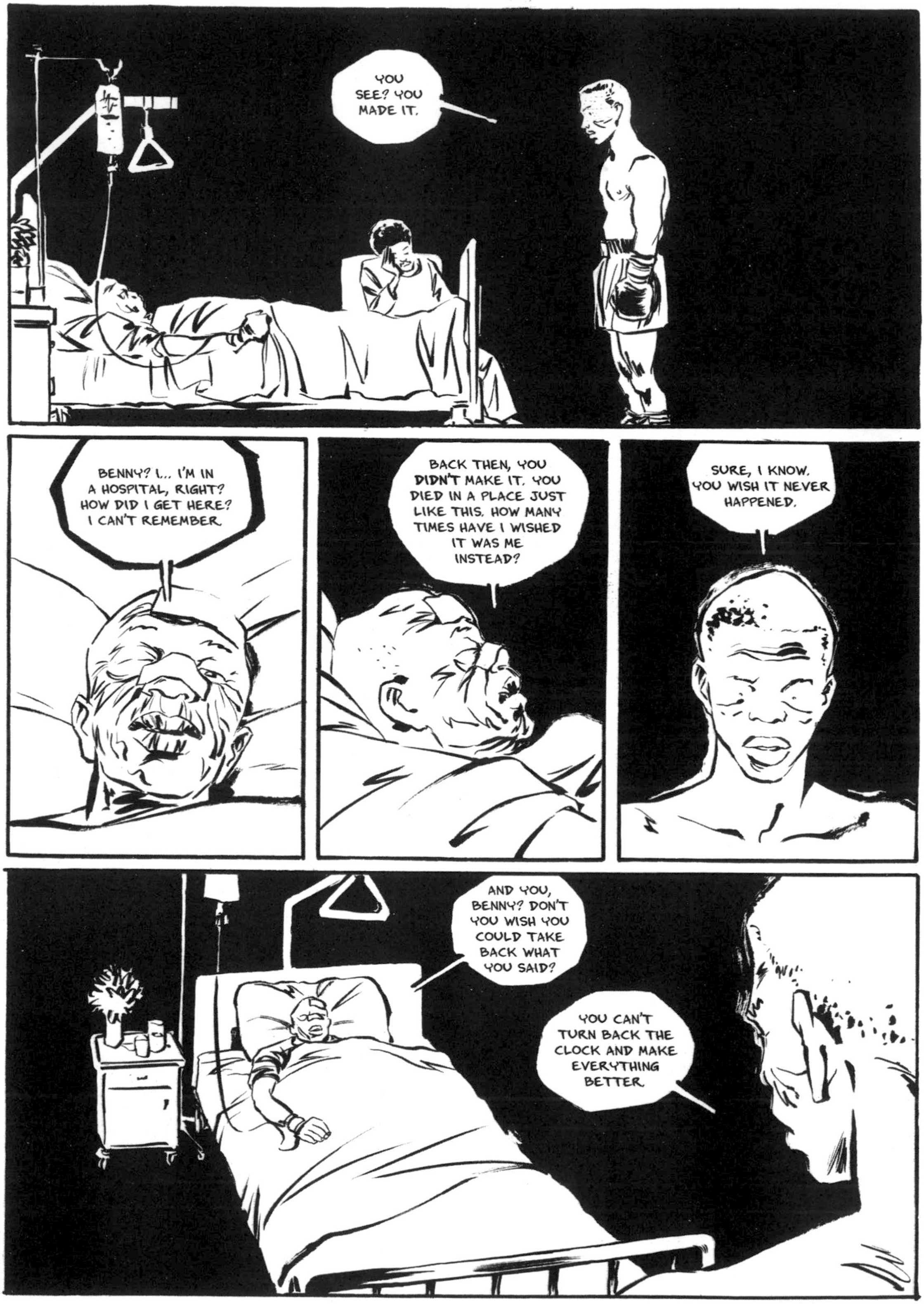
YOU SEE? YOU MADE IT.
BENNY? I... I'M IN A HOSPITAL, RIGHT? HOW DID I GET HERE? I CAN'T REMEMBER.
BACK THEN, YOU **DIDN'T** MAKE IT. YOU DIED IN A PLACE JUST LIKE THIS. HOW MANY TIMES HAVE I WISHED IT WAS ME INSTEAD?
SURE, I KNOW. YOU WISH IT NEVER HAPPENED.
AND YOU, BENNY? DON'T YOU WISH YOU COULD TAKE BACK WHAT YOU SAID?
YOU CAN'T TURN BACK THE CLOCK AND MAKE EVERYTHING BETTER.

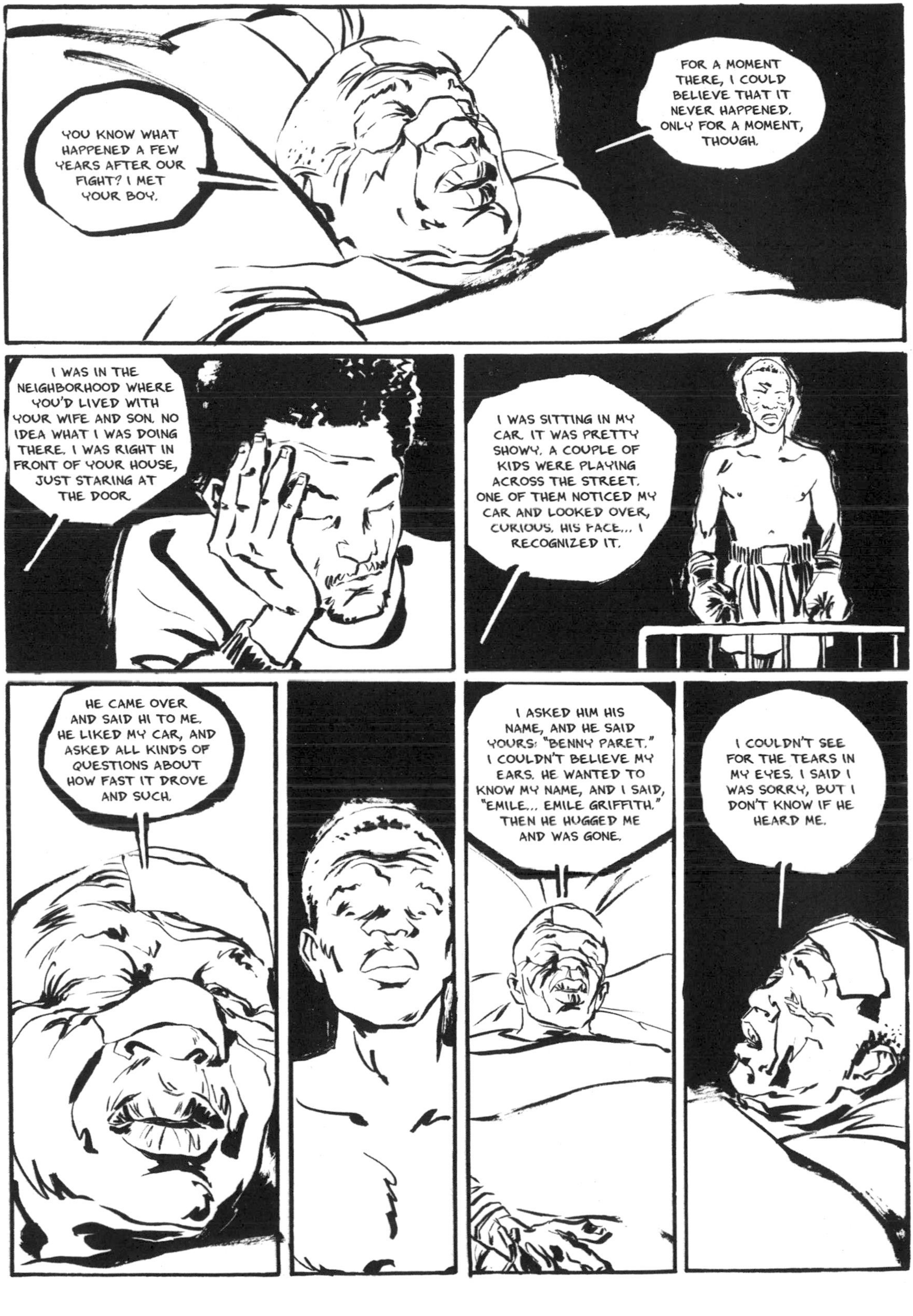
YOU KNOW WHAT HAPPENED A FEW YEARS AFTER OUR FIGHT? I MET YOUR BOY.
FOR A MOMENT THERE, I COULD BELIEVE THAT IT NEVER HAPPENED. ONLY FOR A MOMENT, THOUGH.
I WAS IN THE NEIGHBORHOOD WHERE YOU'D LIVED WITH YOUR WIFE AND SON. NO IDEA WHAT I WAS DOING THERE. I WAS RIGHT IN FRONT OF YOUR HOUSE, JUST STARING AT THE DOOR.
I WAS SITTING IN MY CAR. IT WAS PRETTY SHOWY. A COUPLE OF KIDS WERE PLAYING ACROSS THE STREET. ONE OF THEM NOTICED MY CAR AND LOOKED OVER, CURIOUS. HIS FACE... I RECOGNIZED IT.
HE CAME OVER AND SAID HI TO ME. HE LIKED MY CAR, AND ASKED ALL KINDS OF QUESTIONS ABOUT HOW FAST IT DROVE AND SUCH.
I ASKED HIM HIS NAME, AND HE SAID YOURS: "BENNY PARET." I COULDN'T BELIEVE MY EARS. HE WANTED TO KNOW MY NAME, AND I SAID, "EMILE... EMILE GRIFFITH." THEN HE HUGGED ME AND WAS GONE.
I COULDN'T SEE FOR THE TEARS IN MY EYES. I SAID I WAS SORRY, BUT I DON'T KNOW IF HE HEARD ME.

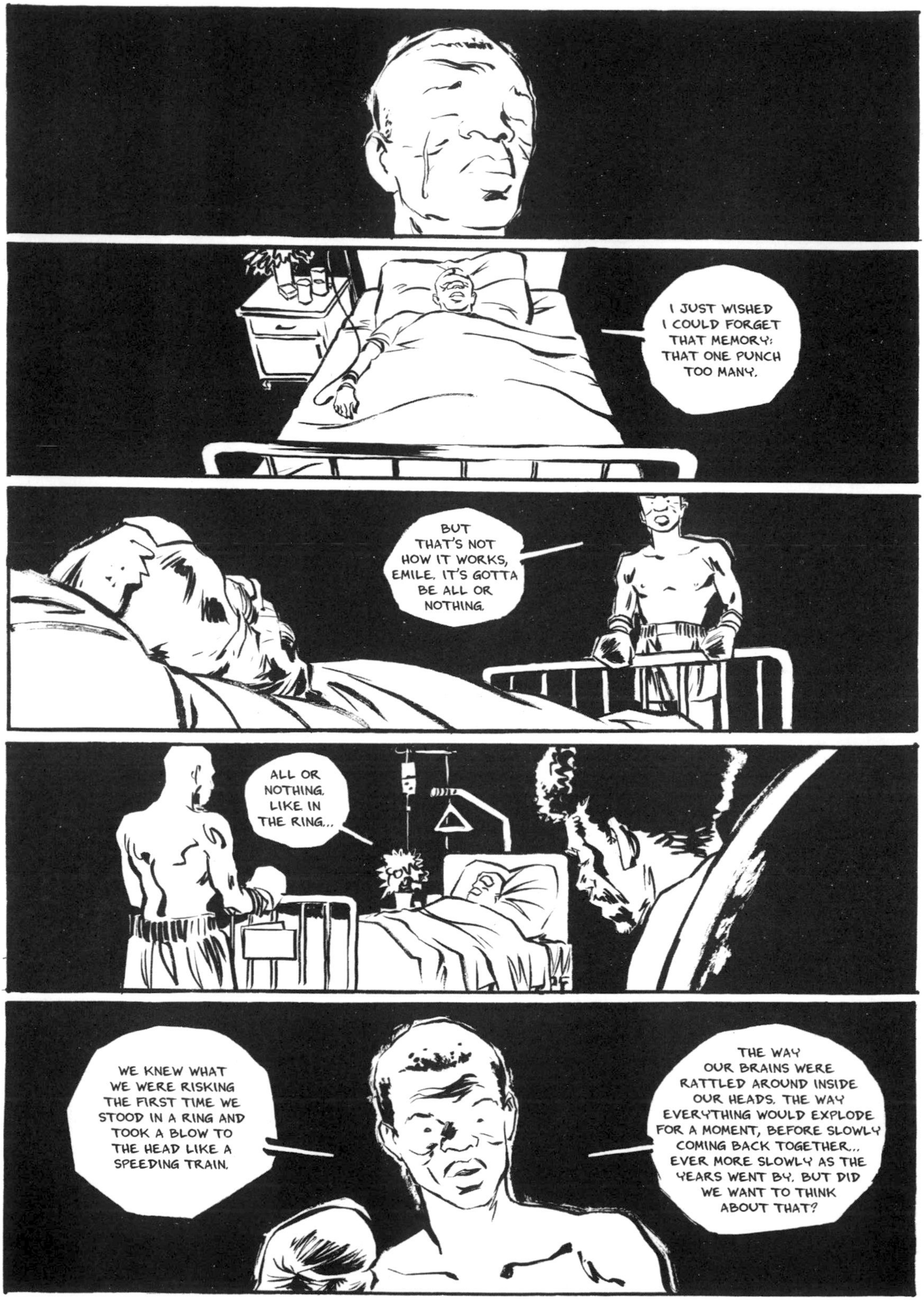
I JUST WISHED I COULD FORGET THAT MEMORY: THAT ONE PUNCH TOO MANY.
BUT THAT'S NOT HOW IT WORKS, EMILE. IT'S GOTTA BE ALL OR NOTHING.
ALL OR NOTHING. LIKE IN THE RING...
WE KNEW WHAT WE WERE RISKING THE FIRST TIME WE STOOD IN A RING AND TOOK A BLOW TO THE HEAD LIKE A SPEEDING TRAIN.
THE WAY OUR BRAINS WERE RATTLED AROUND INSIDE OUR HEADS. THE WAY EVERYTHING WOULD EXPLODE FOR A MOMENT, BEFORE SLOWLY COMING BACK TOGETHER... EVER MORE SLOWLY AS THE YEARS WENT BY. BUT DID WE WANT TO THINK ABOUT THAT?

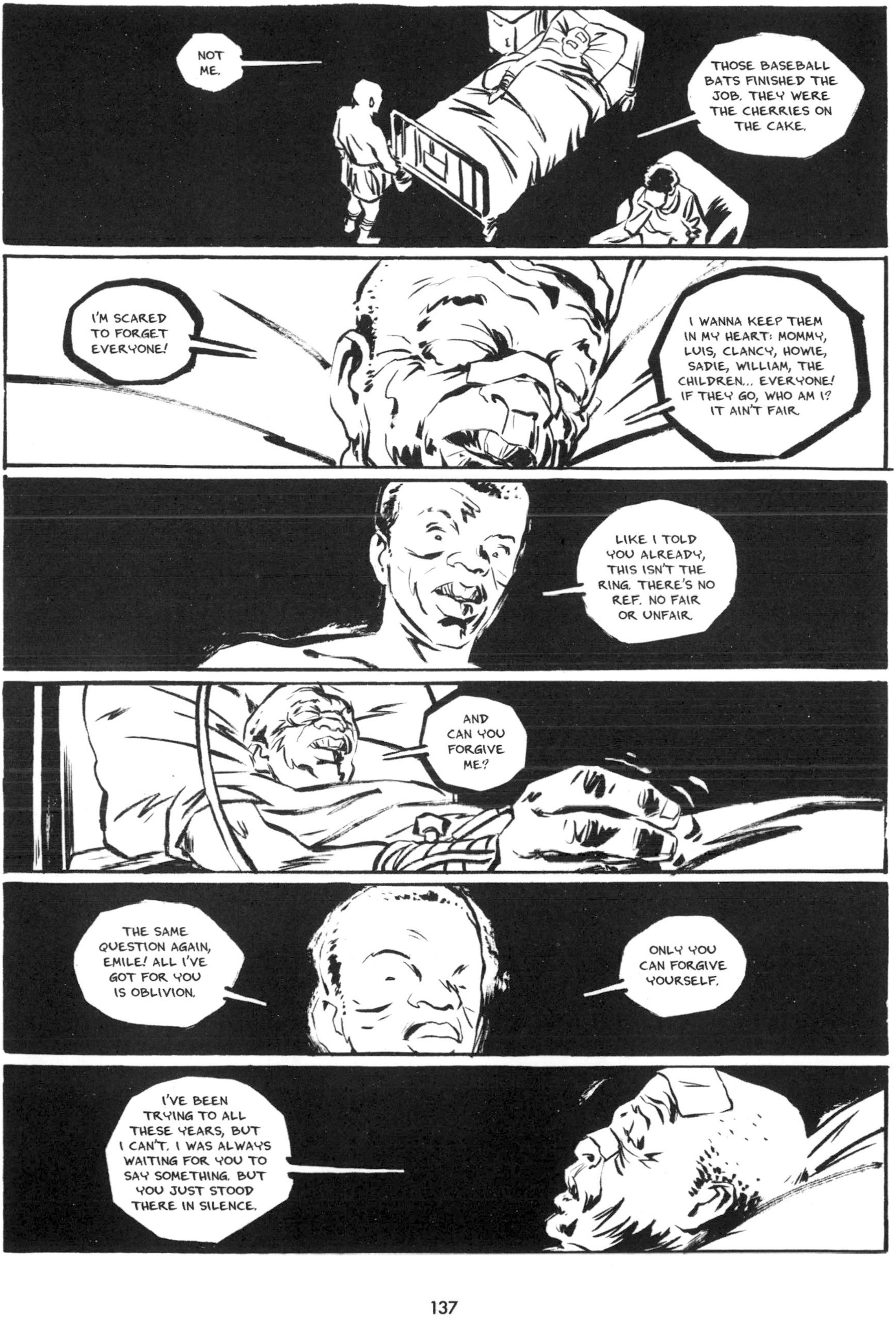
NOT ME.
THOSE BASEBALL BATS FINISHED THE JOB. THEY WERE THE CHERRIES ON THE CAKE.
I'M SCARED TO FORGET EVERYONE!
I WANNA KEEP THEM IN MY HEART: MOMMY, LUIS, CLANCY, HOWIE, SADIE, WILLIAM, THE CHILDREN... EVERYONE! IF THEY GO, WHO AM I? IT AIN'T FAIR.
LIKE I TOLD YOU ALREADY, THIS ISN'T THE RING. THERE'S NO REF. NO FAIR OR UNFAIR.
AND CAN YOU FORGIVE ME?
THE SAME QUESTION AGAIN, EMILE! ALL I'VE GOT FOR YOU IS OBLIVION.
ONLY YOU CAN FORGIVE YOURSELF.
I'VE BEEN TRYING TO ALL THESE YEARS, BUT I CAN'T. I WAS ALWAYS WAITING FOR YOU TO SAY SOMETHING. BUT YOU JUST STOOD THERE IN SILENCE.

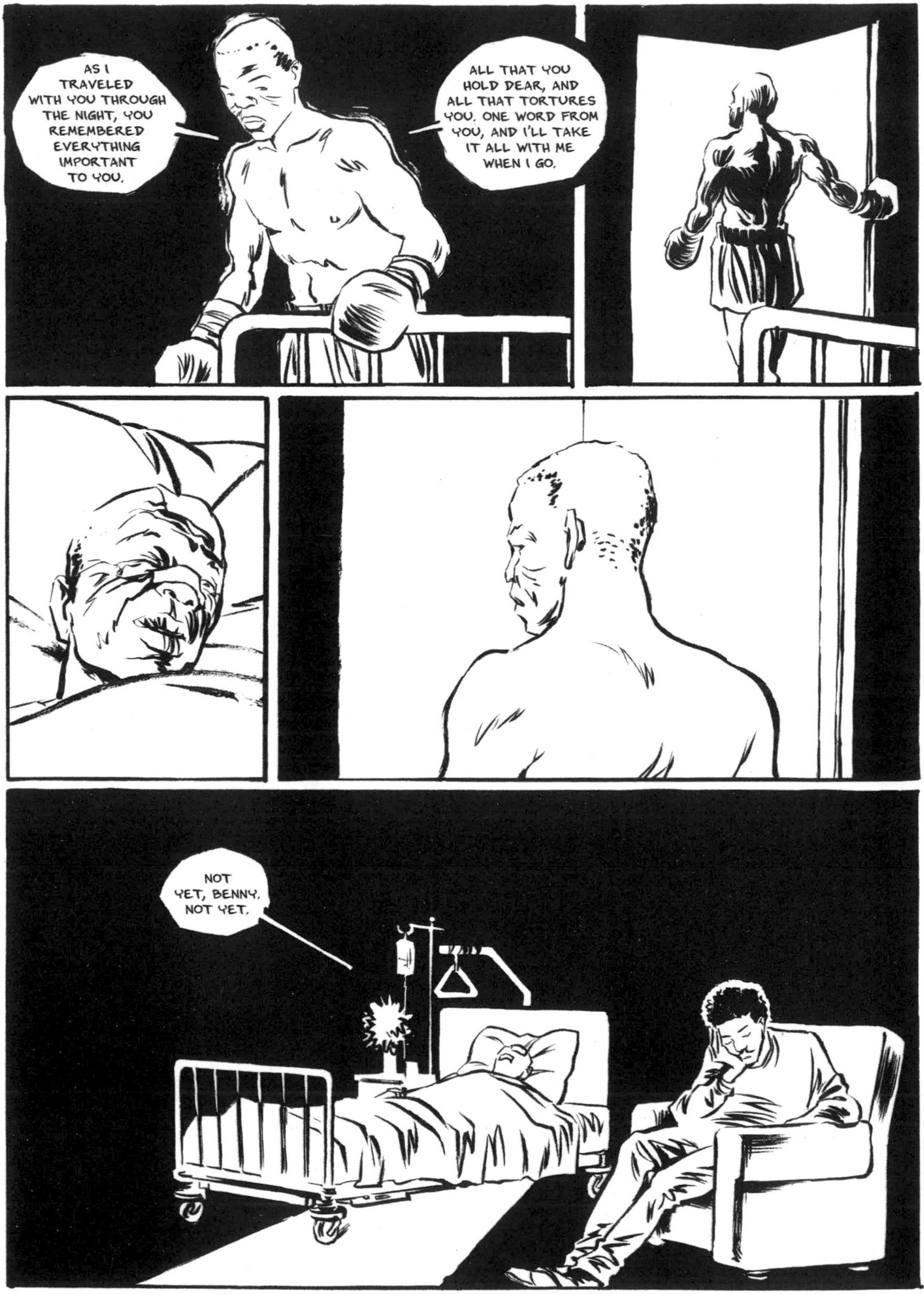
AS I TRAVELED WITH YOU THROUGH THE NIGHT, YOU REMEMBERED EVERYTHING IMPORTANT TO YOU.
ALL THAT YOU HOLD DEAR, AND ALL THAT TORTURES YOU. ONE WORD FROM YOU, AND I'LL TAKE IT ALL WITH ME WHEN I GO.
NOT YET, BENNY. NOT YET.

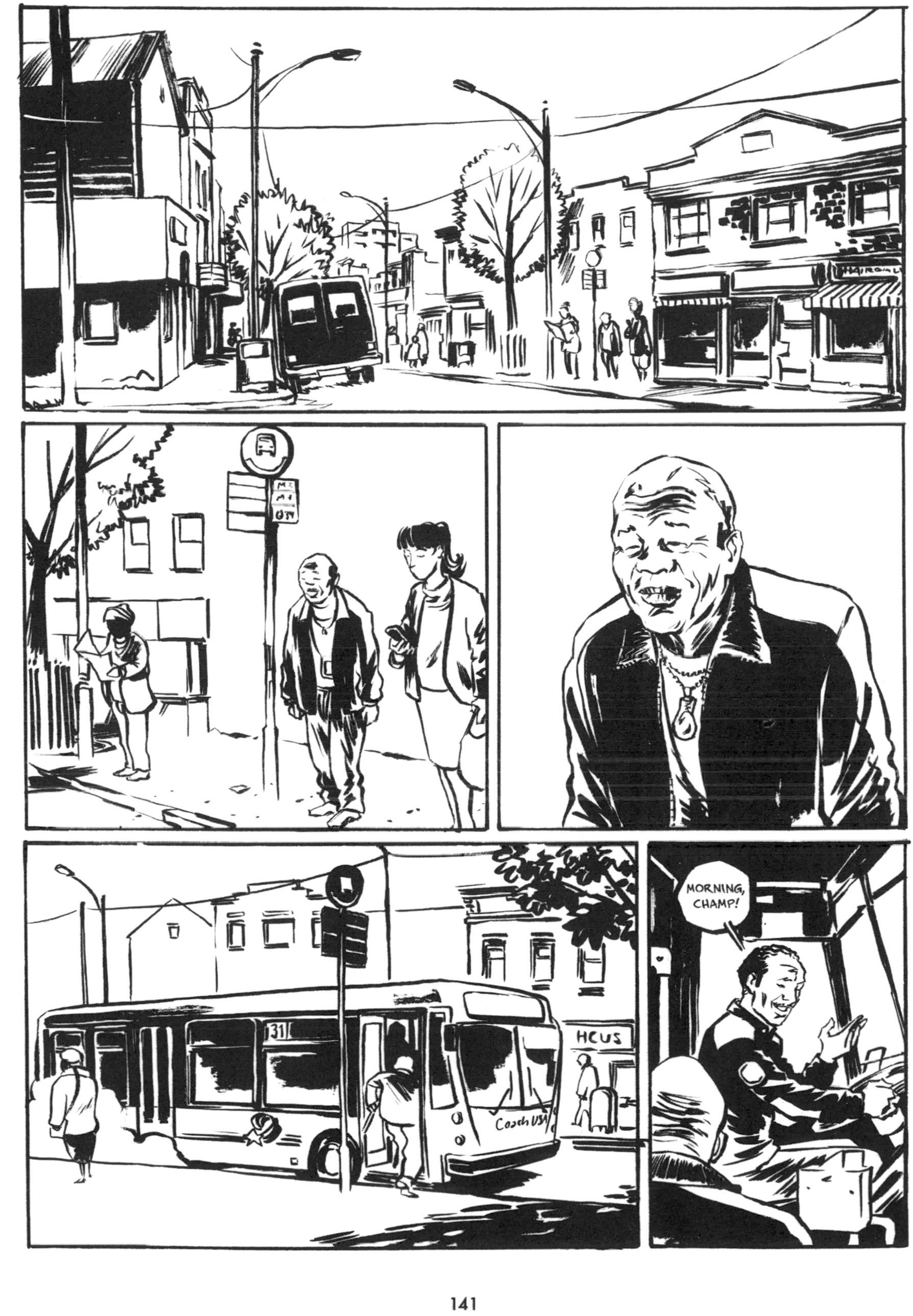
31
Coach USA
MORNING, CHAMP!

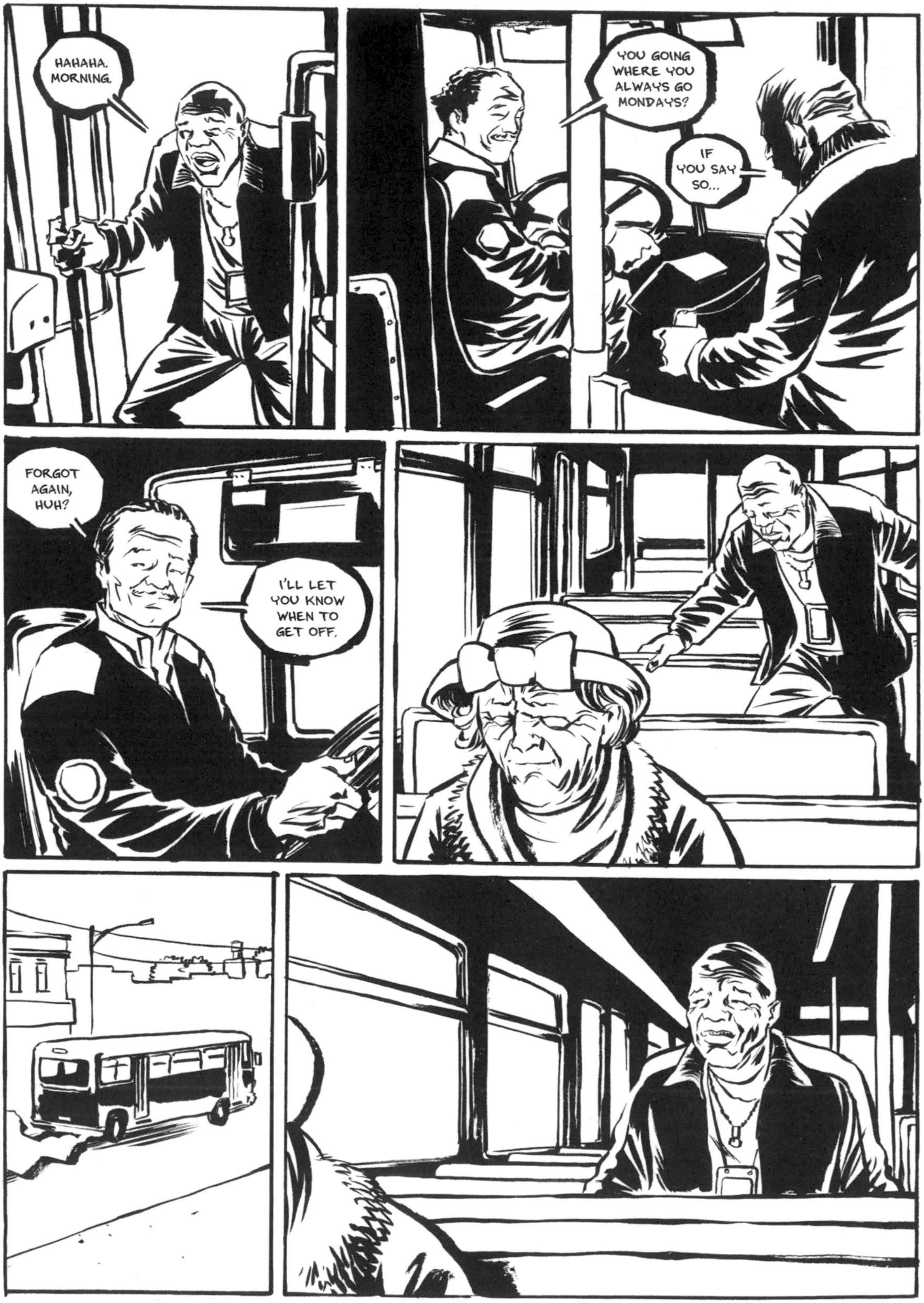
HAHAHA. MORNING.
YOU GOING WHERE YOU ALWAYS GO MONDAYS?
IF YOU SAY SO...
FORGOT AGAIN, HUH?
I'LL LET YOU KNOW WHEN TO GET OFF.

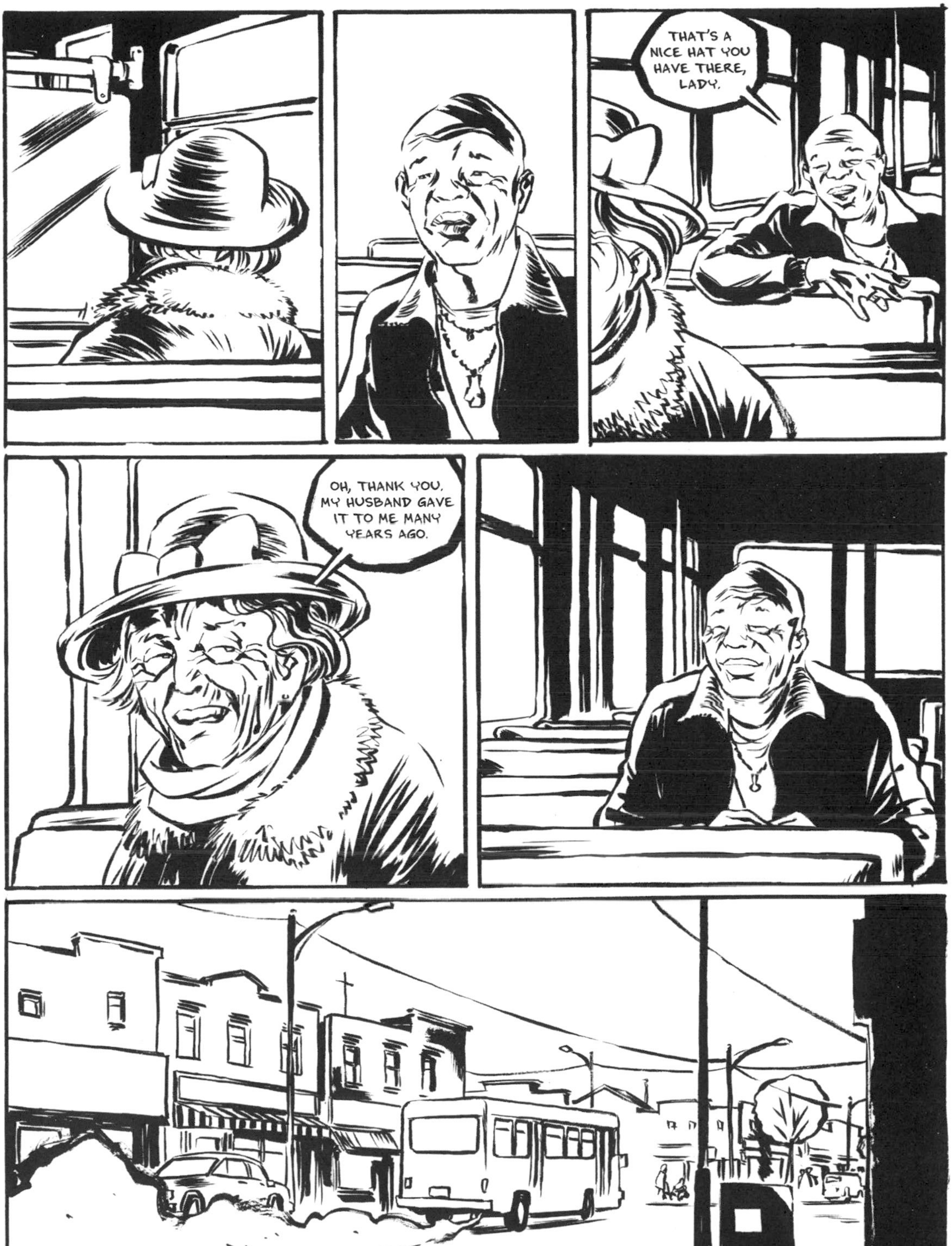
THAT'S A NICE HAT YOU HAVE THERE, LADY.
OH, THANK YOU. MY HUSBAND GAVE IT TO ME MANY YEARS AGO.

EMILE GRIFFITH was born on February 3, 1938, on the Caribbean island of St. Thomas. He boxed from 1956 until 1977, and was welterweight, junior middleweight, and middleweight world champion.

He died in Hempstead, New York, on July 23, 2013.

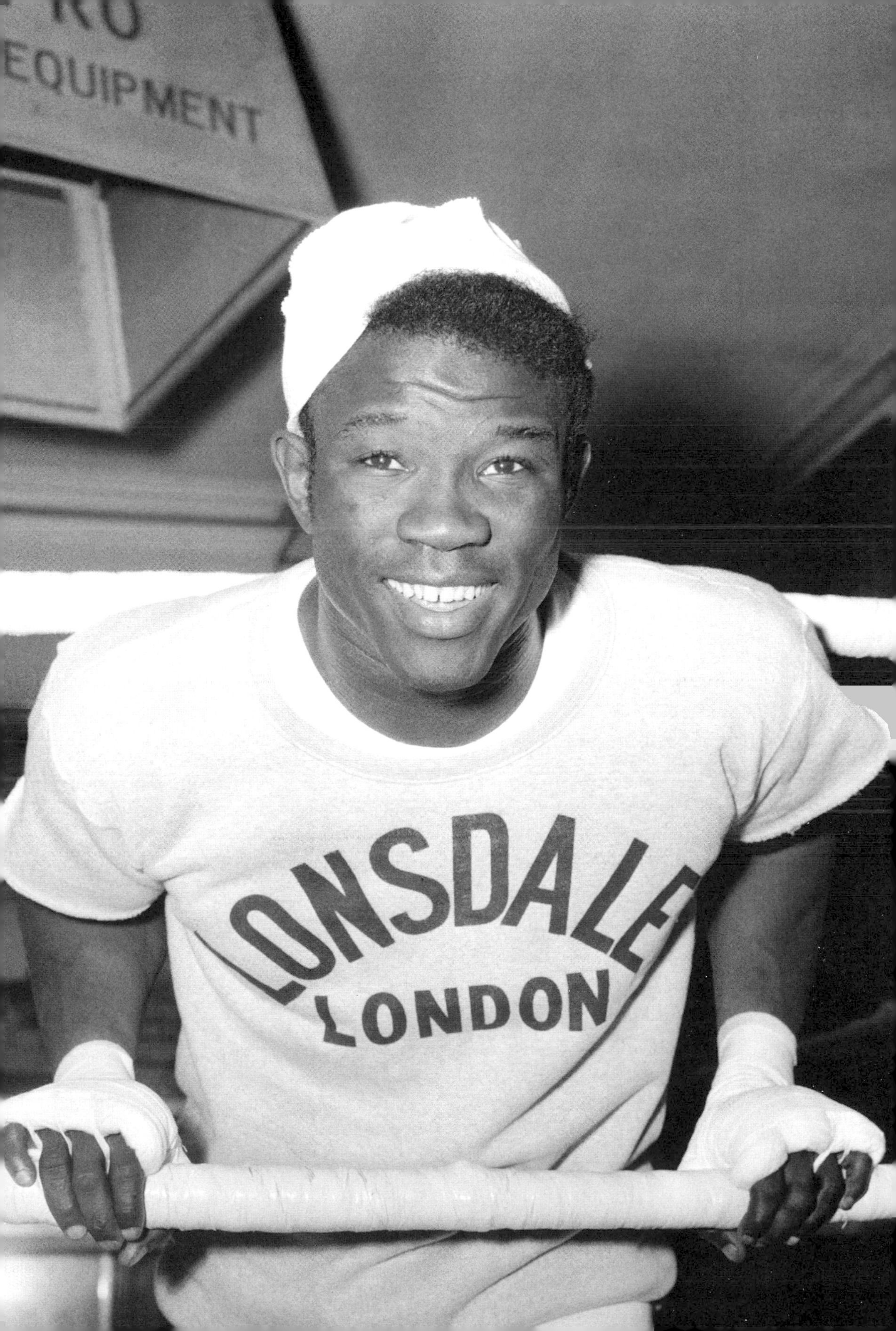
EQUIPMENT
LONSDALE
LONDON

EMILE GRIFFITH – FIGHTING ON TWO FRONTS

by Tatjana Eggeling

A naive young man from the US Virgin Islands ventures out into the big wide world. In New York, he learns to box and goes on to have a successful professional boxing career with several world championship titles. Summarized thus, Emile's life is a typically American story of a self-made man, the kind of story that fascinates so many of us. A rags-to-riches story with plenty of scope for dreams, desires, and romanticized imaginings.

However, Emile's story is potentially far more explosive than the idealized versions of such careers would lead you to believe. His story bore two attributes that made his journey a particularly rocky one. While it's true that his poor educational background and difficult family life would fit the typical mold, these were not the attributes in question; they were his skin color and homosexuality. Emile began his boxing career when the civil rights movement was still in its infancy and before the gay liberation movement had even been born (its birth was marked by the Stonewall riots, protesting against police brutality, that began in front of The Stonewall Inn on Christopher Street, New York, in 1969). Their fight for equality and recognition later led to the creation of a political home and social network for all the people they fought for. In so doing, they allowed people to bolster their self-confidence and empower themselves to no longer perceive themselves as inferior for their differences from the dominant white heteronormative society. They forged role models, called upon others to accept their differences as being integral to their persons, and demanded the required respect.

"BROWN BOMBER" AND "BLACK BEAST"

Successful Black boxers have been a paradigm of clichés and stereotypes ever since the white-dominated media began reporting on their title fights in the US. In the 1930s, they described Joe Louis as the "Brown Bomber" or "Dark Destroyer" who had "come from the jungle" – a choice of words that was typical of the decade. The legendary fight between Muhammad Ali and George Foreman in Kinshasa in 1974, in which two Black boxers fought in the "dark continent" for the world championship title, has been firmly established in history as the "Rumble in the Jungle." This tagline and Muhammad Ali's nickname of "Black Beast" or "Cannibal" serve as clichés evoking the animalistic, exotic, and primitive associations made with Black men and their "roots" in Africa, and remain powerful to this day.

The history of boxing in the US is part of the history of racism. Sport in the US is organized differently than in European countries. There, it is primarily associations that organize popular and competitive sports all the way up to professional levels. In the US, universities are important actors in the running of sports. Anyone wishing to pursue a professional sports career doesn't just need to be accepted by a university; they also have to either pay the expensive tuition fees or, with a little luck and a lot of talent, win a scholarship. In contrast, boxing has been built on the foundations of private enterprise, and runs in parallel to the university model. This historically offered Black people (and other marginalized immigrant groups) in the US the opportunity to achieve social recognition and to secure their own livelihood, regardless of their social background, by competing in the sport and even helping to organize it. The fact that both boxing promoters and boxers themselves were often closely tied (to varying degrees) to criminal activity reflects how marginalized groups are forced to the fringes of society. They took over and exploited the realms of action available to them that existed parallel to the structures built and dominated by white normative society. That society, which warily observed and condemned this, forgot that it itself was made up of people who had originally belonged to underprivileged or discriminated-against groups that had emigrated out of need and who had eventually created the dominant elite of the US.

The Black descendants of slaves had few opportunities to participate in society in the 1950s and '60s. The biographies of Black boxers not infrequently feature similar markers: an educational background with breaks or discontinuation, an early start in the working world with few chances for improvement. Boxing offered them opportunities that other occupations didn't.

They made the best that they could out of the social and cultural disadvantages presented to them. Emile Griffith, the Black man from the Virgin Islands with a difficult family life, was lucky to find work at a hatmaker's and discover his talent for

boxing. His dream of competing in the white sporting world of ping-pong would have hit a glass ceiling, as was the case for other Black athletes of his era. As a Black man, boxing was at least somewhat socially acceptable and expected – a societal niche.

A TECHNICAL K.O. – GAY IN SPORTS

Such niches didn't exist for gay athletes in Emile's day, as they were forced to hide their homosexuality. Even today, open homosexuality is still not a matter of course in a mainstream sport that has existed since the 19th century and still carries all of its associated traditions, values, and perceptions with it. Over the last 40 years, boxing has developed an LGBTI (lesbian, gay, bisexual, transgender, and intersex) movement with its own clubs, associations, venues, and even international competitions. However, in a sports world defined by heteronormative codes, athletes in competitive and professional sports can only engage in *mainstream* sports. Heteronormativity is based on two fundamental assumptions: firstly, that there are two clearly defined sexes (male and female), and secondly, that these are, of course, heterosexually oriented. Both sexes are assigned different characteristics and abilities: men are strong, passionate, aggressive, achievement-oriented, and assertive; women are emotional, sensitive, weak, and balanced. Because sports often value the highest performance and because this is usually achieved by men, the guiding values of a sport are also defined by characteristics associated with masculinity. A fact that is overlooked is that performance discrepancies between men and women are due to physiological differences. Men can't help being the ultimate record-holders. In addition, the more that a sport is perceived as being typically male, the fewer the deviations from the norm that are accepted. This is one reason why women were prohibited from participating in sports that were considered particularly male, why they continue to the present day not to be recognized as equal, and why their athletic performances are not judged on their own merits and are rewarded with smaller financial prizes in professional sports. The more they adapt to the heterosexual male values and rules of a sport, the greater the distrust they are regarded with. Homosexual men fall into the same trap because they are assigned "female" characteristics: they are delicate, bitchy, easily hurt, lacking in assertiveness – and therefore are not "real" men.

Boxing is generally viewed as a sport for tough, powerful men who are, of course, heterosexual. Accordingly, a gay boxer still seems like a contradiction to many people, because the characteristics they are assigned do not fit the general picture of the sport. Naturally, there have been, and are, gay athletes in all kinds of sports who go unnoticed. In contrast to being Black, homosexuality is not visible. It can, therefore, be hidden, easily ignored, and even hushed up – what we do not see does not exist. Homosexuality is also something that is usually physically experienced only once puberty is reached. This has far-reaching consequences for lesbians and gays, and their personal social environments. In contrast to people of color, they are not familiar with being different to the norm from birth. They are forced to go through the socialization process of being "other" without the help of personal role models, and they frequently have to undergo this laborious development alone. They generally grow up in heterosexual families, in which the potential homosexuality of a child is paid little consideration and spoken of even less. This means that they are confronted with something that they are initially unable to even name, and for which they can expect little understanding or support. They discover through thoughtless remarks, gay jokes, and derogatory comments that homosexuality is something negative. Hiding and disavowing their homosexuality in everyday situations – whether in the family, at school, in the workplace, or even in sports – is an obvious reaction. Under such conditions, it may be difficult for lesbians and gays to accept as positive something that sets them apart from the others in their life.

Being gay in sports is particularly precarious, because in sports it is the body that is the central medium of experience and communication, as it is in sexual activity. As long as homosexuality is primarily seen as a sexual activity and not as a way of life, it stands to reason that direct contact with homosexuals is especially feared in sports, more so than in other areas of society in which the body and physicality play lesser roles. Fear of contact is very real to people, even if it is unfounded. Sport is seen as something pure, healthy, and beneficial, and unrelenting effort is spent on excluding anything sexual. Representations of eroticism and desire, such as in figure skating, are merely aspects of the athletic display, and reinforce the naturally accepted heterosexuality of the athletes. In contrast, homosexuality (especially male homosexuality) has associations with dirtiness and impurity, and is associated with the enactment of unnatural urges. Many heterosexuals consider it alien and even dangerous, giving rise to tropes such as showering with one's ass to the wall for safety. Homosexuals quickly learn to hide their sexual orientation in mainstream sports. In doing so, they may waste a lot of energy that would be better spent on training and competition. Many present themselves as heterosexually as possible, competing in the ring or on the field with particular toughness, entering into sham heterosexual relationships, and even joining in with the homophobic harassment of others.

Coming out in competitive sports entails many uncertainties. It may mean expulsion from the team or training group, bullying, and loss of sponsorship or the like. In professional sports, the matter of "homo" or "hetero" is, to a certain extent, one of survival. Those who come out usually do so once their sports career is over; some dare not come out for their whole lives.

Emile Griffith's late coming out at the age of 70 (five years before his death in 2013) is typical for an athlete of his generation. He is due particular respect for enduring the double burden of racism and homophobia without breaking.

LESBIAN AND GAY BOXERS

PANAMA AL BROWN (1902–1951) was the first ever Latin American boxing world champion. His father, an emancipated slave from Tennessee, emigrated to Panama in 1880, where he worked on the construction of the Panama Canal. He died when Panama Al Brown was 13 years old. Panama began boxing to help

feed his family. He went to New York after a series of successful fights and having won the Panamanian championship. There, his success continued, but because of the color of his skin and despite being the best in his class, he was not given a world championship fight until 1929. He won his first K.O. fight in Paris in 1926. He felt more at home there than in New York, and enjoyed life in the local bars and dance halls. He befriended Jean Cocteau, danced in Josephine Baker's La Revue Nègre, and performed in the cabaret Caprice Viennois. He enjoyed great popularity as an athlete in France. He fought in more than 40 fights in Europe, and continued to be successful despite having had a drug addiction for many years and becoming infected with syphilis in the 1930s. Cocteau unsuccessfully tried to persuade him to get sober. Panama fought his last fight in Paris in 1938, after which he wanted to end his career. He returned to New York at the outbreak of the Second World War. There, he entered the ring again to earn a living until 1942. He then spent a year in prison for cocaine abuse. Up to that point, Panama Al Brown had maintained a successful win rate: 161 fights with 129 victories (59 of which were K.O.s). He earned a living as a sparring partner until his death in 1951. He died of tuberculosis.

The Canadian boxer MARK LEDUC (1962–2009) boxed from the age of 12 years old. His parents separated when he was 15 and he ended up on the streets, where he got by committing petty crimes. His talent for boxing was discovered during a prison stint. Mark began a successful amateur career, became light welterweight Canadian champion three times, and won silver at the Olympic Games in Barcelona. After that, he attempted a professional career, but had only five fights. In 1993, he spoke anonymously about his life as a gay athlete in the radio broadcast *The Last Closet* by the Canadian radio broadcaster CBS Radio. The Canadian swimmer Mark Tewksbury also spoke in the broadcast, and later came out in 1994. Marc Leduc came out the same year in the TV documentary *For the Love of the Game*, and subsequently became actively involved in Toronto's lesbian and gay youth schemes and in the AIDS Foundation. He earned a living as a movie set builder. His death in a "hotel sauna" was the source of many rumors, although officially he died of heatstroke. Many reports of the time concealed the fact that the St. Mark's Spa was a well-known gay sauna in Toronto.

YUSAF MACK, born in 1980, attracted more attention for his life outside the ring than for his professional fights (2000–2014: 41-31-17): a year after it became known that he had performed in a gay pornographic film in 2014, he initially claimed that he had been drugged and had been an unwilling participant in the film. He later retracted these claims, explaining in interviews that he had been in the film for financial reasons and that he was bisexual. 48 hours later, he admitted that he had lied again, and came out as gay. The father of 10 had kept his secret for eight years because he hadn't known how to tell his children, which had provoked suicidal thoughts. The people in his life reacted overwhelmingly positively to his coming out. In a later interview,

Yusaf declared his interest in transgender men and women, because he didn't like muscled people like himself. He received criticism following this, especially from transgender people, because he'd used the word "tranny," which is considered a slur.

LIZ CARMOUCHE, born in 1984, was the first lesbian boxer to be put under contract by the US-based UFC (Ultimate Fighting Championship). The UFC organizes mixed martial arts (MMA) competitions – fights which pit different martial arts against each other in octagonal cages. In contrast to boxing, this allows full body contact. Prior to her professional career, Liz was a marine in the US army and served three tours in Iraq. As a soldier, she was subject to the homophobic guideline that forced lesbian and gay soldiers to keep their sexuality secret. This was abolished by President Obama. As a professional athlete, she refused to hide anymore and became an activist against homophobia. She would enter the octagon wearing a rainbow-colored mouthguard, and in 2013 became the spokesperson for an anti-HIV campaign for lesbian and gay youths, supported by the UFC. Today, she campaigns for medical marijuana products. Her win rate as an MMA fighter attests to her success: 19-13-6.

Englishwoman MICHELE ABORO, born in 1967, is one of the most successful female boxers of all time. Together with Regina Halmich and Michelle Sutcliffe, she has been a trailblazer for the recognition of women's boxing. When Michele began boxing, it was still illegal to train women boxers in England; trainers ran the risk of losing their license. Women were only officially permitted to box professionally as late as 1996. Unable to find a promoter in England who would sign her, Michele

boxed for a German boxing stable. Her win rate as a boxer is impressive: 21 fights and 21 victories (12 of which were K.O.s), including seven world championship titles. She was equally successful as a kickboxer: 36-32-23. From a performance perspective, there was no reason to end her career. However, following her last victory against Nadja Debras in 2001, Michele simply wasn't offered any more fights because she was no longer marketable as an openly lesbian woman. Women's boxing was targeted at heterosexual men, who had put up with the fact that women had broken into a conventionally male domain. However, promoters were not brave enough to present them with an openly lesbian woman. After retiring, Michele Aboro followed her Dutch-Chinese wife to Shanghai. Unable to find any training opportunities there, she opened her first boxing school, which led to the creation of the Aboro Academy. There, Michele Aboro offers her wards high-level boxing and kickboxing training, regardless of gender or social background. The school is, in her own words, her legacy.

ORLANDO CRUZ, born in 1981, came out as a "proud gay man." He described the

time before this as "living in an armored shell" and as psychologically torturous and traumatizing – a path creeping toward suicide. Due to discrimination against homosexuals, he was unable to come out in his beloved homeland of Puerto Rico. It was only while living in the US, and with the help of a psychologist, that Orlando was able to take this step at the age of 31. This made him the first openly gay professional boxer. For him, it was a moment of great liberation: now, at peace with himself, he firmly believed he could become an even better boxer and be respected as the person he truly was. He saw this as necessary to fulfilling his grand dream of winning a world championship title. He knew that coming out in the tough world of men's boxing would be especially difficult. However, he received huge recognition for his courage and honesty. As an openly gay man, he also no longer felt vulnerable to hurtful and derogatory slurs. Knowing the hide-and-seek nature of gay life so well, he regretted that Emile Griffith hadn't found the courage to come out earlier. In 2013, he dedicated his world championship fight against the Mexican Orlando Salido to Emile Griffith and his family. Orlando Cruz considers coming out to be a highly personal matter, but he hopes to embolden others to follow his example. Because: "Nothing can scare me anymore. I'm free, I've learned to fight, and I'm ready to win."

Apart from her fight statistics (14-7-0), very little information is available on the origin and life of the Brazilian fighter HALANA DOS SANTOS. In a short interview for a German tabloid paper before her third world championship title fight against Ramona Kühne in Potsdam in 2013, she stated that she would like to be the first lesbian boxing world champion; the time was ripe for her to come out. Aged 23 at the time, she lost her fight against Kühne.

The biographies of lesbian and gay boxers attest to how difficult it still is to come out in sport. This is as true for individual sports like boxing as it is for team sports. The more "masculine" a sport is considered, the greater the fear of the negative consequences of coming out. Further "battle lines" exist when the athlete is also Black and/or a woman, and is therefore held in low esteem. The athletes portrayed here have fought against both internal and external obstacles, and have all earned recognition.

Dr. Tatjana Eggeling, born in 1963, is a European ethnologist and an expert in homosexuality and homophobia in sport. She offers consultation and training on the topic for clubs, associations, and people working in sport. In her youth, Tatjana was a competitive rower, and she has been an ardent recreational athlete for over 25 years. She lives in Berlin.

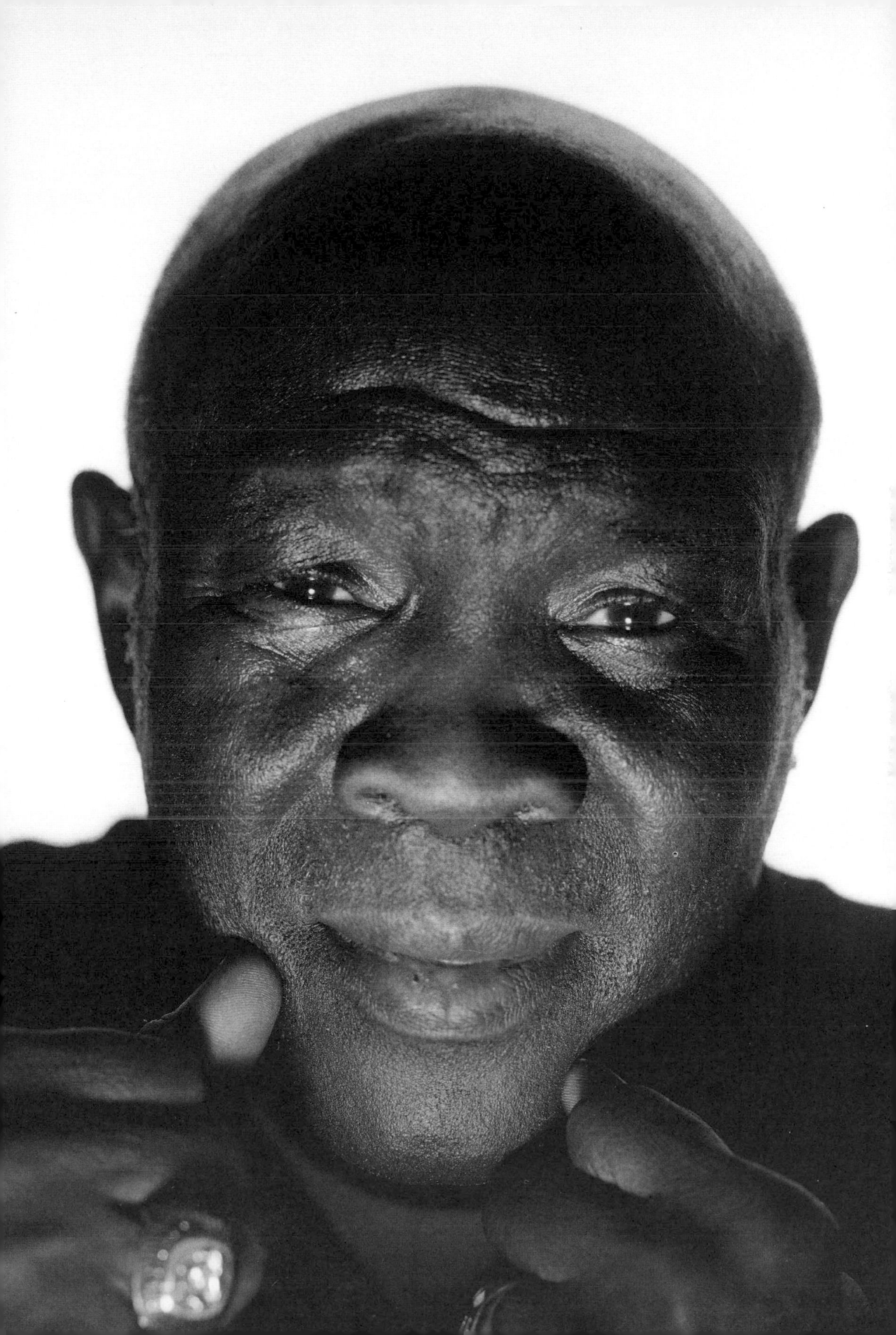

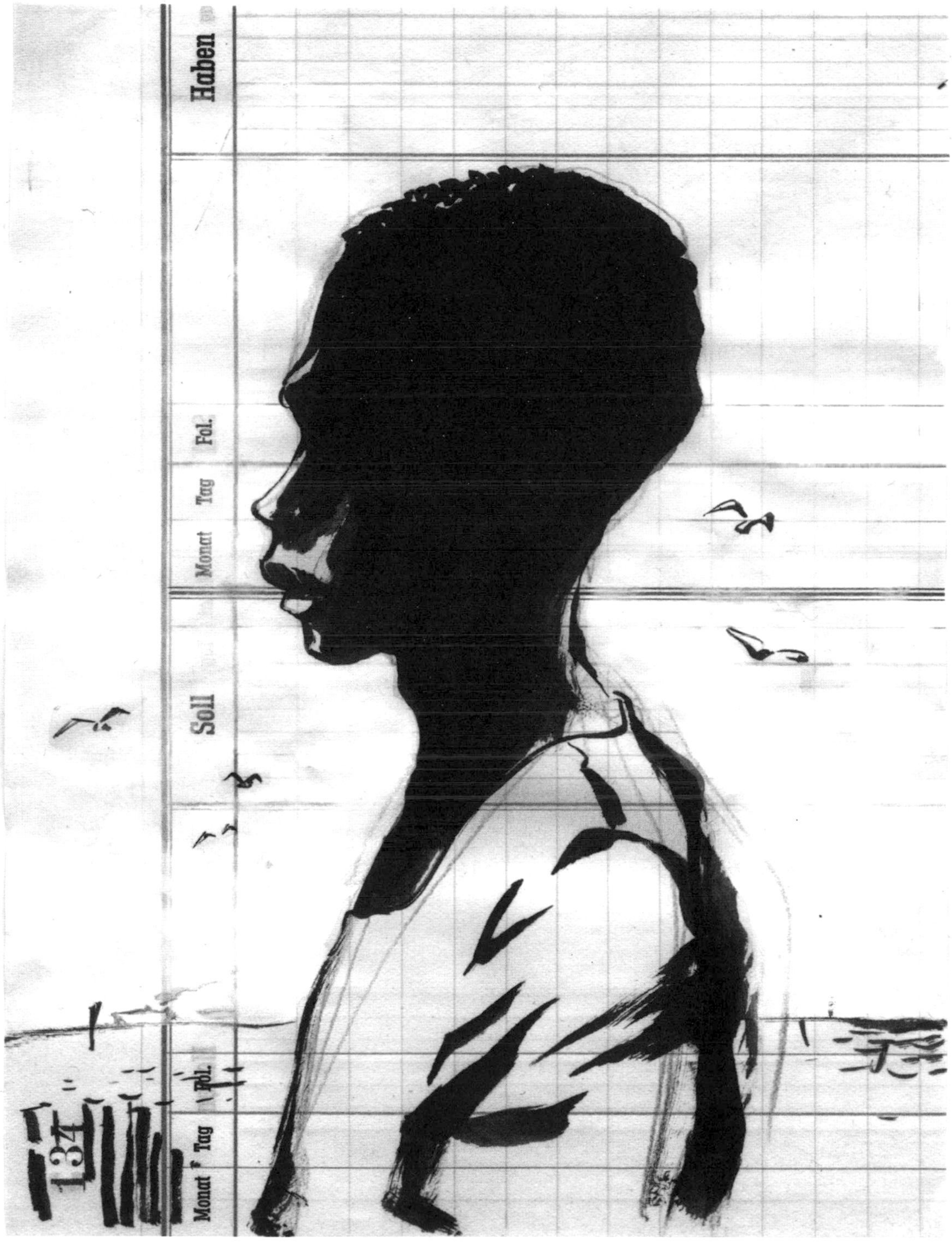
Haben
Monat Tag Fol.
Soll
134
Monat Tag Fol.

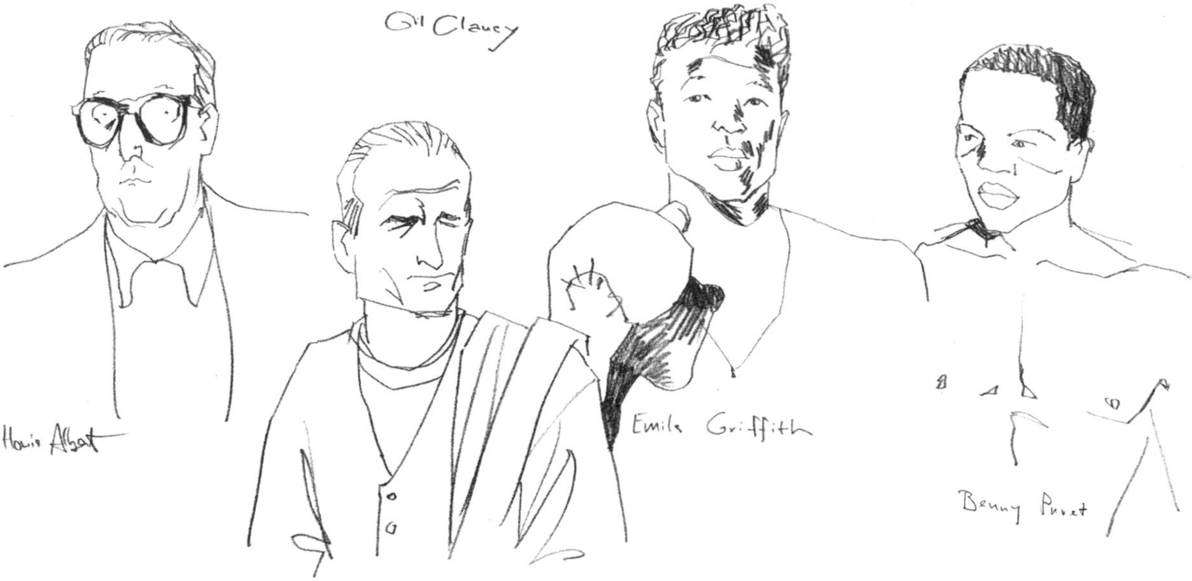
Gil Clancy
Howie Albert
Emile Griffith
Benny Paret

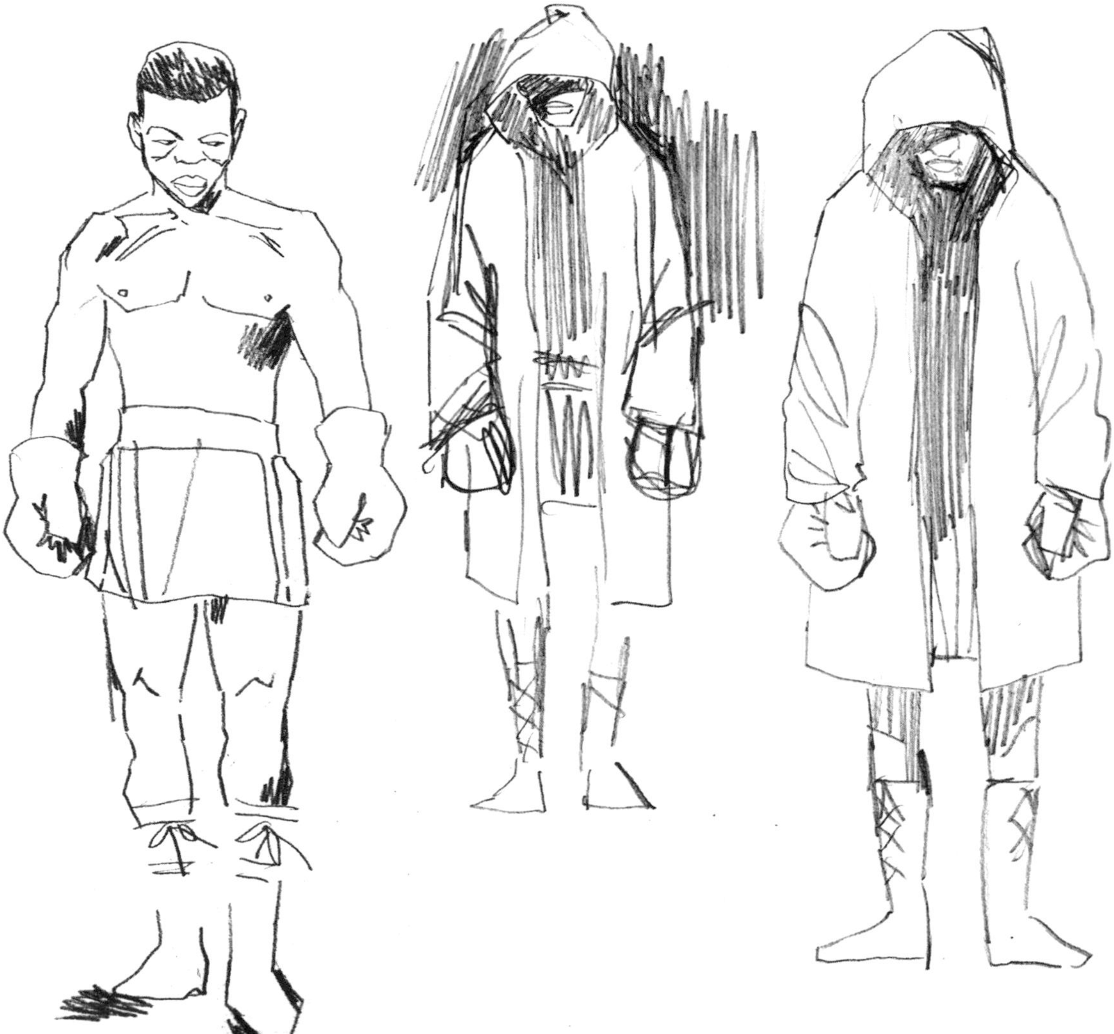

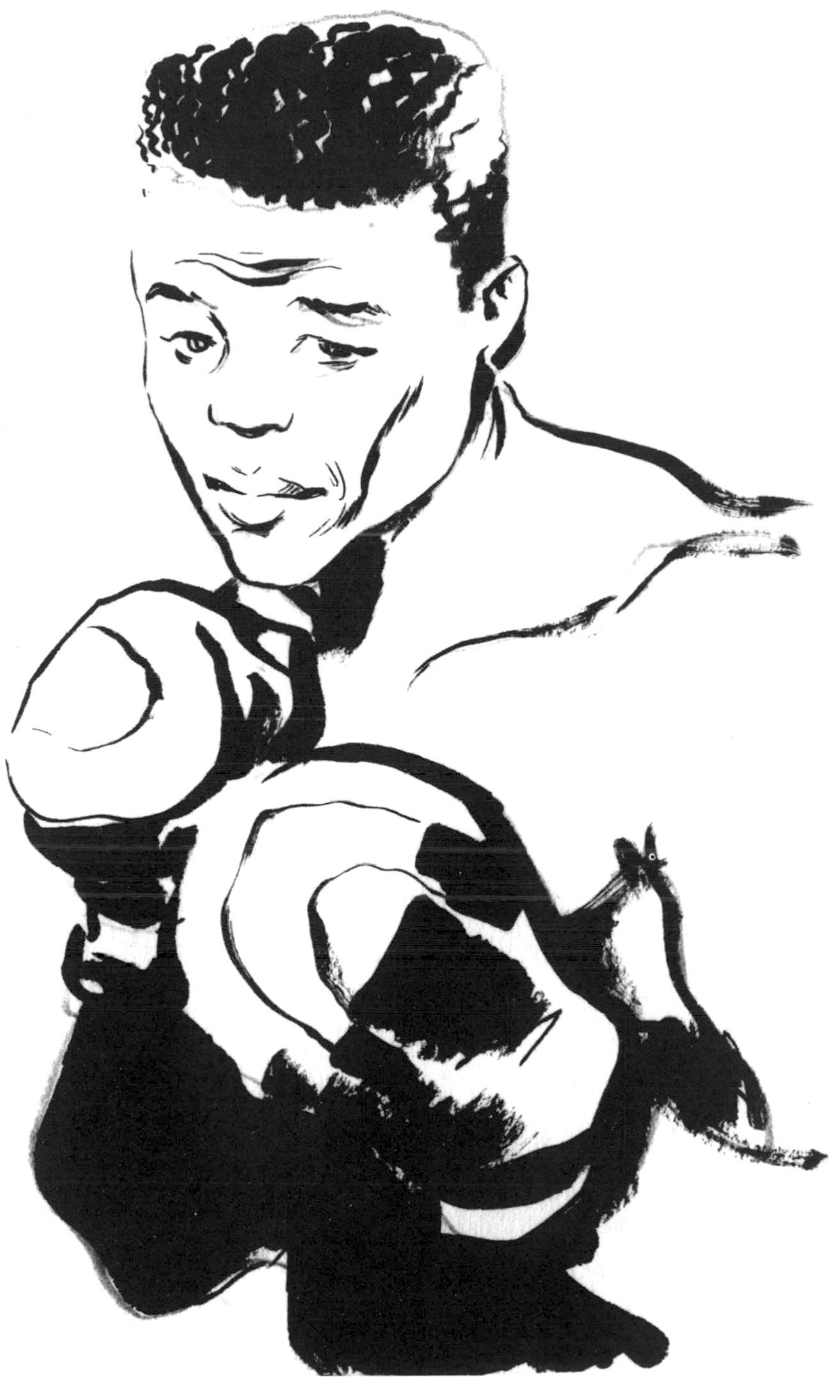

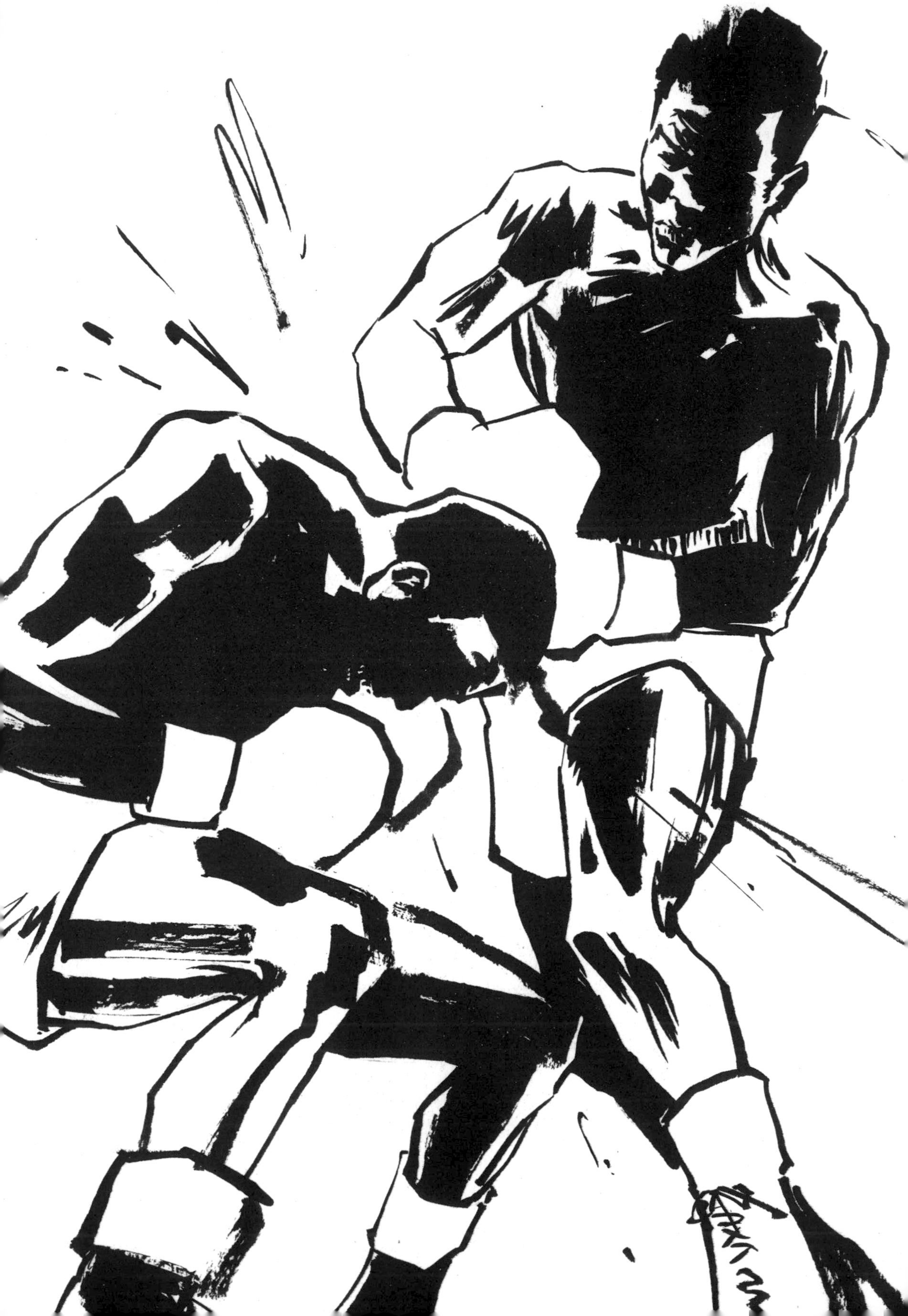

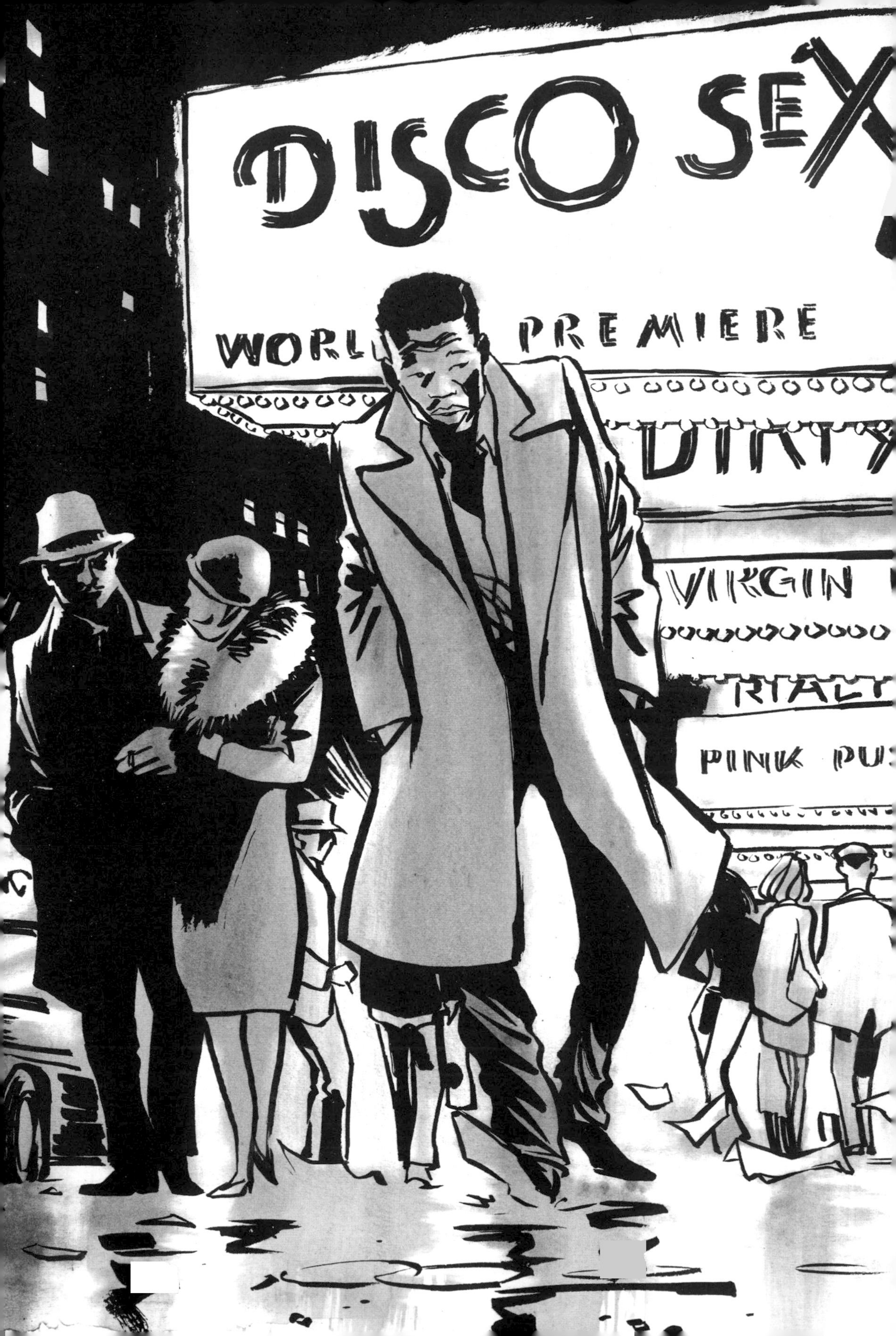
DISCO SEX
PREMIERE
VIRGIN

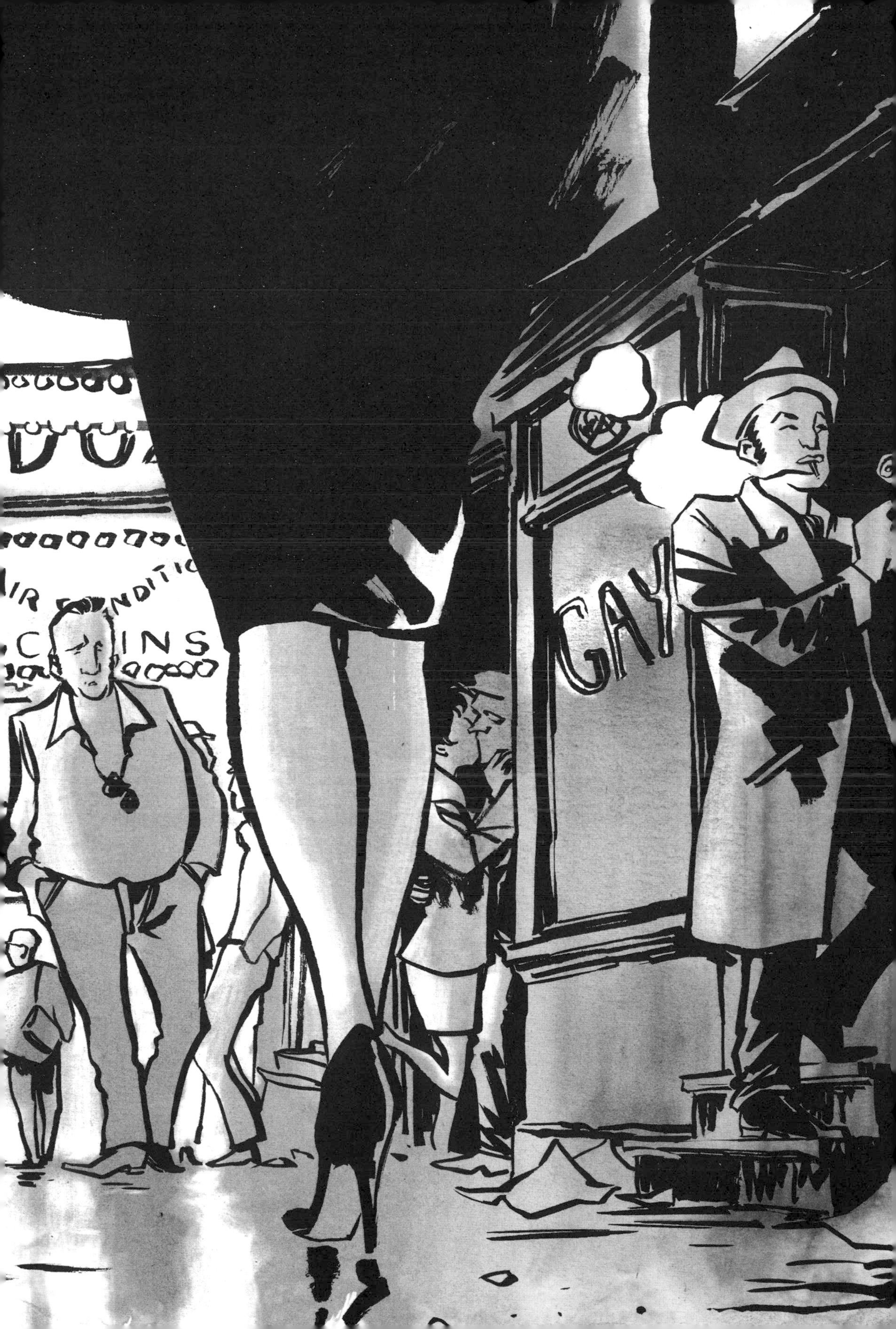
GAY

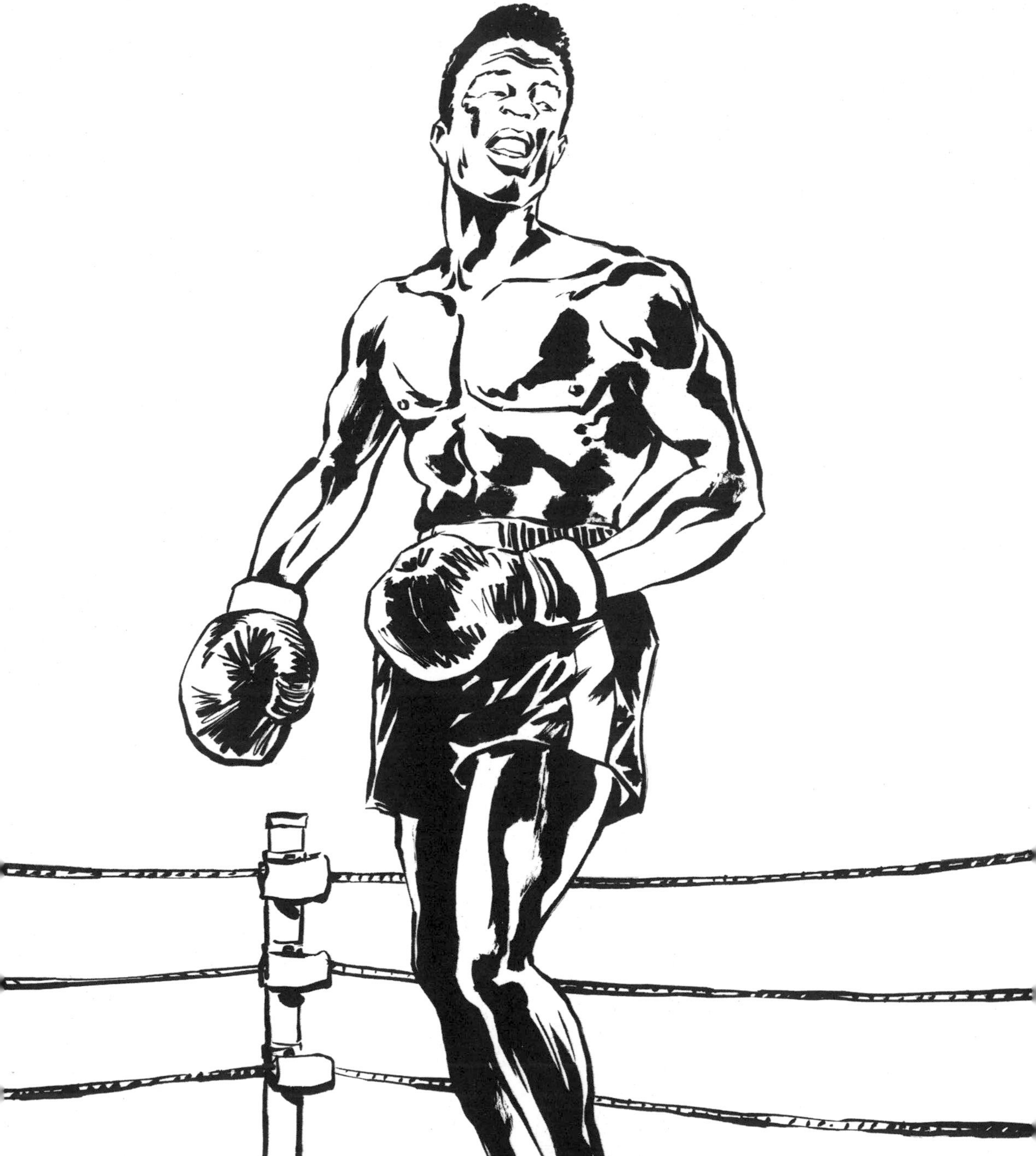

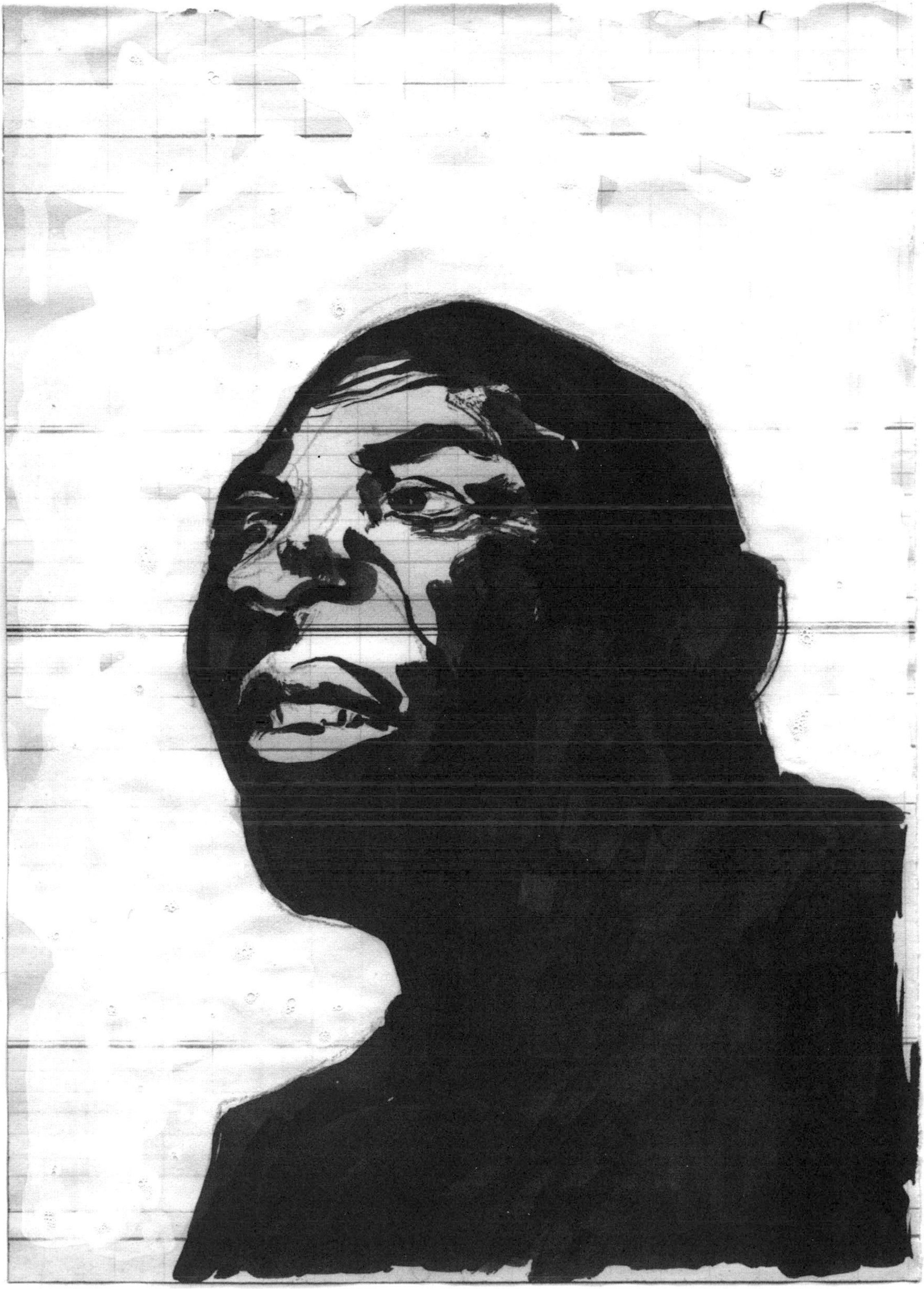

THANKS

My thanks to:

Michael Groenewald
Claudia Jerusalem-Groenewald
Bettina Oguamanam
Minou Zaribaf
Olav Korth
Thomas Gilke
Carlsen Verlag
My parents
Ron Ross
Isabel Kreitz
Carlos A. Marin
Mark Nevins
Robert D. Moran
Naomi Fearn
The Schomburg Center for Research
in Black Culture, NY
Tatjana Eggeling
Tanaquil Enzensberger and Jan
Sparstad
Marianne Enzensberger
K77-Studio
Roland Hüve
Lars von Törne
Frank Bachner

Please help campaign for love and equality:

allout.org

All Out mobilizes thousands of people around the globe to help bring about a world in which no one has to sacrifice family, freedom, safety, or dignity to be themselves or to love whichever person they choose.

– Reinhard Kleist

BIOGRAPHY

Reinhard Kleist, born in 1970 in Hürth, Cologne, has worked and lived as an illustrator and comic book artist in Berlin since 1996.

He became known to a wide audience in 1994 with the book *Lovecraft*, and made his international breakthrough in 2006 with the biographical comic book *Johnny Cash: I See A Darkness*. Both books were awarded the renowned Max and Moritz Prize. Kleist received the German Children's Literature Award for *The Boxer* in 2013. In 2016, *An Olympic Dream* was awarded the Luchs-Buchpreis, the Katholischen Kinder- und Jugendbuchpreis, and the Gustav-Heinemann-Friedenspreis. In 2017, Kleist once again tackled one of music's great storytellers in *Nick Cave: Mercy on Me*, which was simultaneously released in many languages. In 2018, Kleist was honoured for his work with the Max and Moritz Prize for Best German-Language Comic Book Artist.

In addition to his graphic novels, Reinhard Kleist has illustrated many books and record and DVD covers, and has worked for the *Süddeutsche Zeitung Magazin*, **FAZ**, and the TV channel **ARTE**. He holds workshops all around the world, and regularly performs live drawing events on stage.

www.reinhard-kleist.de